Vehicles

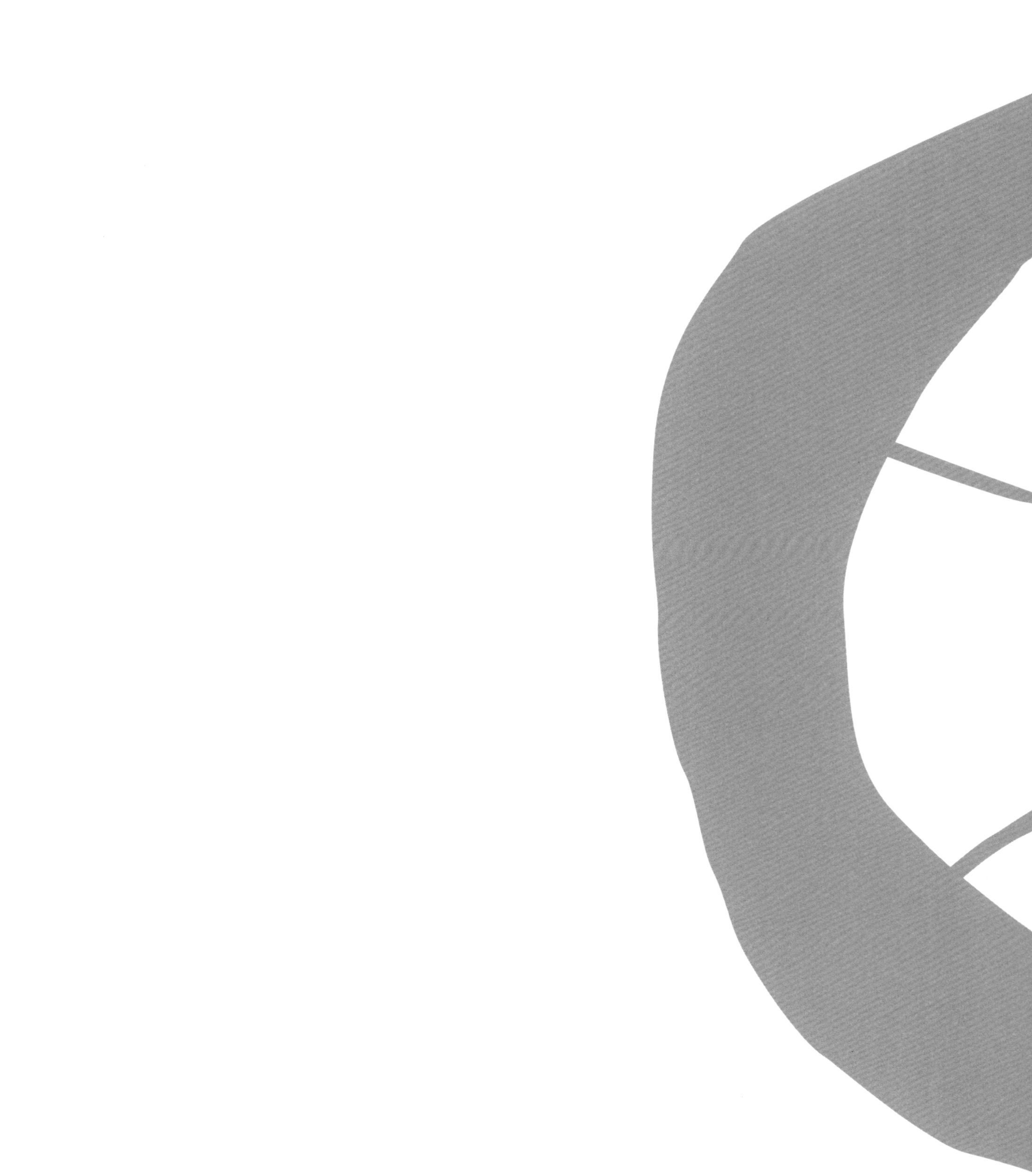

ART BRUT
The Collection

Vehicles

COLLECTION DE L'ART BRUT LAUSANNE

5 CONTINENTS

Contents

6 Preface Sarah Lombardi

9 Travellers without Tickets Anic Zanzi

19 Move Along! Michel Thévoz

31 CATALOGUE

ANNEXES

154 Biographies

162 Selected Bibliography

167 Photo Credits

Preface

Vehicles is the first in a new series of exhibitions at the Art Brut Collection, a biannual event presenting works from our collection only. These 'Art Brut Biennials' will give the public an idea of the wealth of our collections, which now number over 60,000 paintings, drawings, sculptures, textile works, and writings. They will feature works collected by Jean Dubuffet, which constitute the historic core of the museum opened on 26th February 1976, alongside later purchases.
These shows will either be thematic, like this one, or focus on a technique common to several artists. A multitude of graphic languages, all unique and personal, are expressed through the filter of the same subject.
Each exhibition will be accompanied by a bilingual catalogue, entitled *Art Brut, the Collection*, co-published with 5 Continents Editions (Milan). I would like to take this opportunity to thank the publisher, Eric Ghysels, who has participated enthusiastically in this adventure, demonstrating a real passion for the works in our institution. This book is the first in a new series offering visitors a virtual visit to the museum through the chosen theme. I am also grateful to Michel Thévoz, the first curator of the Art Brut Collection, who graciously accepted to write an essay to begin the series. For this first exhibition, Anic Zanzi, curator of both the museum and the exhibition, has chosen the theme of vehicles, a subject explored by many Art Brut artists.

Whether they are designed to travel through the air, over the sea, or across the land, vehicles have always fascinated people in general, and Art Brut artists in particular. They are associated with the world of childhood, with which these artists have kept special ties, but they also incarnate an idea of physical and sexual power that extends human capacities.
The artists perhaps try to assert themselves through these pictures or regain a certain control over their lives after a somewhat battered start. The act of drawing (cars, boats, aircraft, trains, bicycles, and rockets) allows some escape from their everyday lives or explore inner territories. In this case the journey may be long and does not always reach its destination. Others choose vehicles as an ultimate means of locomotion, like the African artist Ataa Oko, who died last year: he asked to be buried in a wooden coffin representing a Ghanaian train, in keeping with the tradition of figurative coffins in his country, like the ones he made in his youth.
The exhibition brings together about forty artists, all men except for Lorna Hylton. Among them are some historic figures, such as Benjamin Arneval,

Slavko Kopac, Michel Thévoz and Jean Dubuffet at the Art Brut Collection, February 1976.

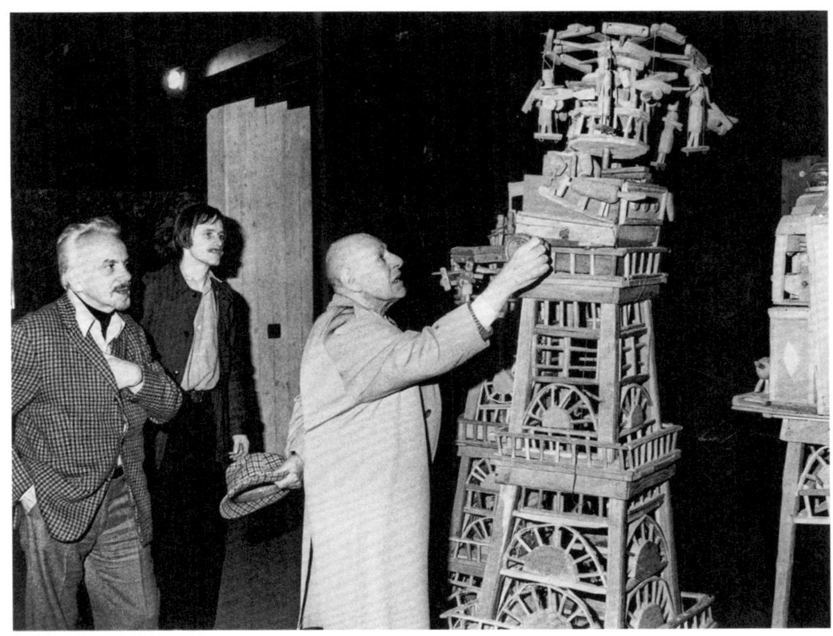

Auguste Forestier, and Sylvain Lecocq, whose works were bought by Jean Dubuffet, alongside more recent artists, such as Fausto Badari, whose drawings of agricultural machinery and trucks with anthropomorphic features entered the museum collection in 2013.

May this journey through our collections transport you to another land, as Jean Dubuffet was fond of saying, leaving behind territories sometimes over-accustomed to cultural art!

Sarah Lombardi
DIRECTOR OF THE ART BRUT COLLECTION

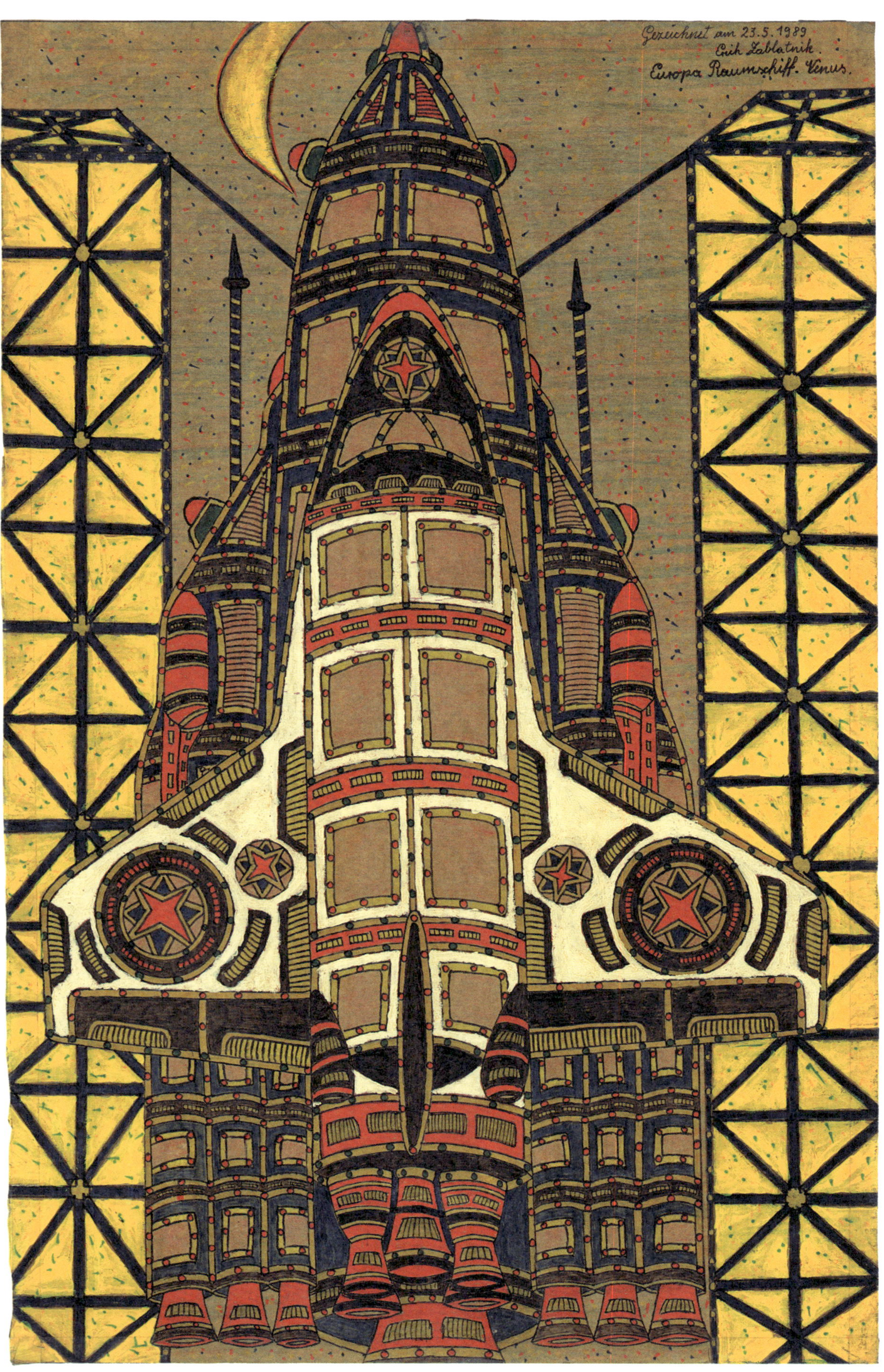
Gezeichnet am 23.5.1989
Erih Zablatnik.
Europa Raumschiff. Venus.

Travellers without Tickets

Erich Zablatnik
Europa Raumschiff Venus, 1989
felt pen and acrylic paint on cardboard
60.5 x 39.2 cm

When the Art Brut Collection opened its doors to the public in Lausanne in 1976, shortly after Jean Dubuffet's donation, it numbered nearly 5,000 works that the French painter had collected over a period of thirty years. Other drawings, paintings, sculptures, assemblages, textiles, and writings have since enriched the museum, either the work of new artists or works by artists already in the Collection. The first step in preparing a theme exhibition is to choose the exhibits. This is a crucial stage, and it is particularly exciting when the institution holds thousands of works. 'Vehicles' is a theme which enabled us to put works never shown before alongside more familiar pieces displayed in a new context. The process of discovering or rediscovering these works refreshed our view of the collections. Art Brut artists often draw inspiration from their childhood or their immediate surroundings. Their work is therefore closely intertwined with their lives. And as locomotion is part of their everyday lives, means of transport loom large in the Art Brut Collection. For the exhibition *Vehicles* we have chosen about forty artists and over two hundred works featuring machines for travelling on land, over the sea, or through the air.

Some artists have made vehicles their sole subject; their entire production therefore consists of variations on a single motif. This is the case of Motooka Hidenori[1] and David Braillon who draw trains obsessively or of the Québec artist Philippe Lemaire, who paints nothing but his father's 'char',[2] and the French artist Jean Tourlonias, who has produced a picturesque, colourful array of different cars and motorbikes. Francis Mayor, combining collage and drawing, likes to sail on Lake Geneva or take us out to sea, often a choppy sea, in boats. Erich Zablatnik propels us into space with his rockets and flying machines straight out of science fiction. Other artists take a broader interest in the transport world, such as Willem Van Genk, who makes models of buses, as well as drawings of railway stations and airports.

When humans settled in sedentary groups they roamed over an area only a few kilometres from their home base, but when the means of locomotion evolved their horizons opened up. The rapid development of transport in the nineteenth century was a symbol of progress and caused great social upheaval. Initially reserved for the elite, bicycles and then cars were soon within reach of the masses. The distinction between social classes then shifted to the vehicle itself: the make, the

[1] Refer to the Catalogue section (pp. 31–151) for the authors and illustrations of the works mentioned in the article.
[2] Not a 'tank' but Québec slang for a 'car'.

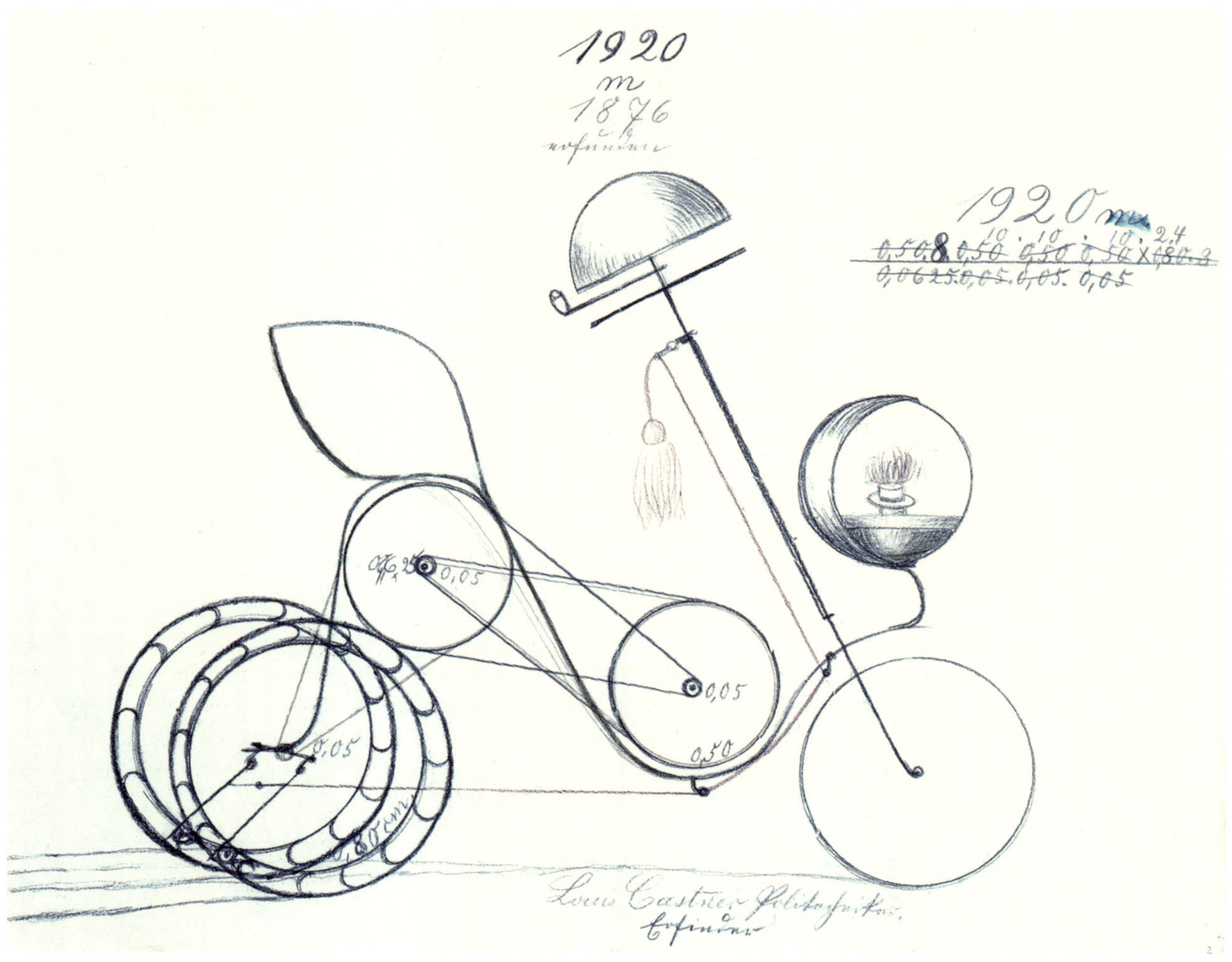

Louis Castner
« 1920 », 1920
pencil, indelible pencil, colored pencil on paper
33 x 21 cm
Prinzhorn collection, Heidelberg

engine size, and the horsepower. The multiplicity, abundance, and variety of models of vehicles fascinated many Art Brut artists. They built up their own documentation, accumulating magazines, catalogues, and specialised publications with a view to drawing up inventories of their own. Willem Van Genk, Motooka Hidenori and Helmut Nimczevski supplemented these archives with their own photographs; Gregory Blackstock drew on his phenomenal memory and took inspiration from dictionary illustrations. Motooka Hidenori and David Braillon sought to draw up an exhaustive list of all the types of trains they knew. Han Ploos Van Amstel and Serge Delaunay were captivated by four-wheeled vehicles. They all drew up lists, series, and repertories in which each type of aircraft, car or train is arranged in an orderly, precise manner. Repetition, juxtaposition and alignment often bring out the subtle differences between the various models they draw, but can also create a mass effect making distinctions hard to perceive. The almost maniacal classification and rigour that seem necessary to these artists reveal their need to organise or even appropriate the world, and gives them a means of control.

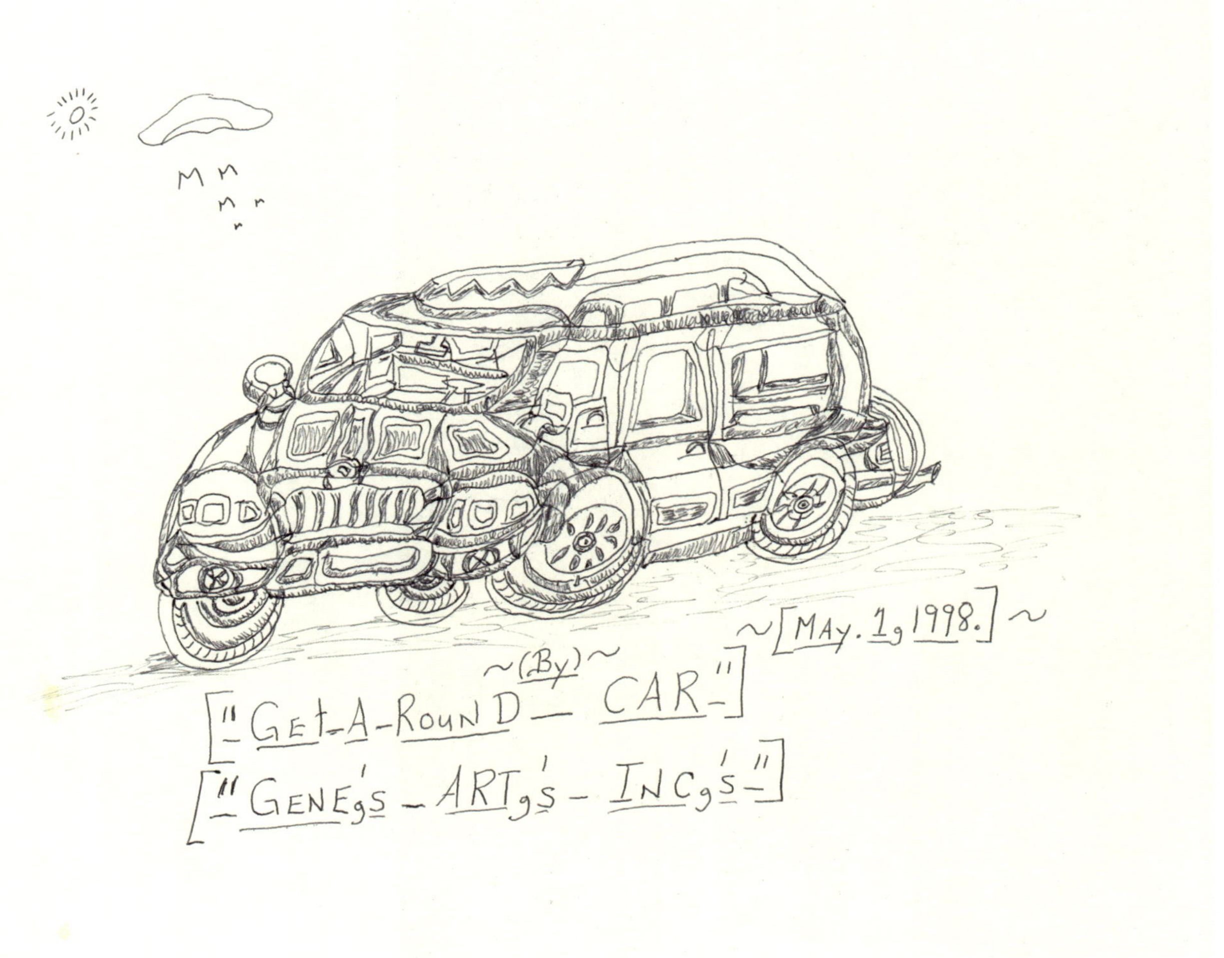

Gene Merritt
Get around Car, 1998
ballpoint pen on paper
27.9 x 35.3 cm

Many of them have striven to revolutionise travel. Crazy inventors, they imagine futuristic constructions, flying machines, and vehicles with propellers or motors. The German Gustav Mesmer, nicknamed Icarus of Lautertal, was constantly designing devices to help him fly. He made wings from umbrellas, a bicycle from all sorts of salvaged materials, added propellers and launched into test flights. Although he pedalled vigorously, he rose only a few centimetres above the ground over a short distance. But he did not give up and spent all his time and energy on his inventions. These dream-ridden utopians turn into avant-garde mechanics. Before Gustav Mesmer, Louis Castner (1863–1920), some of whose drawings are kept in the Prinzhorn Collection in Heidelberg,[3] devised systems which multiplied the movement of bicycles. Later, Benjamin Arneval, whose works were collected by Jean Dubuffet, was also intrigued by wheelworks and drew two-wheelers with great precision. The same interest in mechanics and painstaking detail is found in Serge Delaunay, who was passionately interested in space travel and automobiles. His work concentrates on rockets and cars, with all the parts carefully drawn in felt pen. Like the American artist Gene Merritt, he takes multiple viewpoints,

[3] Hans Prinzhorn, a German art historian and psychiatrist, collected works by patients in psychiatric hospitals which are now in the Prinzhorn Collection in Heidelberg, Germany.

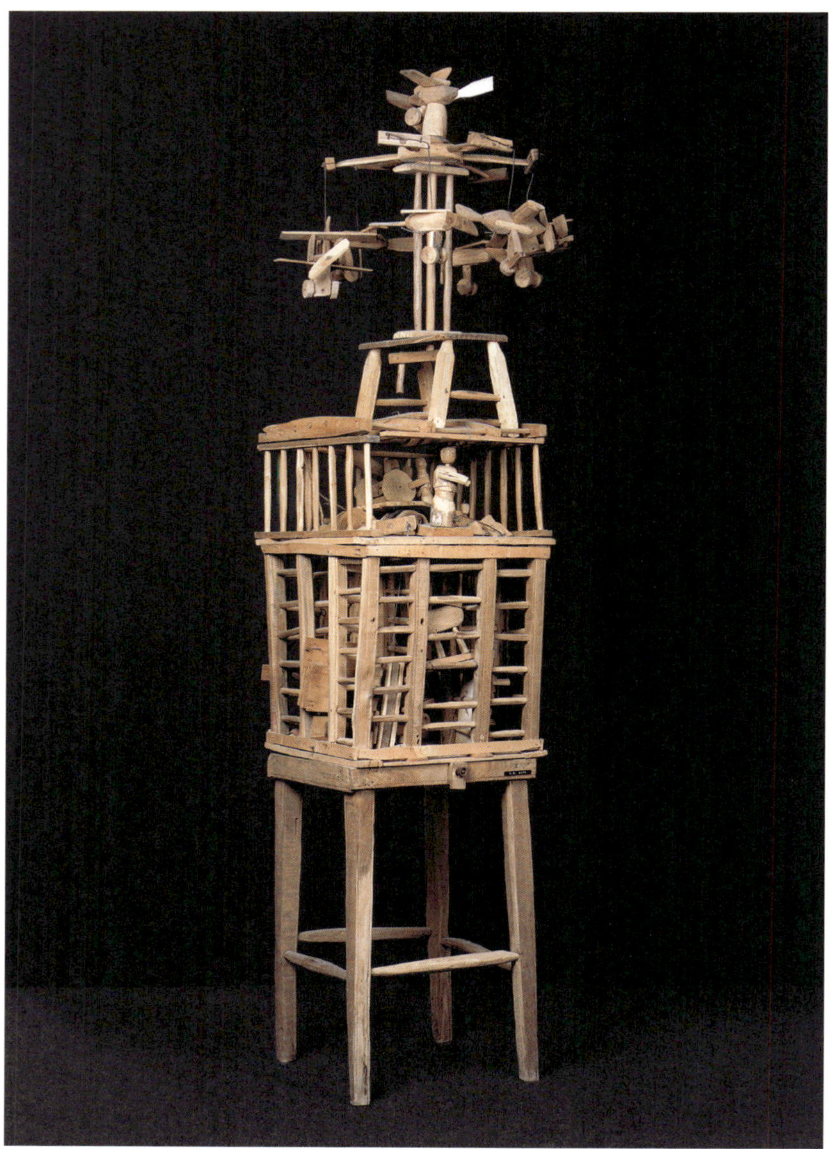

Émile Ratier
Arc de triomphe (Triumphal Arch), 1966
wood and mixed media
H.: 219 cm

showing the roof, the front, the side, the interior and the engine of the car simultaneously, as if his drawings were to be used in an instruction manual for constructing a vehicle. Captions, advertising slogans, and spare parts are often arranged on or beside the vehicle, saturating the sheet to the point of confusion. Fausto Badari also depicts the interior and exterior of his buses, lorries and agricultural machinery. His vigorous strokes even seem to express the movement of the engines. Émile Ratier was fanatic about movement and machinery. All his constructions are articulated and some have hundreds of wooden parts: crank handles, cogs and gears set in motion the structures cleverly crafted from pieces of wood, tin lids, scrap metal, and wire. Although Émile Ratier did not start making his sculptures until he was sixty-five, when his eyesight gradually failed until he went completely blind, he had shown signs of an inventive

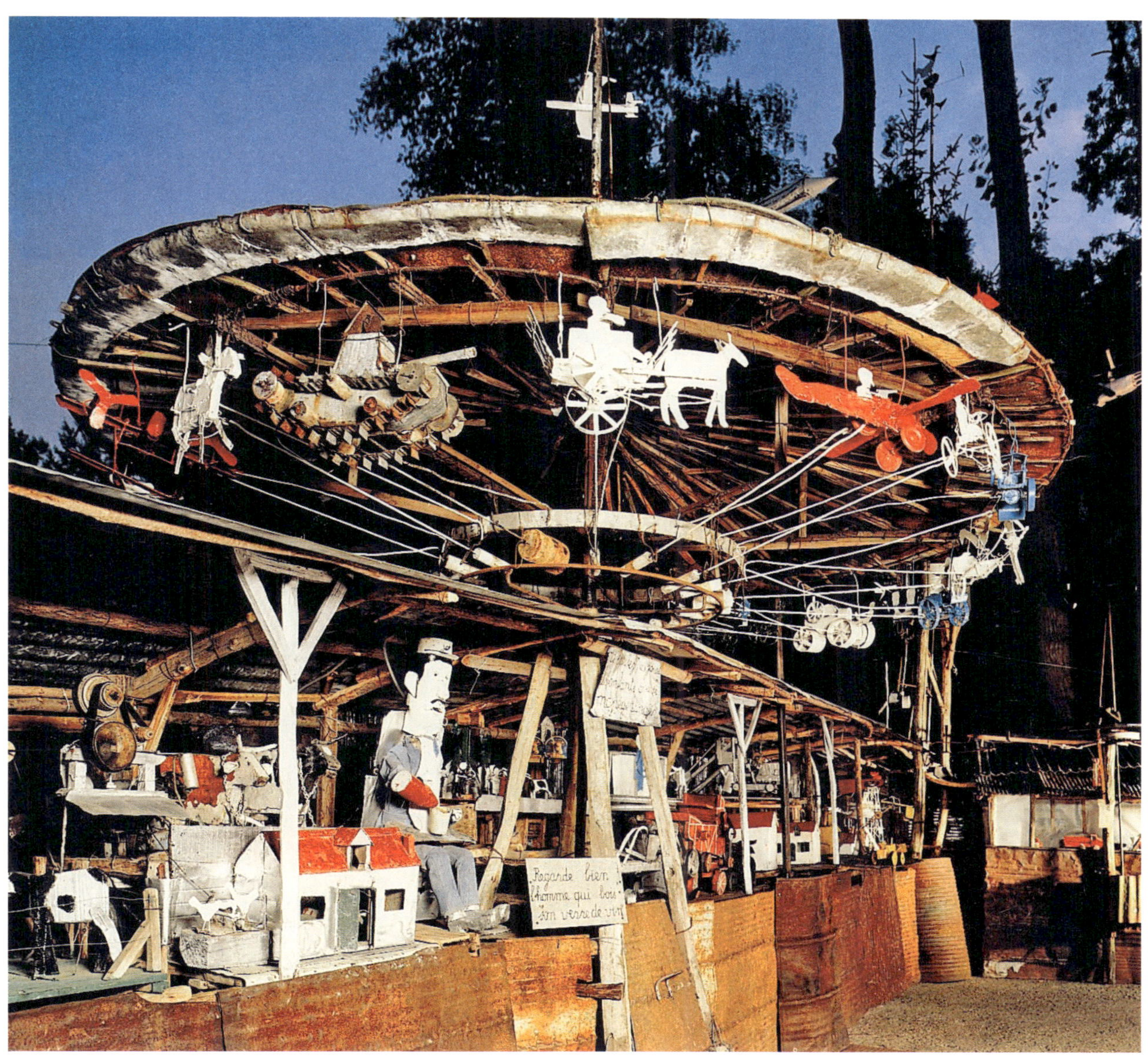

Petit Pierre (Pierre Avezard)
Manège (Merry-go-round)
La Fabuloserie, Dicy

mind and great ingenuity when he was only a boy. He made machines for splitting chestnuts or chopping Jerusalem artichokes, a dog cart for carrying water and bread, a wooden bicycle, and wheelbarrows. He loved merry-go-rounds and incorporated them in his works. Like the whimsical *Manège de Petit Pierre* at the Fabuloserie (Art Brut park) in France, Émile Ratier's merry-go-rounds include vehicles of all kinds. Replicas of fairground attractions are a sure sign of the desire to amuse people and the pleasure it brings. Ratier was delighted to give children the objects he made, mounted on wheels so they could pull them along on a string.[4]

The sculptures in this exhibition are mainly assemblages. Willem Van Genk, Auguste Forestier and François Burland use salvaged materials. Forestier gathered all kinds of waste materials (wood, cloth, glass, metal,

[4] Auguste Forestier, whose boats are in the exhibition, also made toys for the children of the staff of the Saint-Alban hospital where he was living.

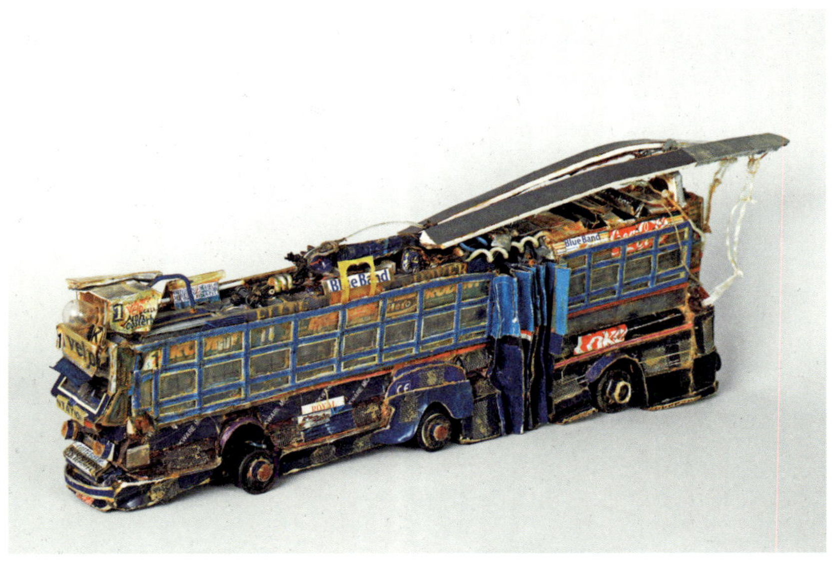

Willem Van Genk
Untitled, undated
salvaged materials
24 x 81 cm

▸
Guillaume Pujolle
Untitled, ca. 1949-1950
wood and mixed media
13 x 27 x 18 cm

François Burland
Atomik Submarine, 2011
wood and painted metal
1,800 x 535 x 376 cm
Author's collection

▸▸
Adolf Wölfli
Le Grand Chemin de fer du ravin de la colère (The Great Railway of Ravine of Fury), 1911
lead and coloured pencil on paper
50 x 37.5 cm

animals' teeth, bits of leather, and string) to make his figures, animals and boats.[5] Fascinated by the world of transport and travel, Willem Van Genk used packaging materials, such as cigarette or medicine boxes, to make his multicoloured buses. François Burland picked up materials from waste-sorting centres to make aeroplanes, boats and cars. In 2011, after a joking bet made one evening with friends, he set about making an eighteen-metre-long submarine. The huge machine was built in France, and then dismantled and taken to Switzerland[6] for an exhibition. Burland, accustomed to solitary labour in his workshop, transformed himself into a company director in order to carry out his crazy project.

Means of transport are indissociable from the idea of travel. Who has not dreamed of taking to the road one day? Everybody nurtures a dream of escape, or a longing for freedom. A journey may be synonymous with discovery and experience, like a metaphor for life. In the first part of his fictitious autobiography entitled *Du berceau au tombeau* (1908–1912), Adolf Wölfli used ideas from magazines, books, atlases, travel stories and postcards to reinvent the past and turn his childhood into a travel diary. He and his family roamed the world and sailed through the cosmos, battling with unexpected events which threatened to bring their trip to an untimely end. For travel also implies risk taking and danger.[7] The adventure may turn into a misadventure and the journey could end in a disaster. Like Guillaume Pujolle's boats thrashing about in a storm, some of the works displayed in the exhibition explore the dangers of travel. André Stanton shows a sinking ship, and George Widener represents the *Titanic*. Lorna Hylton, Feng Shi Yi and Willem Van Genk depict the disquieting chaos generated by hordes of moving machines.

Art Brut artists use art as a way of escaping from an often difficult life and fleeing their condition. For those who are forcibly immobilised, the desire to be elsewhere takes on another dimension: Johann Hauser, Sylvain Lecocq, and Auguste Forestier were institutionalised and locked up, but

[5] Curious to see what happens when wheels crush obstacles, Auguste Forestier once piled stones on a railway track and derailed a train.
[6] *What are you doing after the apocalypse?* Musée d'ethnographie, Neuchâtel, 19 November 2011–24 June 2012.
[7] Note that in 2000, the Swiss railways put quotations from Swiss personalities on the walls of some of their carriages, including this one from Adolf Wölfli: 'O könnte ich fliegen wie ein Vogel, ich wäre nicht hier. Ich wäre sicher schon lange, im Gadalquivier.' (Oh, if only I could fly like a bird, I would not be here. I would certainly long since be in Guadalquivir.)

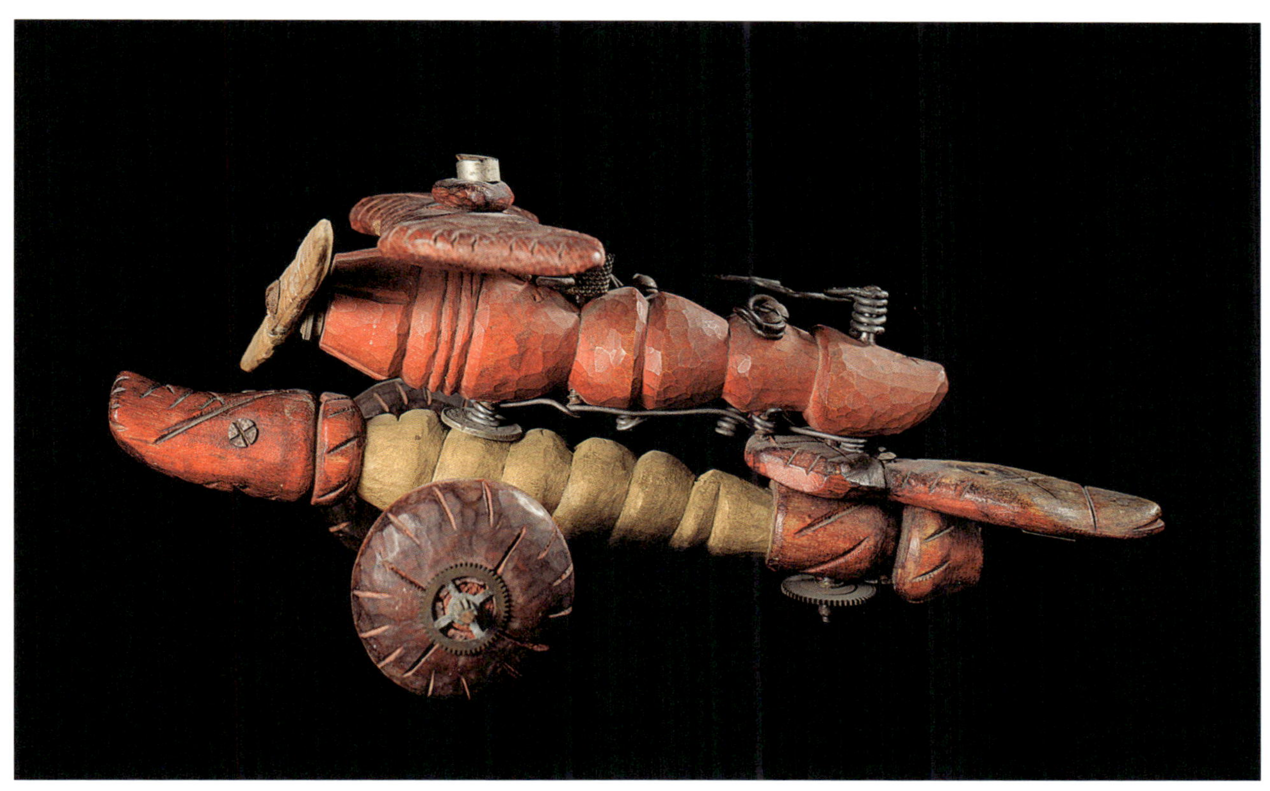

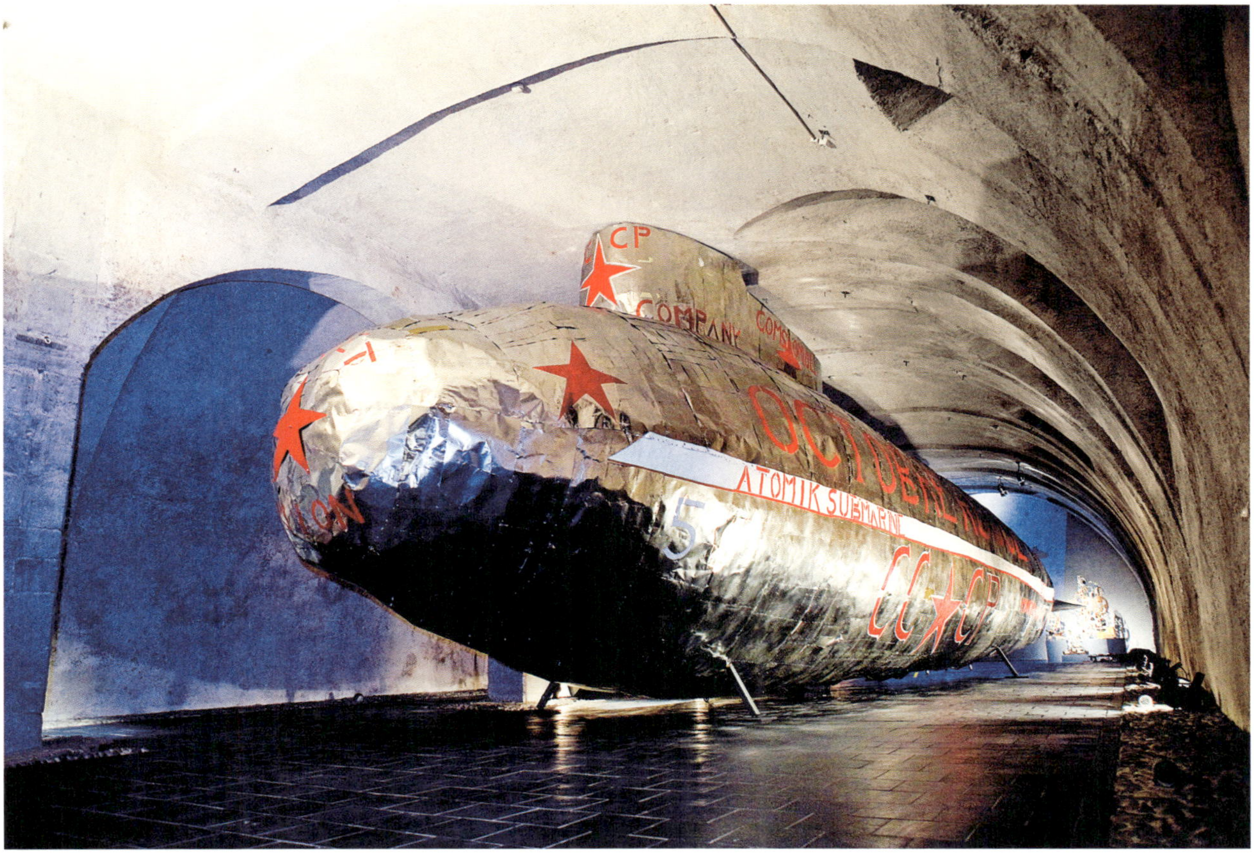

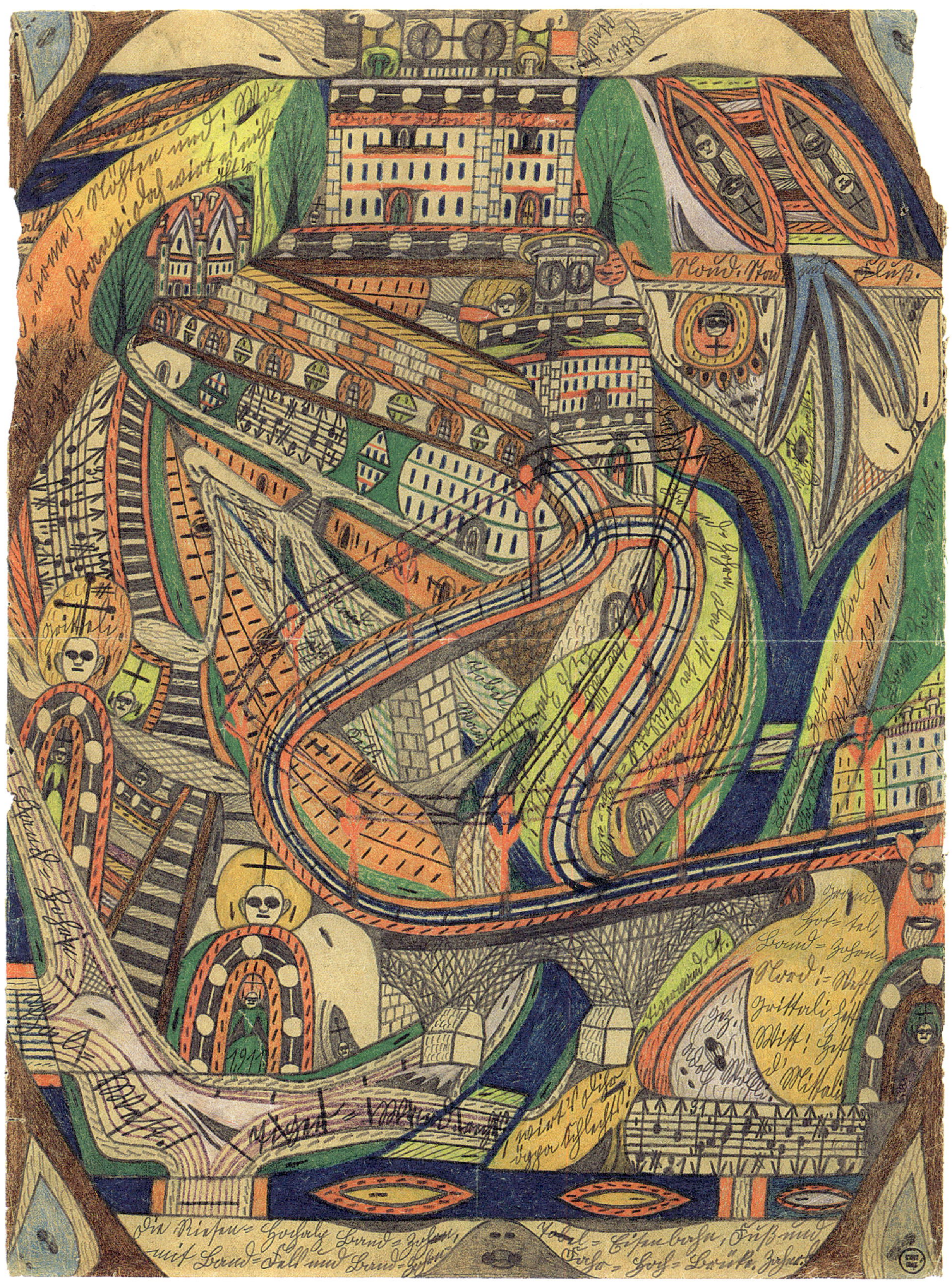

they each ran away several times.[8] Sylvain Lecocq was confined to a hospital and escaped by drawing a 'bocycling'[9] map of the Tour de France on Kraft paper. As the French cycle race was very popular, many people identified with the winners—Coppi, the pork butcher, or Bobet, the baker's boy—whose adventures were a way of rising above the common run of things. Yet François Burland had no illusions, saying: '[Death] mocks my determination to make aircraft, rockets and cars, because he knows I can never escape in them.'[10]

Although women are almost absent from this exhibition, it is a woman who perhaps found the best solution. Aloïse Corbaz transcended her life through drawing, living an imaginary love story. Her lovers ride in carriages, gondolas, trains, and boats. For the transports of love must surely be the way to seventh heaven.

Anic Zanzi
CURATOR, COLLECTION DE L'ART BRUT

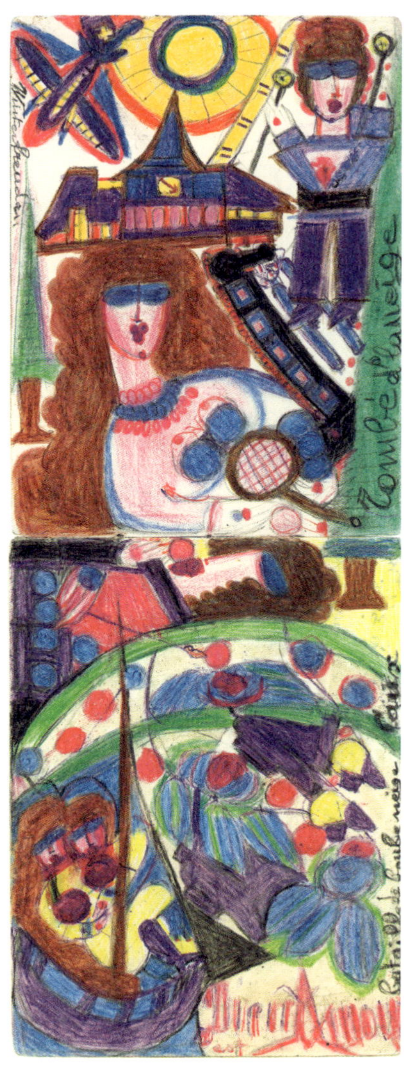

Aloïse
'Voici Noël' (This is Christmas) album,
1941–51
lead and coloured pencil on paper
21.5 x 57 cm (open album page)

[8] Psychiatrists observed a veritable epidemic of mad travellers in the late nineteenth century. Many medical studies looked at the urge to escape from the angle of hysteria or epilepsy as a way of explaining travellers' lack of conscience or amnesia. See Savine Faupin, 'Le voyageur immobile,' in *Trait d'union, Les Chemins de l'art brut à Saint-Alban-sur-Limagnole,* Lille Moderne Musée d'art moderne, Lille, 2007.
[9] Sylvain Lecocq also used invented words in many of his texts. In 1949, the year when he drew his Tour de France, the race went through his home town of Boulogne-sur-Mer.
[10] *François Burland: Space Cowboy, les jouets, die Spielzeuge*, 2009.

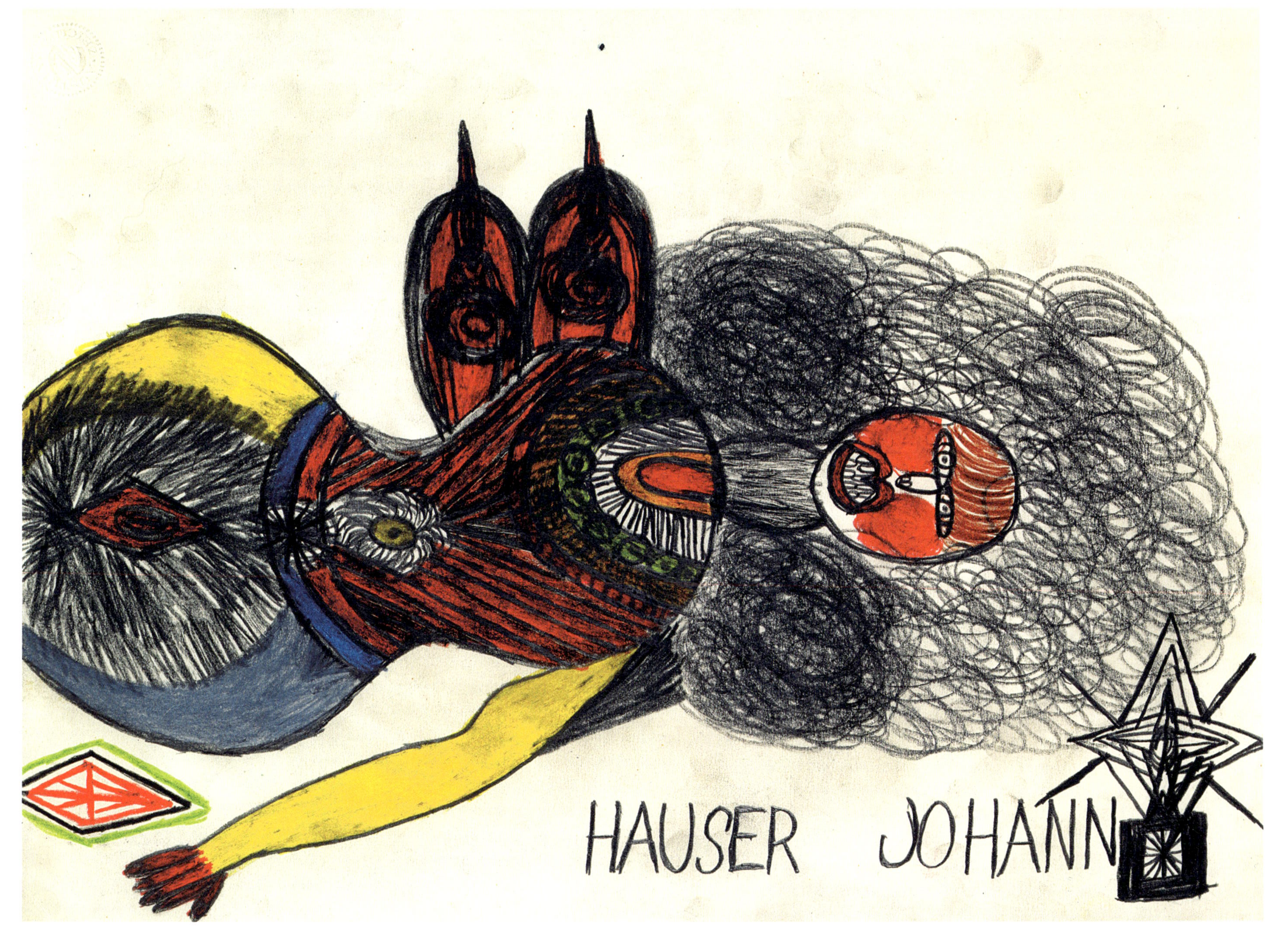
HAUSER JOHANN

Move Along!

◂ **Johann Hauser**
Untitled, 1969
lead pencil, coloured pencil
and crayon on paper
40 x 30 cm

Johann Hauser
Untitled, between 1966 and 1982
lead pencil and coloured pencil
on paper
21 x 29.7 cm

At first glance, we are struck by the number and variety of vehicles in this Art Brut collection, and their resemblance to toys rather than to real machines. It is a marvellous fleet (nothing to do with a parking lot!), that takes us on a jubilant ride back to childhood. But after the initial rush of tenderness, we begin to mull it over. In the age of high speed, technical prowess and global interfaces, why this passion for the auto bodies we have discarded along the way? There is something archaic in this theme that is as much ontogenetic (the child's toy) as phylogenetic (the heroic age of mechanical locomotion) that we are led to interpret in terms of mental regression, fixation or obsessive-compulsive disorder. So be it! Let's go for anamnesis and pathological objectification, and then reverse the perspective when the time comes, on the cinematographic principle of shot/reverse shot.

The archetypal vehicle is obviously the mother's womb. The pushchair is its first avatar: the baby lives in it and is attached to it. It is a uterine prosthesis, needed because the human species is born prematurely, condemning the infant to be wheeled about for the first year of its life, whereas any other mammal can walk after a few days. A human being is originally *carried*. And his first fantasies drive him to reverse this passiveness, to imagine independence before he can achieve it, to bring about the separation. When that happens, perceiving the machine from the outside and pushing it along in play is one of the first formative experiences of self-awareness, objectivity, spatial awareness, and instrumental function.

In any case, if there is one common denominator in all the vehicles in this exhibition, regardless of their diversity, it is their anthropomorphic nature, the pervasiveness of a somatic matrix, the confusion of bodily organs and mechanical parts. Benjamin Arneval, for example, gives us an endoscopic representation of a car or a plane, seen from both inside and out, which mobilises proprioceptive sensitivity. He reminds us that the image starts as a modality of the subject's own body—and the image of the vehicle is the anticipation of independence and mobility. This ambivalence is accentuated in Johann Hauser's work: he composes his drawings from a set of graphic elements, all of verifiable anatomical if not sexual origin: the phallus, which turns into a fuselage or aircraft wings or wings or a rocket; a tuft of pubic hair, whose concentric lines reappear in car wheels or windows; the curve of a breast which may become aerodynamic.

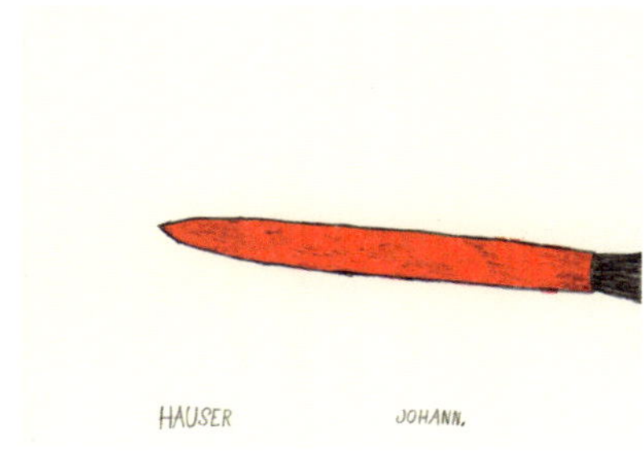

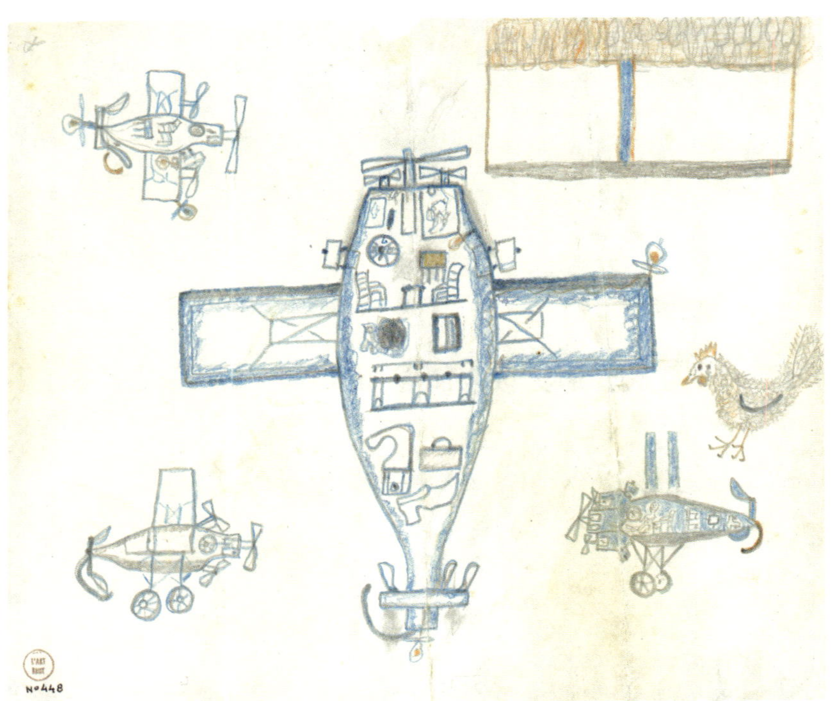

Benjamin Arneval
Untitled, 1948
lead pencil and coloured pencil on paper
21 x 27 cm

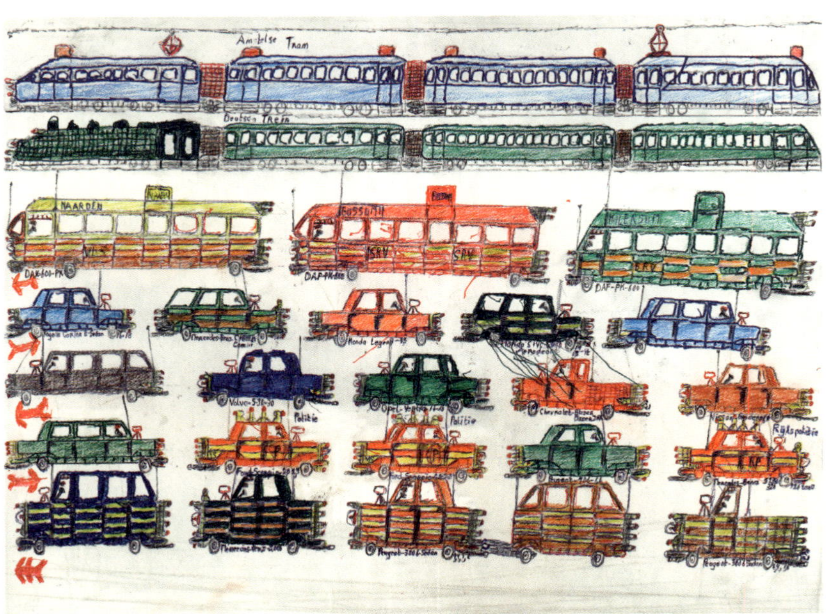

Hans Ploos Van Amstel
Amstelse Tram, ca. 1999
marker, ballpoint pen, lead pencil, crayon and gouache on paper
61 x 85.7 cm

In other words, the representation of a vehicle shows the conversion of the first corporeal fantasies into *signifiers*, in the linguistic and psychoanalytical sense of the term. Vehicles such as bicycles, cars, or trucks are produced on an assembly line. They are put together from prefabricated parts, comparable to the phonemes of language, characters in writing or notes in music. They take their place in a communication network and obey a road code not unlike the rules of syntax. The repetitive insistence on a standard vehicle in many different contexts, its polysemy and its

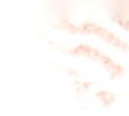

Dominique Bertoliatti
Untitled, ca. 1990
coloured felt pen on paper
27 x 38.5 cm

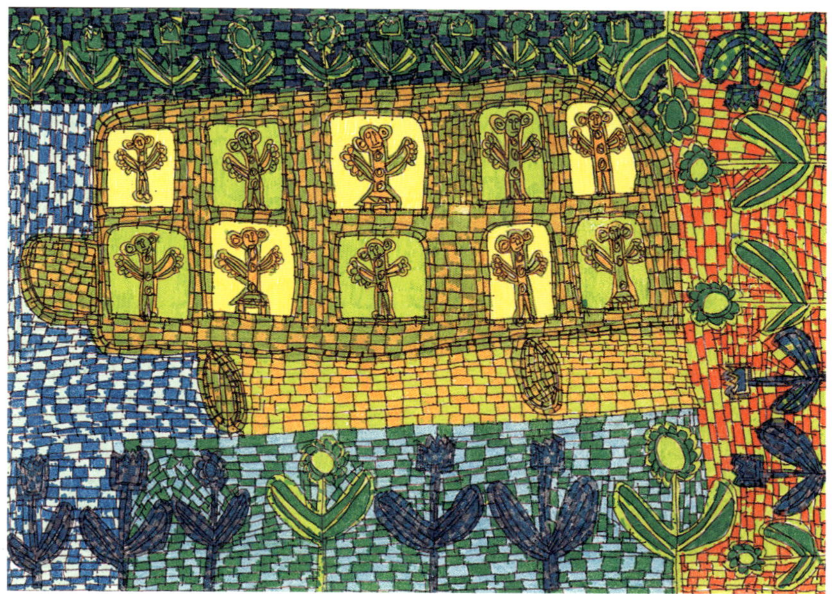

mobility are part of socialisation, exchange, communication, in short, part of what psychoanalysis still calls a symbolic system. At least that is how Lacan describes the individual genesis of symbolism: a return to the primordial maternal objects (womb, breast, milk, etc.), giving rise to terms that set in motion a process of substitution—Lacan calls it 'signifierisation'. The vehicle belongs to a group of preverbal but already 'social' play figures with a metaphorical function—dolls, soft toys, construction sets, and so on—which carry the original maternal pouch into their respective imaginative and symbolic registers.

Dominique Bertoliatti uses drawing as a form of magical incantation: he is transported (literally and metaphorically) in the maternal passenger compartment. He resuscitates the pleasant confusion of life in the womb, the paradise lost in which there was no need to distinguish between the real and the imaginary, between subjectivity and objectivity, inside and outside, stability and movement. Reality is still as labile and ductile as dreams: it is the dwelling that precedes any injunction to realism.

Incidentally, we see here a first significant case of discrimination: the almost total absence of women in this theme exhibition (as in cultural art in general), although it has often been claimed that women have taken their revenge in Art Brut. This 'misogynist' imbalance can probably be explained by the first playful stage of education and the sexist division of toys: dolls for girls (pushchairs, at the limit), but electric train-sets and lorries for boys, in compliance with a diehard division of roles, as old as the human species, which kept women at home by the fire and freed men for hunting and gathering.

In all respects, the vehicle as a signifier takes us from one connection to another (in the sense of logic, poetry, and public transport): a steady stream of conveyance from the pushchair to the hearse, via the tricycle,

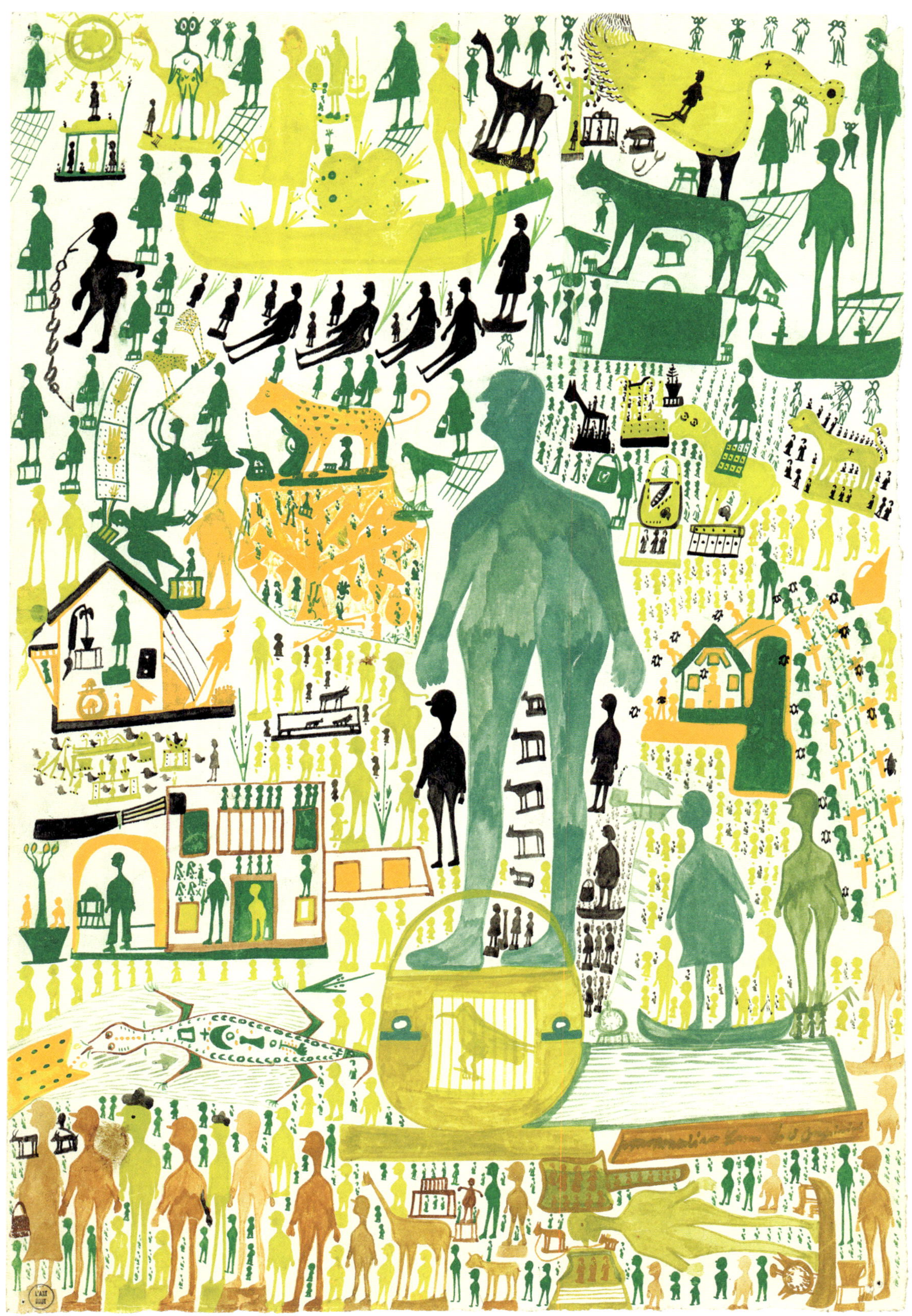

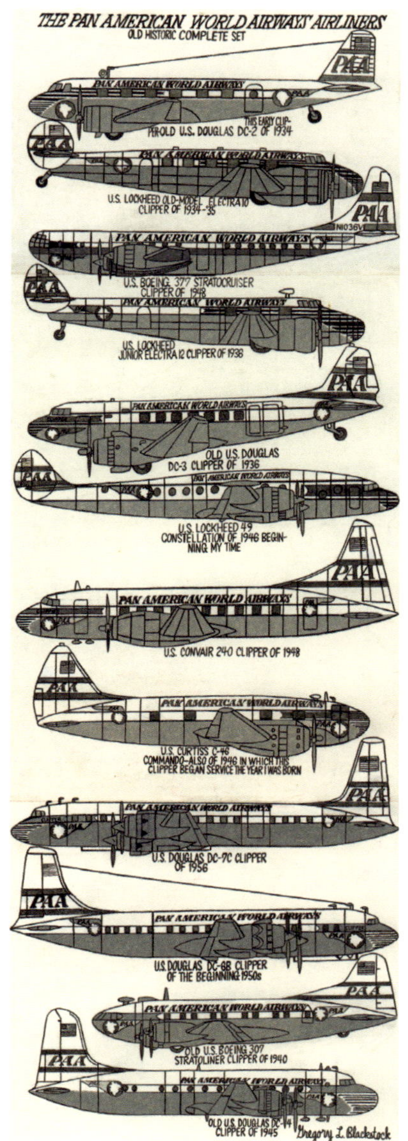

Gregory L. Blackstock
The Pan American World Airways Airliners, 2010
lead pencil, felt pen and crayon on paper
131.8 x 45.1 cm

‹ **Carlo Zinelli**
Untitled, 1960
gouache on paper
35 x 50 cm

bicycle, moped, car, and aeroplane, and it fuels the imagery of locomotion. Through his first toys, then real utilitarian vehicles, Lacan's *hommelette* transits from an anatomical uterus to an engine cockpit, from a diffuse proto-existence to independence, from indissociation to individuation, from nature to the *socius* or individual in society. The various means of locomotion will have carried him from the fusional state to the mastery of a standard, collective technical object—an acquisition effectively comparable to that of language.

Carlo Zinelli is a particularly significant case. He treats the human figure as a stereotype, endlessly multiplied, which makes the machine itself seem more alive. Does that mean he deplores the standardisation of humanity? Perhaps. But in this graphic cloning we sense the dynamism of a series, the poetry of repetition, a syncopated rhythm, the euphoria of locomotion, and ultimately a celebration rather than a denunciation of the machine-man. In his own way, Carlo illustrates Lacan's paradox, which associates man with machines rather than with animals: the beast is imprisoned by its instincts, whereas the machine is open to choices and new uses. It operates in the practical field what language permits in the symbolic order. Depending on the context, it can signify freedom as much as automatism.

We must therefore be wary of a Jungian type of interpretation, assimilating a means of transport to an archetype or giving each sort of vehicle a specific meaning, taken from a dictionary of symbols. On the contrary, the mobile machine should be seen as one of those free-wheeling polysemic figures, devoid of fixed meaning but lending itself to multiple contextual relationships, like a face, a person, a house, etc. If ever there were a signifier that stays true to itself, but is always on the move, conveying all possible meanings, it is indeed the vehicle. Move along, nothing to see here, because it is Lacan's *voyure* itself which reveals the signifiers that structure it.

That helps explain the encyclopaedic verve of artists such as Gregory Blackstock or Han Ploos van Amstel: they catalogue vehicles of the same type, distinguished only by brand, colour, and so forth, on the principle of a paradigm, and arrange them in rows or columns, in a syntactic succession. The signifying process is clear, taking us in this case from the cortège of vehicles to the linear order of the written page, that is, once again from the imaginary to the symbolic. Incidentally, Han Ploos van Amstel occasionally practises *boustrophedon*, switching the direction of the traffic on alternate lines, as in texts in Ancient Greece. What better way to bring out the correspondence between the file of vehicles and the order of words on the page?

Polysemy is particularly strong for rail transport. Thus Clément Fraisse articulates the antithetic meanings of a railway wagon. Kept in close confinement in a psychiatric hospital, he carved obsessively on the wooden wall of his cell a figure of a person locked in a compartment, which could be interpreted as the *mise en abyme* of his own situation.

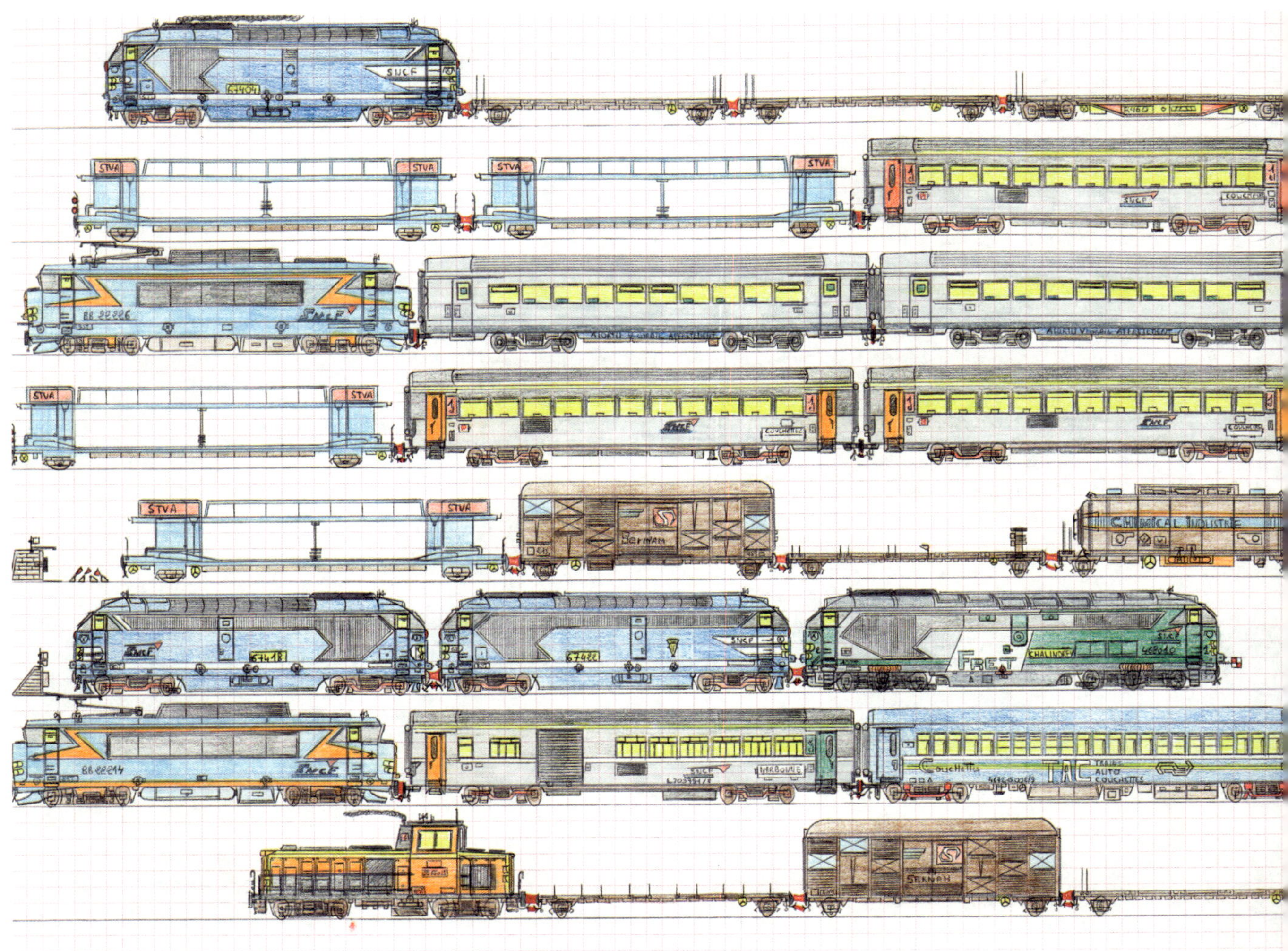

David Braillon
MAESRK, 2002
ballpoint pen and coloured pencil on paper
29.7 x 83.5 cm

But the wagon wheels that he scratched under this concentration-camp composition symbolise freedom. Willem van Genk uses transportation as an exploration of his inner space, warding off his fears by projecting them into metal monsters that rush through the world's megacities and plunge into the depths of the subconscious in a furious din.

Public transport can also surface in the punitive register of the superego. In the 1980s, Martial, called the 'bus-man', roamed through the streets of Lausanne pushing a handcart that he had ingeniously converted into a mock trolleybus, complete with catenaries and a dashboard crammed with switches and indicators. Puffed up with importance, he paraded about the streets, manifestly feeling he controlled the very symbol of power, order, and public service, treating the pedestrians like low life in the barnyard. He berated the passers-by, calling them to order and exhorting them to keep to the line as scrupulously as he did himself, on pain of derailment. Unlike 'a streetcar called desire', his trolleybus called *duty* illustrated the principle of the ordering of the world and social life. Apart from constructing his trolleybuses, most of which alas! he finally destroyed, Martial drew the

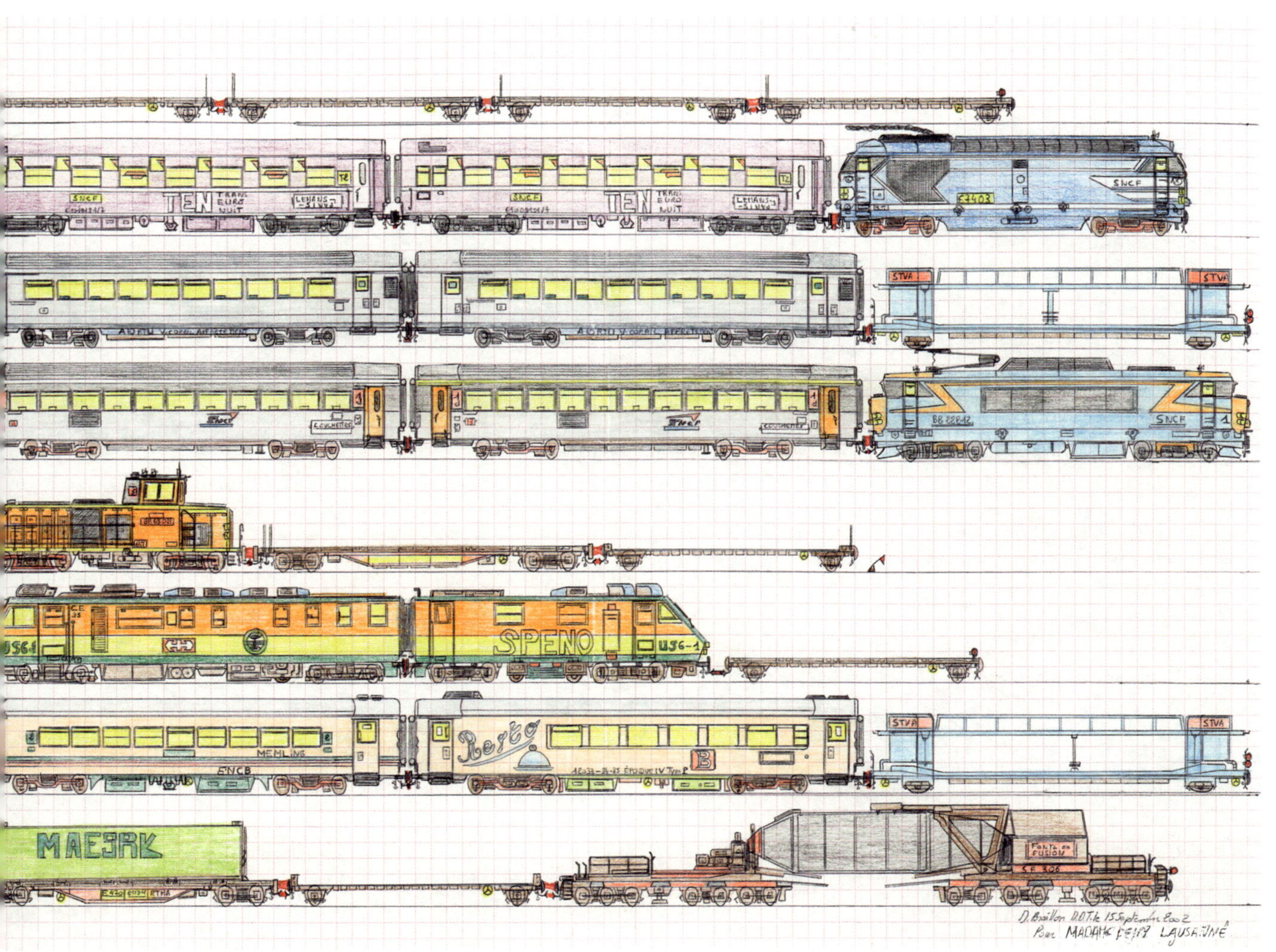

mesh of overhead wires, stark against the sky, like a city transport map and, at the same time, prison bars. Railway lines also often appear as a visual metaphor for rectitude, especially in the work of David Braillon, a long-term prisoner, who rebuilt his life through his drawings, shunting his carriages along the rails like a string of signifiers.

We suddenly realise that the incredibly rich, inventive imagery of locomotion in Art Brut takes us back to the forgotten sources of what we mean by 'art': magic, possession, incantation, therapy, game-playing and all the premises of objectivity. Undoubtedly a regressive step—but regression is unjustly taxed with indigence. Infantile archaism takes us back to the stage of potentialities, to the promise of a crossroads, to the richness of beginnings, to unexploited anthropological reserves, to luxuriant cultural wastelands. Walter Benjamin talked of the 'leaven of the unfinished'; finishing comes down to eliminating the competing virtualities that would have been worth lingering over. And linger is exactly what these 'laggards' do.

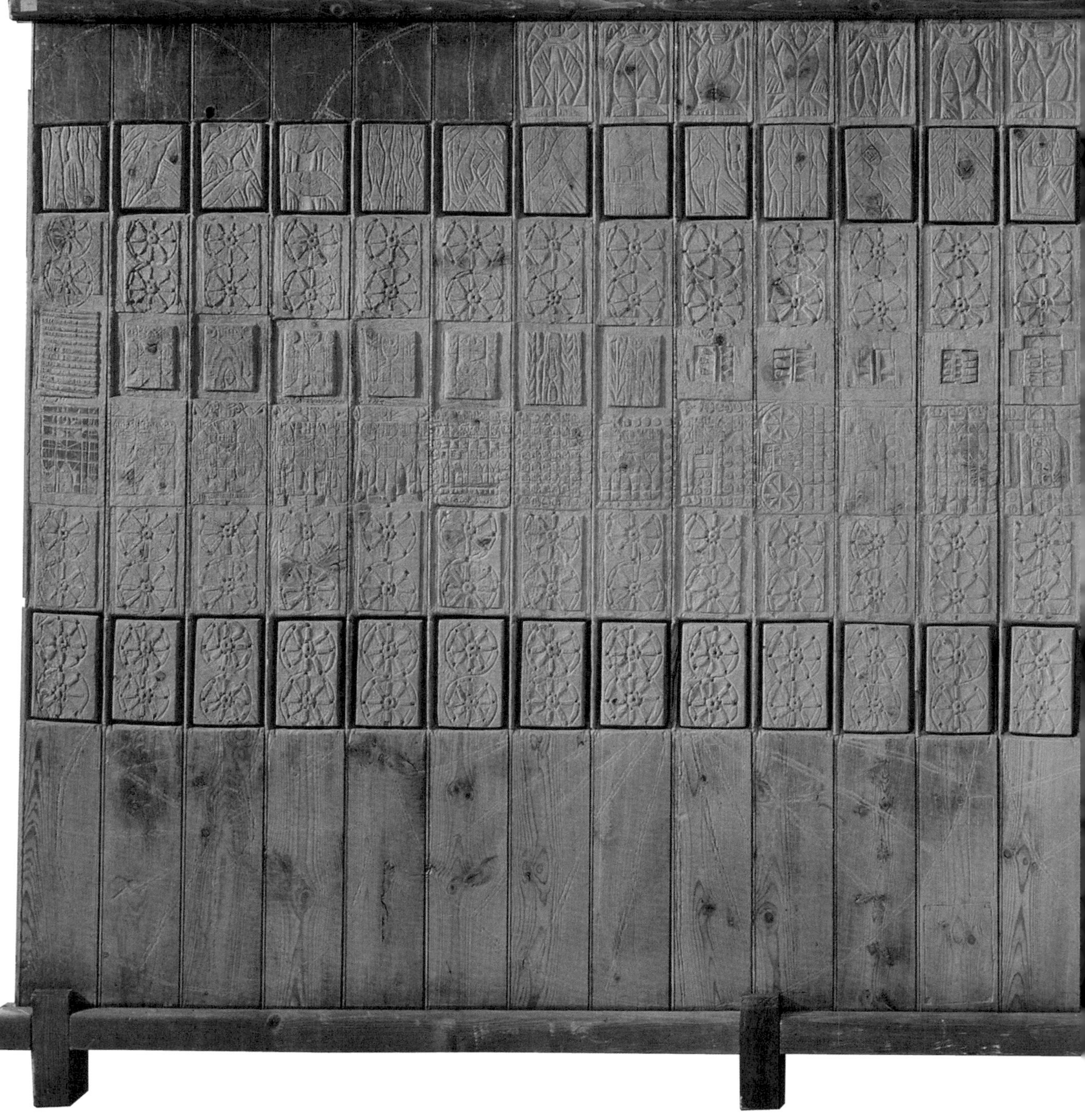

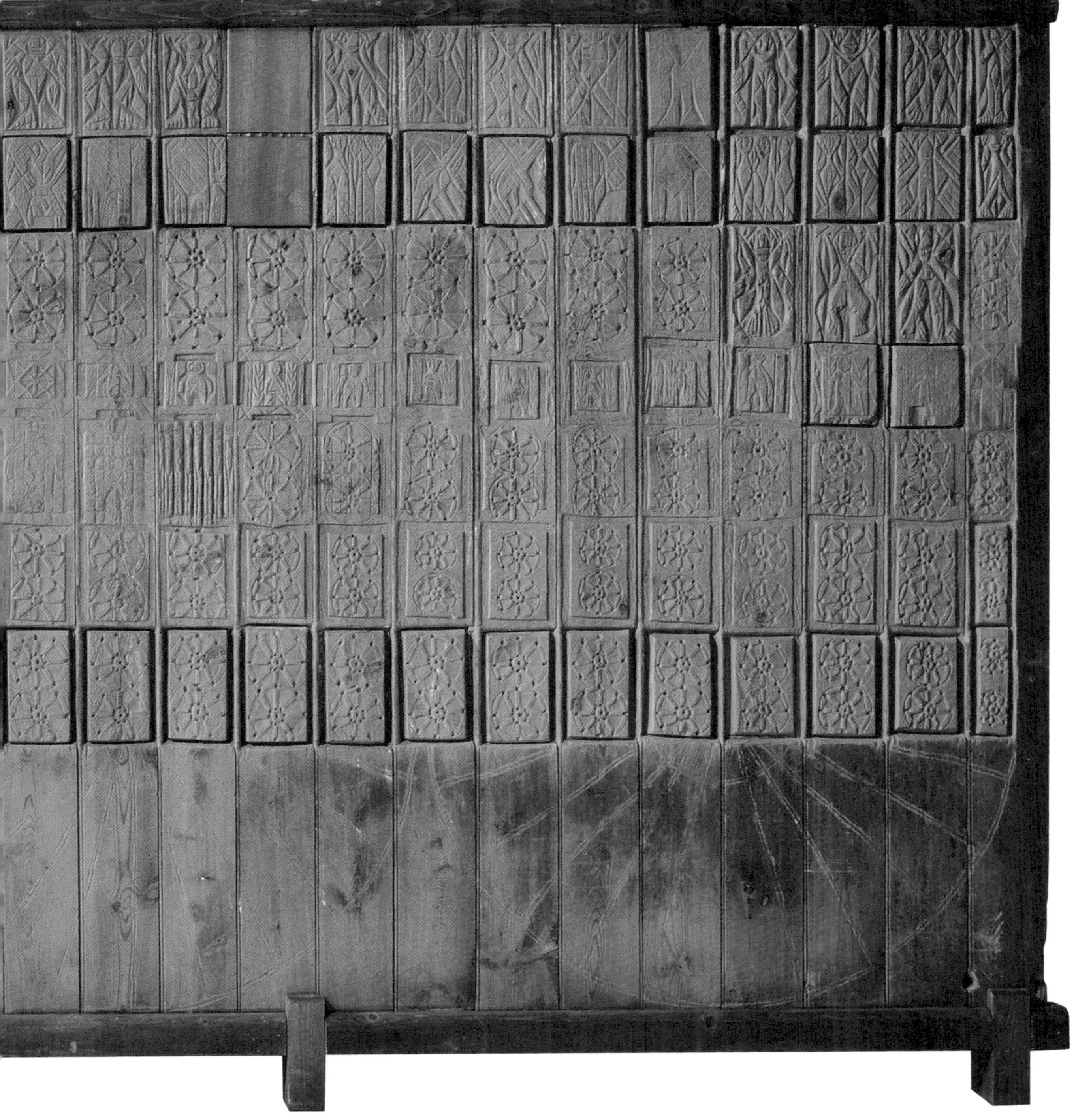

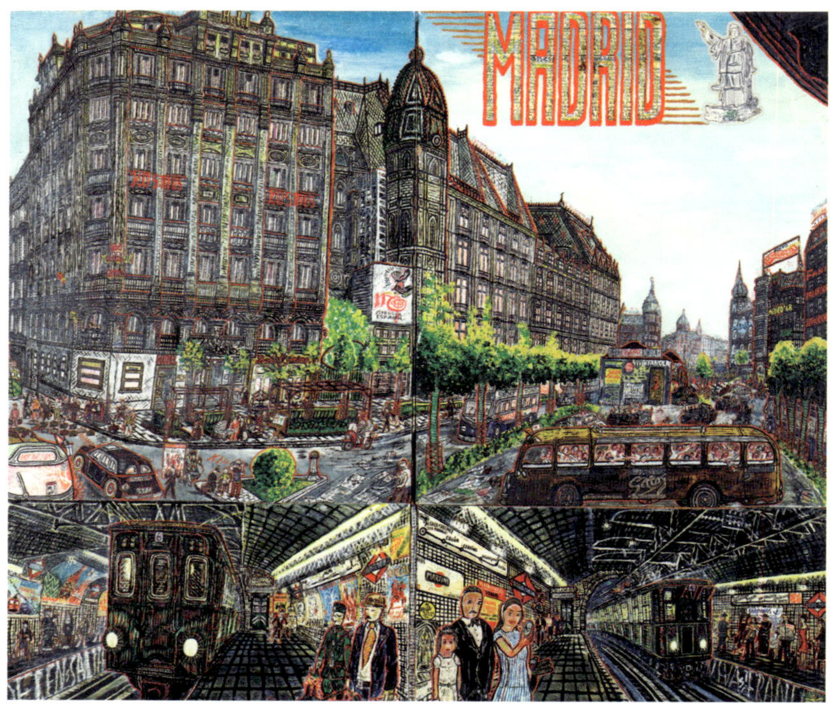

◂◂ Clément Fraisse
Untitled, between 1930 and 1931
wood
170 x 383 cm

Willem Van Genk
Madrid, 1968
paint on pavatex
86.5 x 105.6 cm

Historically and paradoxically, the vehicle as we commonly understand it, that is, a mechanical means of transport, appeared with sedentarisation. And the fantasies linked to it show, in a way, that the Neolithic revolution has not yet happened—at least, it has not yet realised all its virtualities, it has miscarried, it has been betrayed, it insists. The imagery of locomotion, in its most primitive forms, is still potential. So, Art Brut artists, those anthropological dissidents, those Neolithic retards, those anamnestic intruders, maintain and obstinately cultivate the memory of mobility full of infinite promise, which we have led off the track. They board the omnibus or the oxcart, and do not necessarily reach their destination, but they explore regions of which we, in our high-speed train, can only catch a glimpse.
It must be our techno-fascist arrogance that makes us smile in tenderness or commiseration: could these be deranged or retarded beings obsessively reproducing their childhood toys? The answer comes from our nebulous modernity, from air pollution, from the clouds of kerosene, and the globalisation of traffic congestion on the ground and in the air. Once it crosses a certain threshold of consumer hysteria, the automobile – originally a symbol of freedom and the fetish of Western prosperity – chokes our exchanges and brings disillusionment. All it signifies now is the breakdown of the symbolic chain of which it is the cause.
We suddenly see that the primitiveness, fetishism, totemism—in short, savageness—which we used to situate in the past and somewhere in Africa, has only just begun. It is more nightmarish than we thought, because it is taking on a global dimension. The private cars that jam the roads, the sports cars that cretinise, the SUVs emblematic of economic fascism, the tourist charters that will soon have put an end to travel, the

Martial Richoz
Untitled, ca. 1983
ballpoint pen and coloured pencil
on paper
22.1 x 20 cm

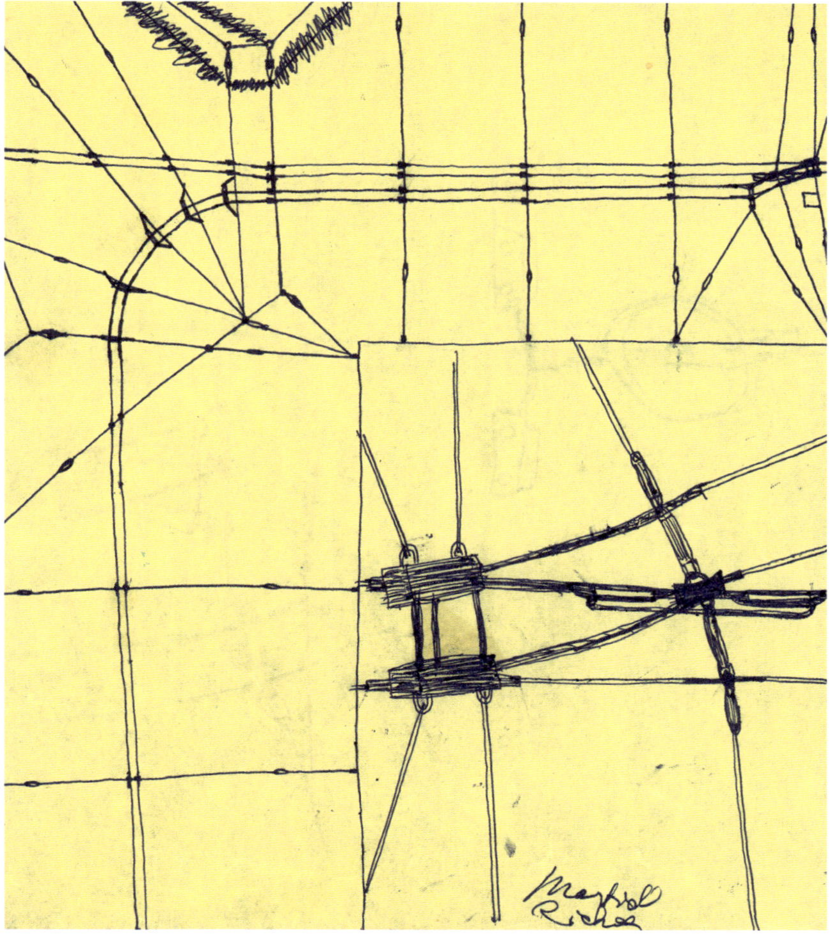

private jets of wealthy villains, fighter planes, the ridiculous Gripen, the killer drone—do we need to go on? If we want to investigate vehicle-related disorders, this is where to look! And this exhibition will have achieved one of its objectives if it leads us to such a counter perspective: to envisage mobility from the standpoint of childhood, the childhood that we leave like an illness, as the poet ironically commented. Plainly, the real illness is not where we think it is.

Michel Thévoz
FIRST CURATOR, COLLECTION DE L'ART BRUT

Catalogue

Abrignani, Giovanni p. 34
Arneval, Benjamin p. 38
Bachler, Josef p. 40
Badari, Fausto p. 42
Bertoliatti, Dominique p. 46
Blackstock, Gregory L. p. 50
Braillon, David p. 52
Burland, François p. 56
Byam, John p. 60
Carlo [Zinelli] p. 62
Delaunay, Serge p. 66
Di Giovanni, Curzio p. 68
Dobay, Anton p. 70
Feng Shi Yi p. 72
Forestier, Auguste p. 74
Hauser, Johann p. 78
Helmut [Nimczewski] p. 82
Hylton, Lorna p. 86
Kernbeis, Franz p. 88
Lecocq, Sylvain p. 92
Lemaire, Philippe p. 94
Mackintosh, Dwight p. 96
Mayor, Francis p. 100
Merritt, Gene p. 104
Motooka Hidenori p. 106
Pauzié, Alain p. 108
Ploos Van Amstel, Han p. 110
Pujolle, Guillaume p. 114
Ratier, Émile p. 118
Richoz, Martial p. 122
Robillard, André p. 124
Saletmeier, Hans p. 128
Sawada Shinichi p. 130
Stanton, André p. 132
Tourlonias, Jean p. 136
Van Genk, Willem p. 138
Vignes, Pépé p. 142
Widener, George p. 144
Zablatnik, Erich p. 148

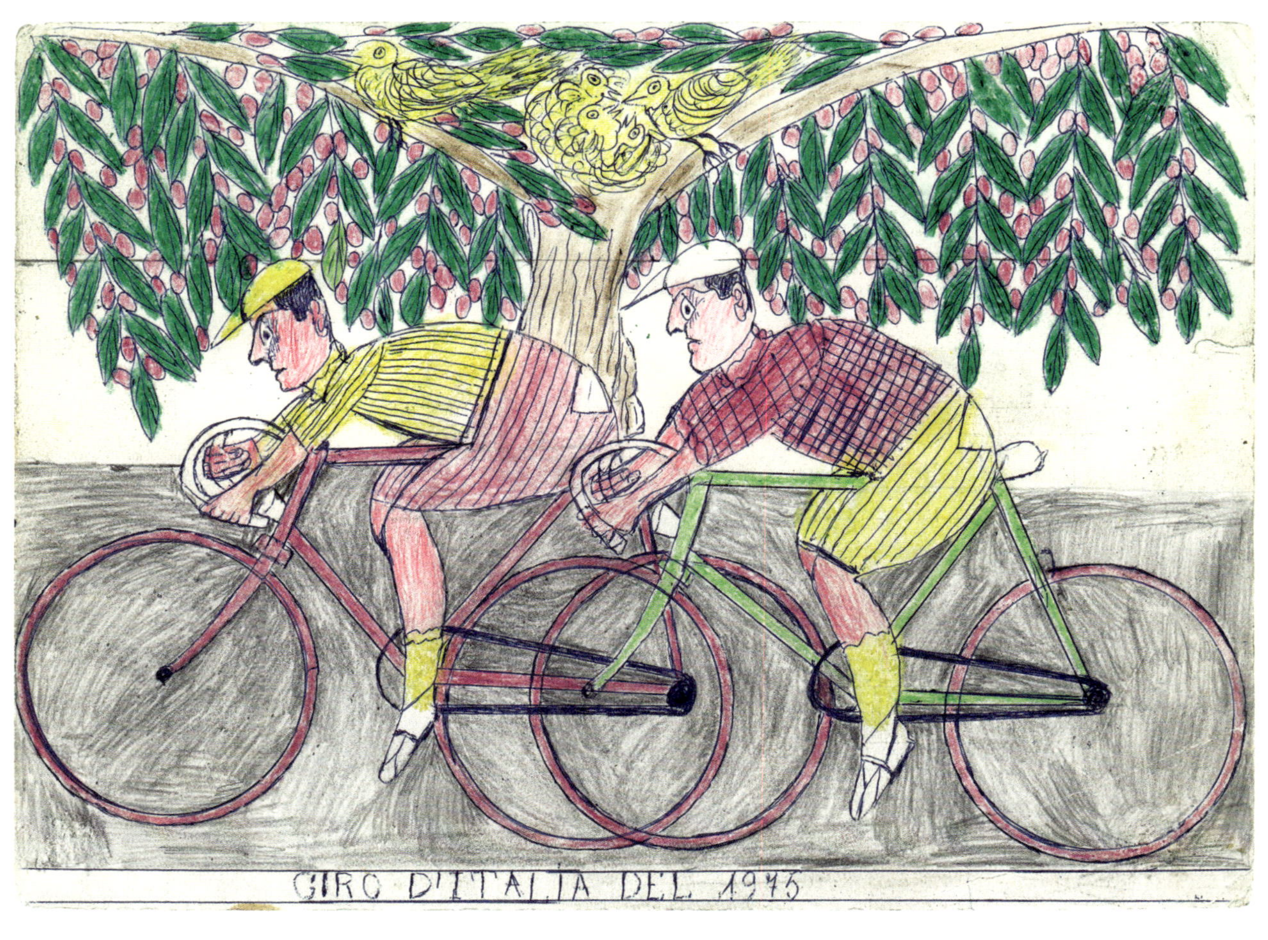

Giovanni Abrignani
Giro d'Italia del 1975, 1975
stylo-bille et crayon de cculeur sur papier
ballpoint pen and coloured pencil on paper
25 x 34,8 cm

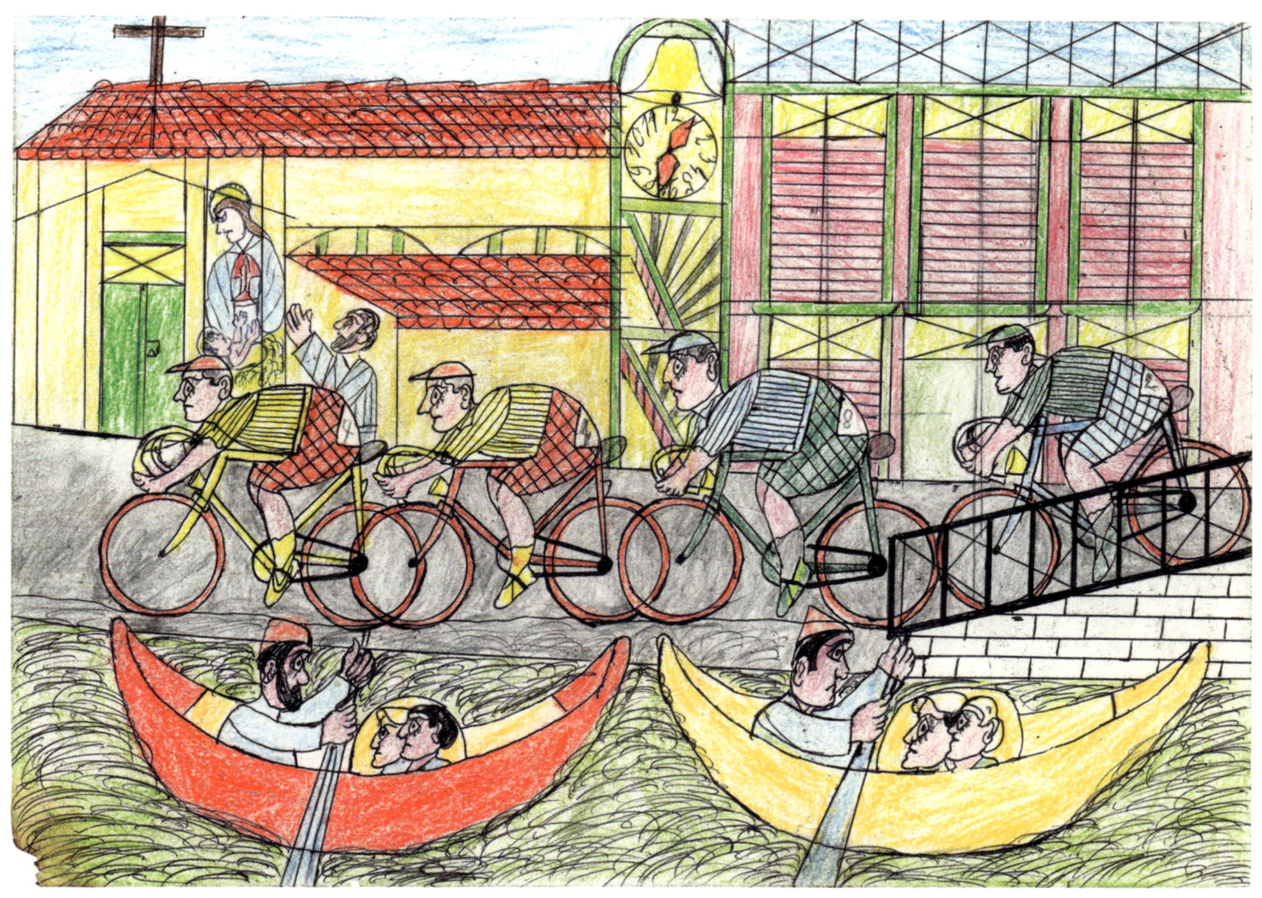

Giovanni Abrignani
Sans titre untitled, ca. 1967-1975
stylo-bille et crayon de couleur sur papier
ballpoint pen and coloured pencil on paper
21 x 33 cm

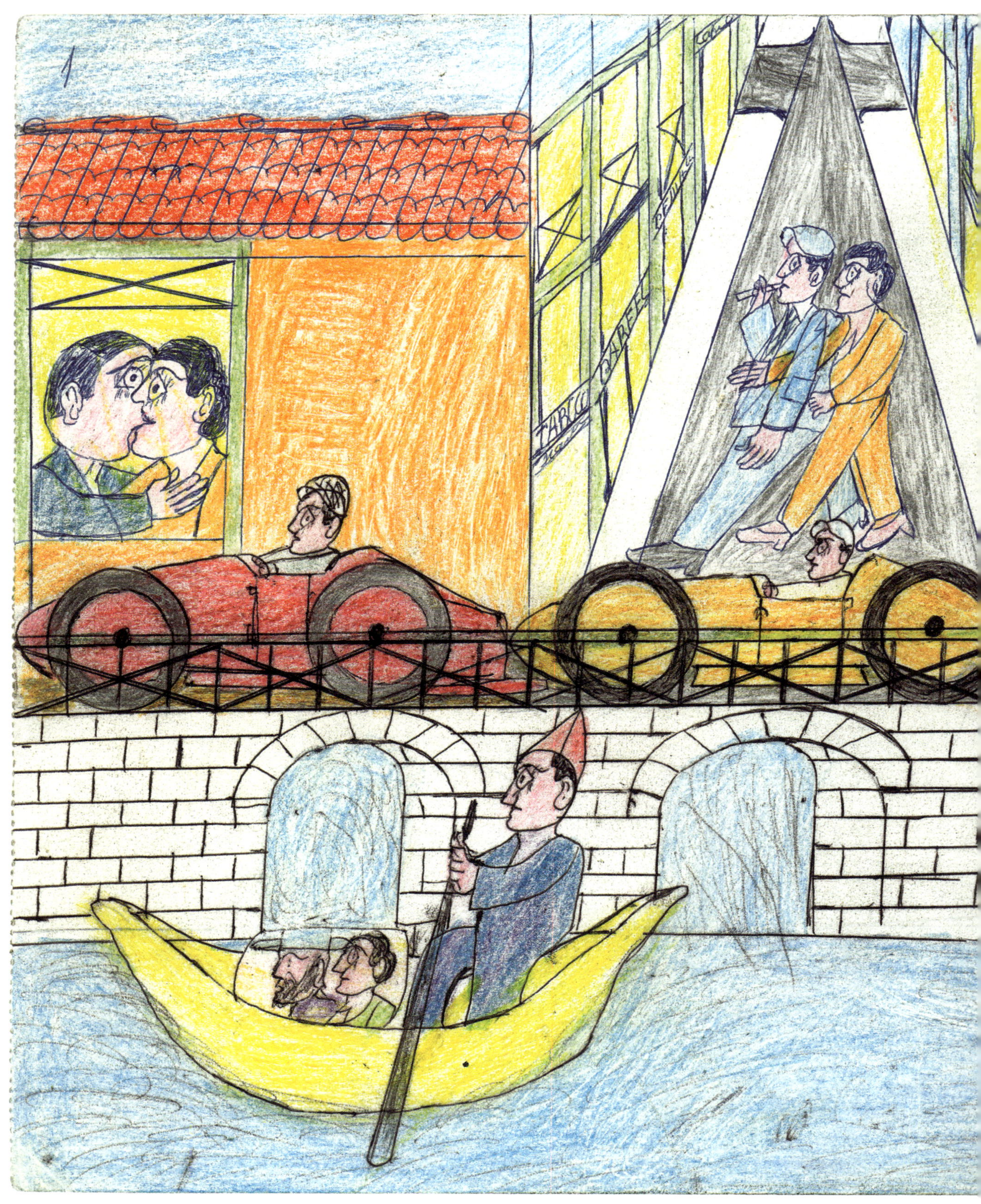

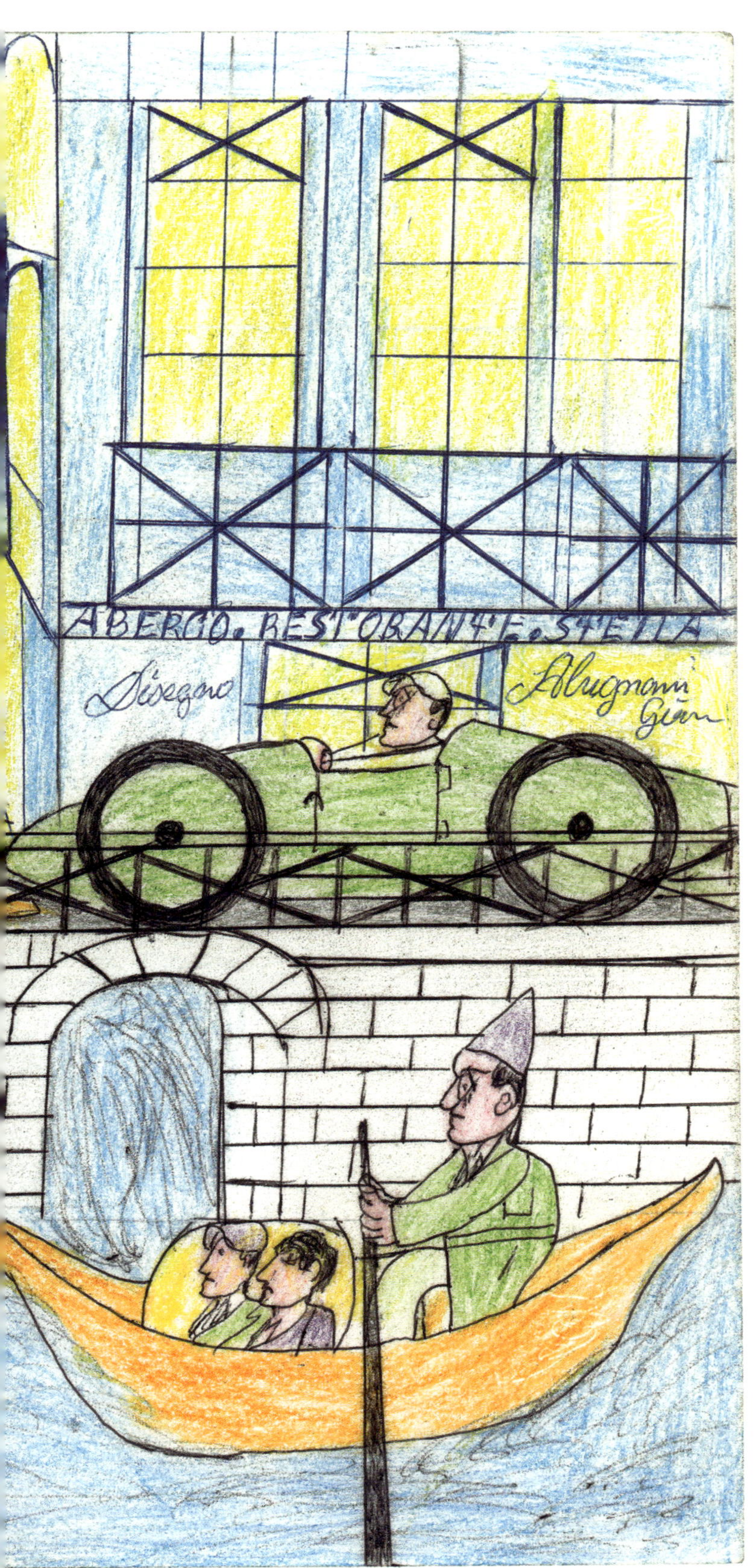

Giovanni Abrignani
Sans titre untitled, ca. 1967-1975
stylo-bille et crayon de couleur sur papier
ballpoint pen and coloured pencil on paper
24 x 33 cm

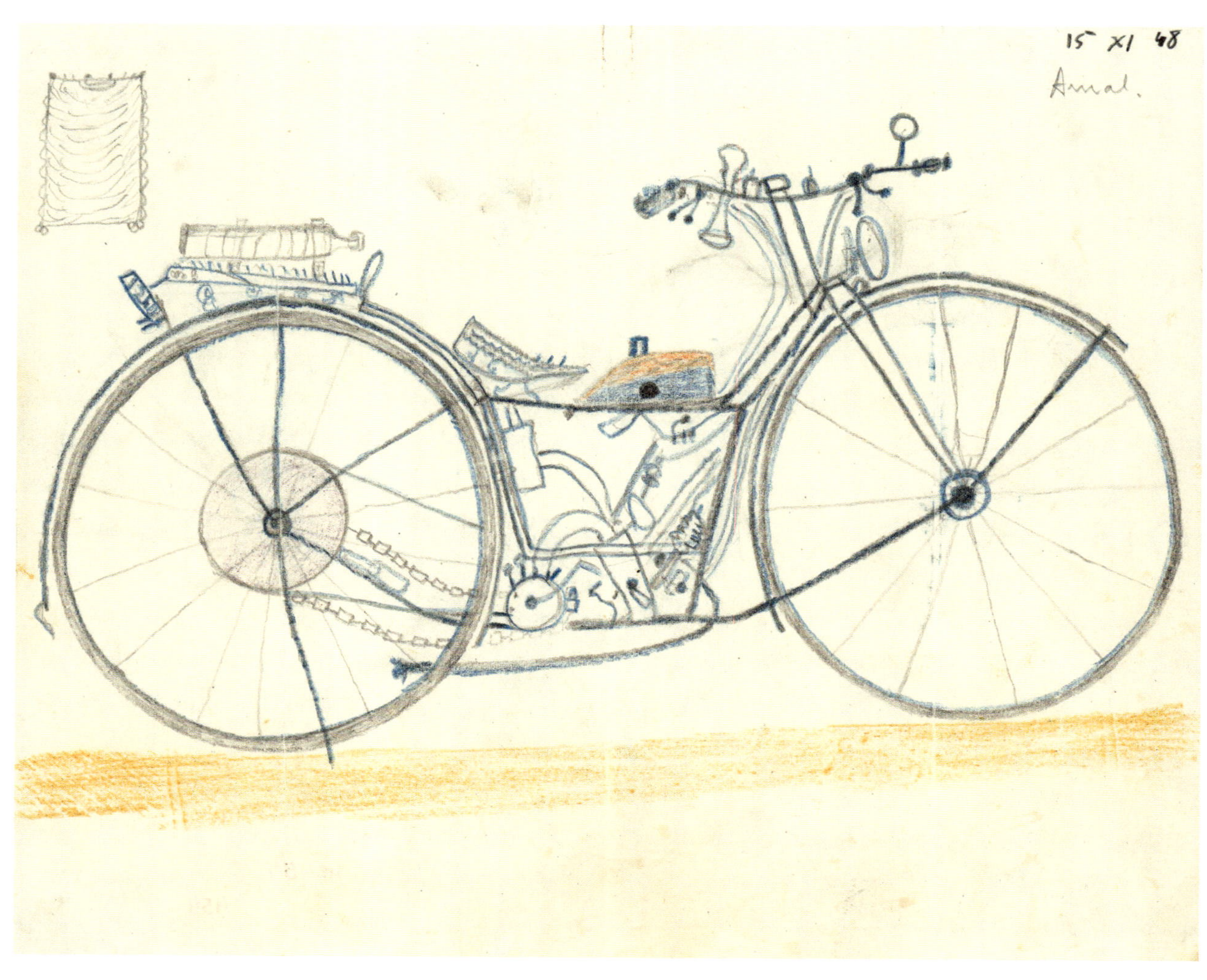

Benjamin Arneval
Sans titre untitled, 1948
mine de plomb et crayon de couleur
sur papier lead pencil and coloured
pencil on paper
21 x 27 cm

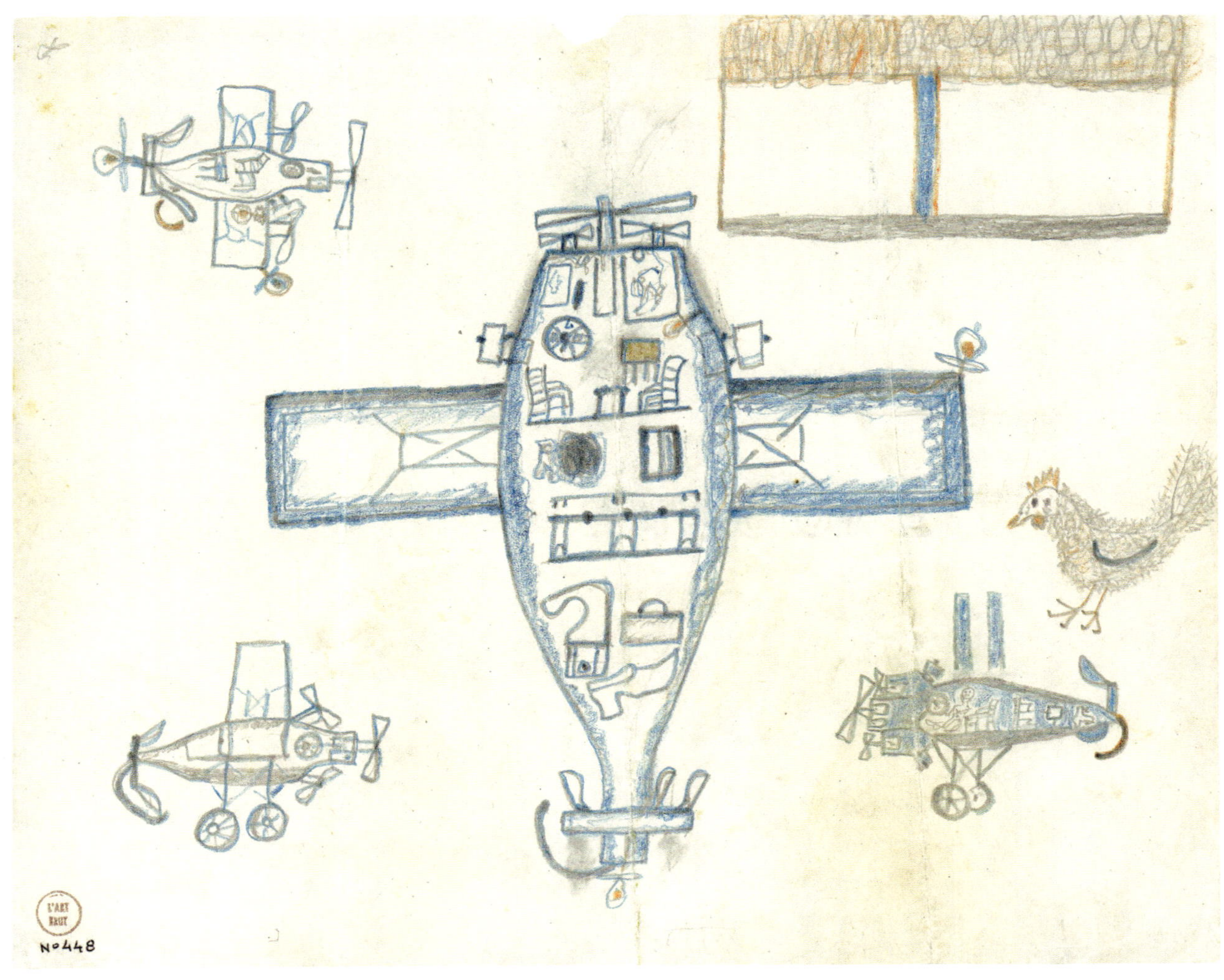

Benjamin Arneval
Sans titre untitled, 1948
mine de plomb et crayon de couleur sur papier lead pencil and coloured pencil on paper
21 x 27 cm

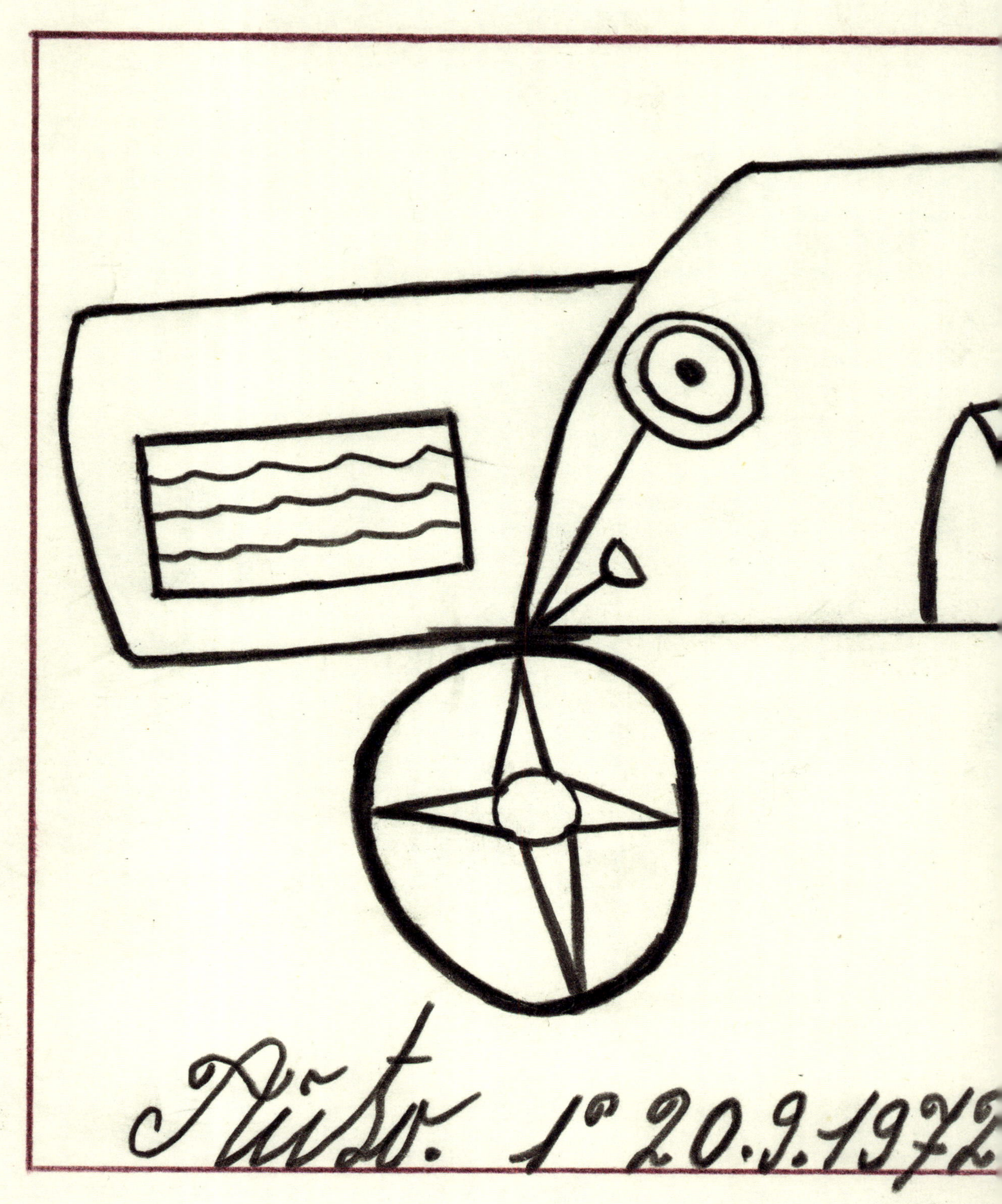
Auto. 1° 20.9.1972

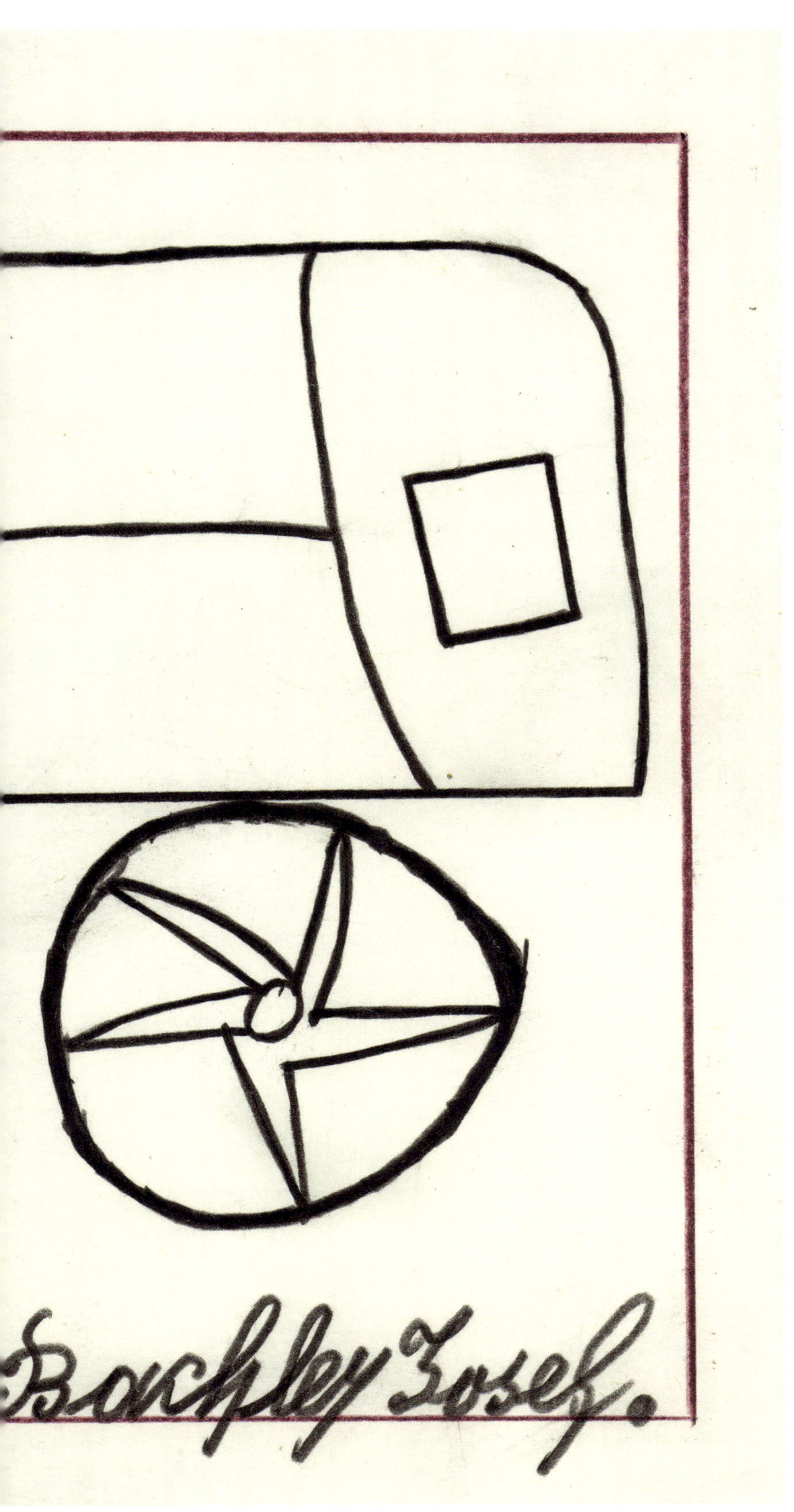

Josef Bachler
Auto 1, 1972
mine de plomb et crayon de couleur sur papier lead pencil and coloured pencil on paper
14,8 x 21 cm

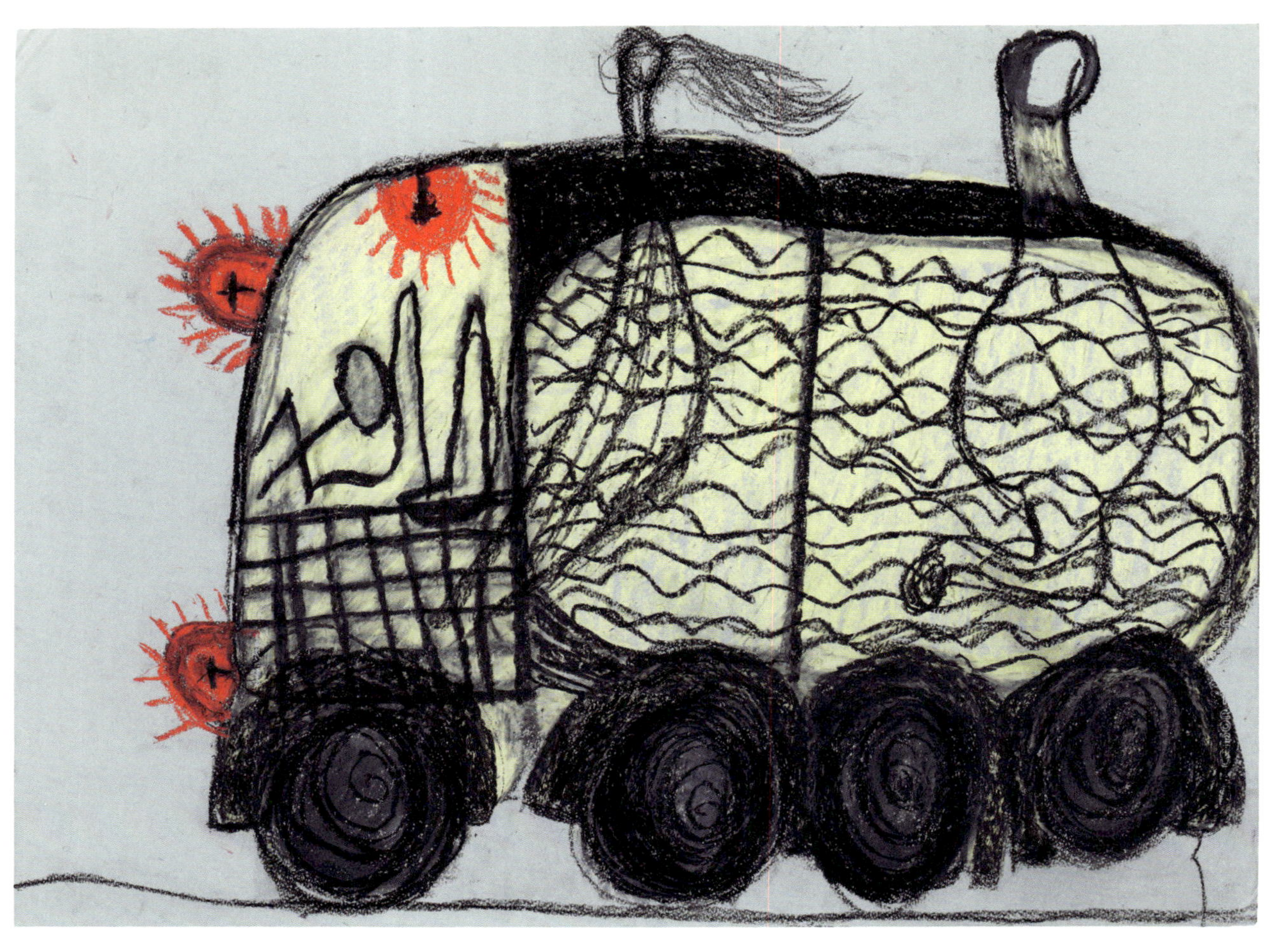

Fausto Badari
Sans titre untitled, 2011
craie grasse sur papier
crayon on paper
50 x 70 cm

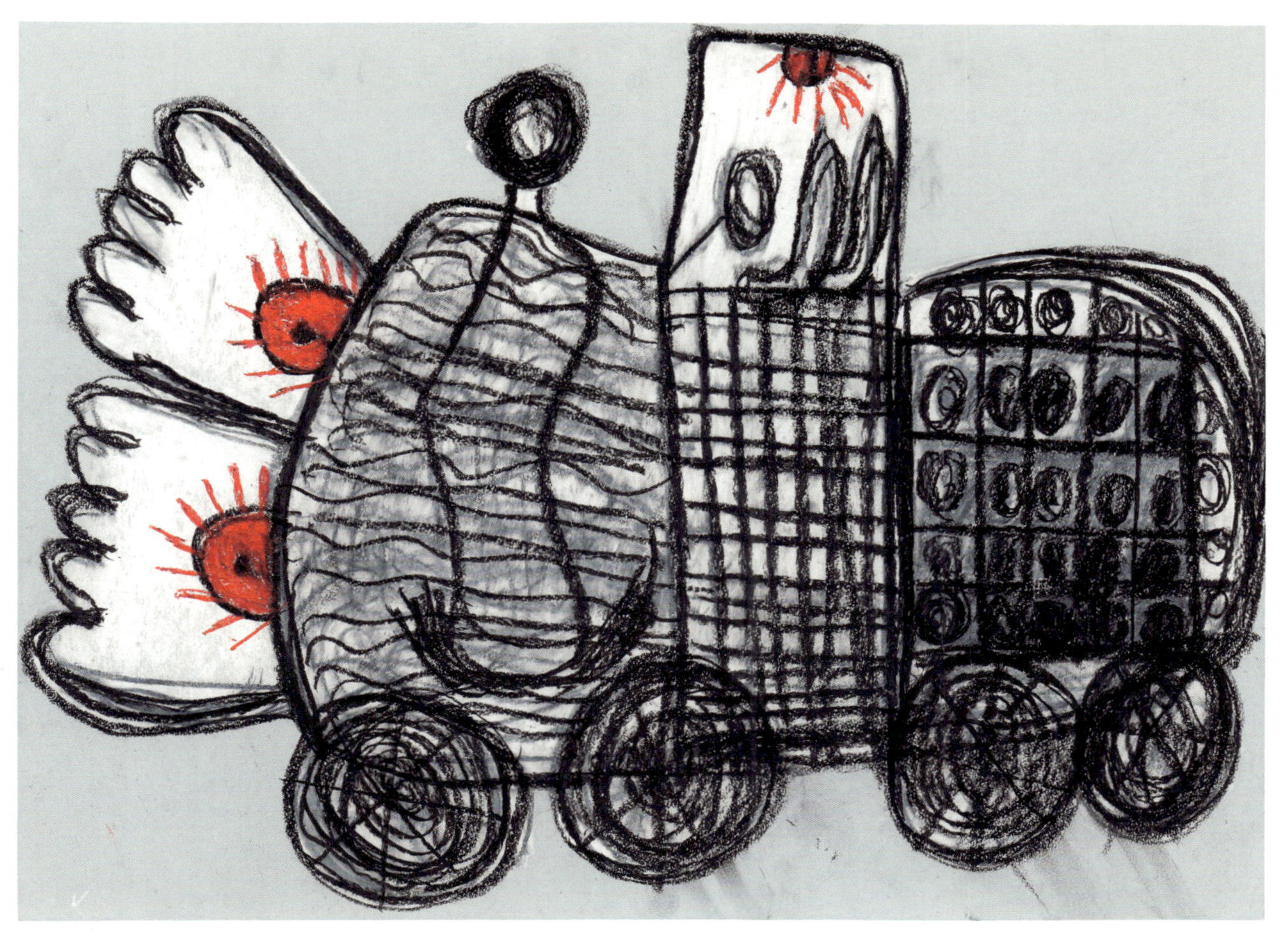

Fausto Badari
Sans titre untitled, 2011
craie grasse sur papier
crayon on paper
50 x 70 cm

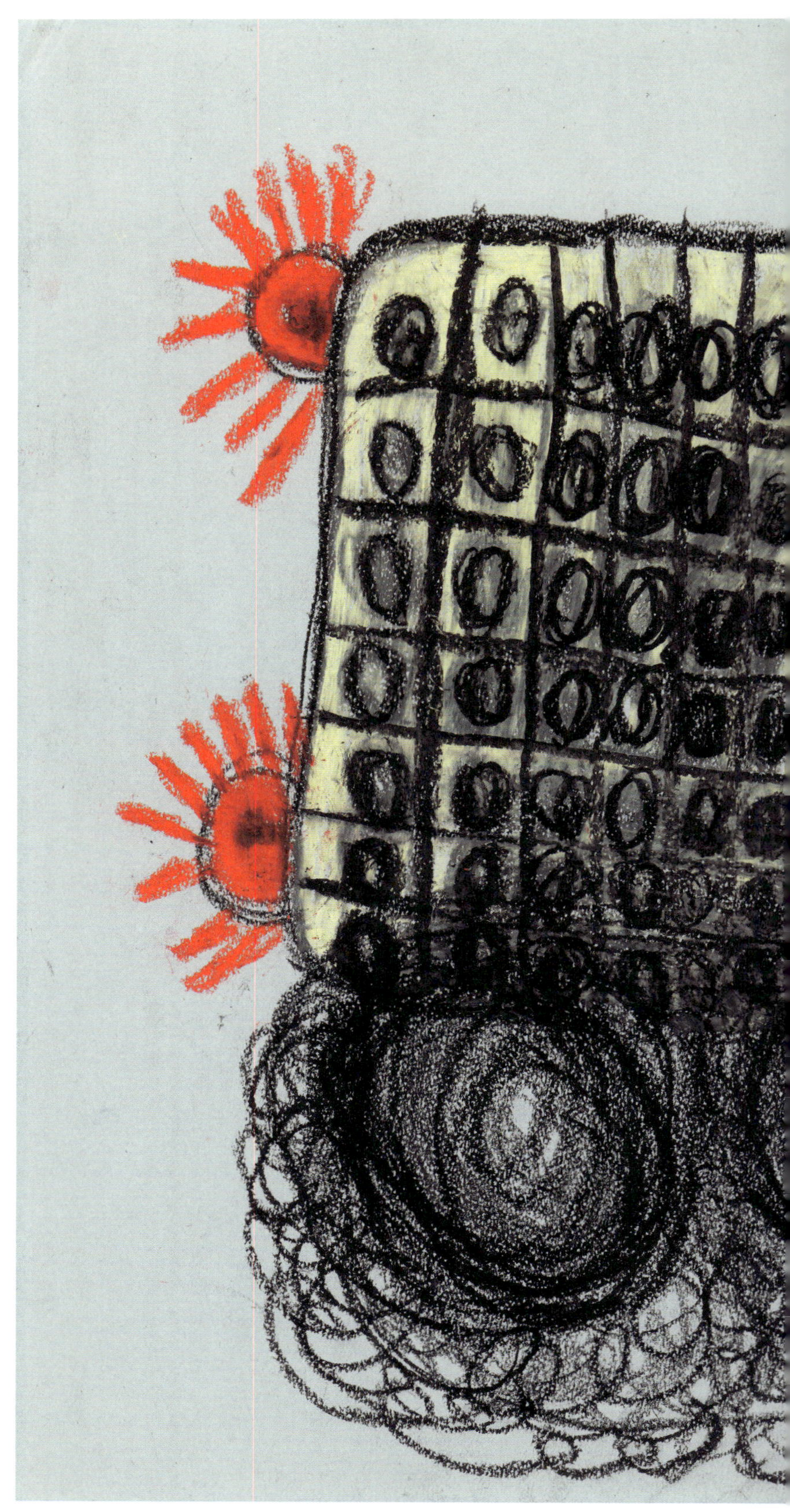

Fausto Badari
Sans titre untitled, 2010
craie grasse sur papier
crayon on paper
50 x 70 cm

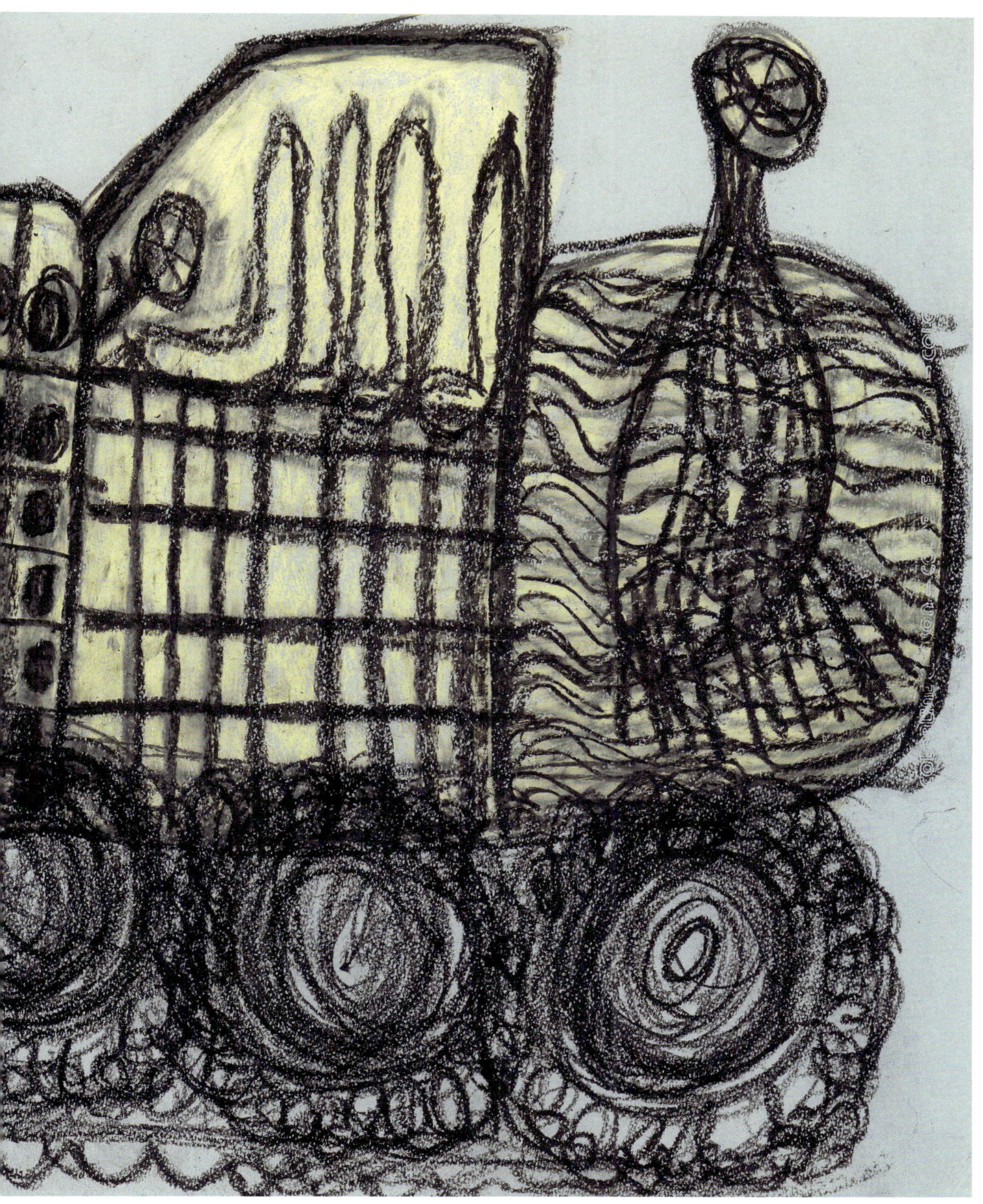

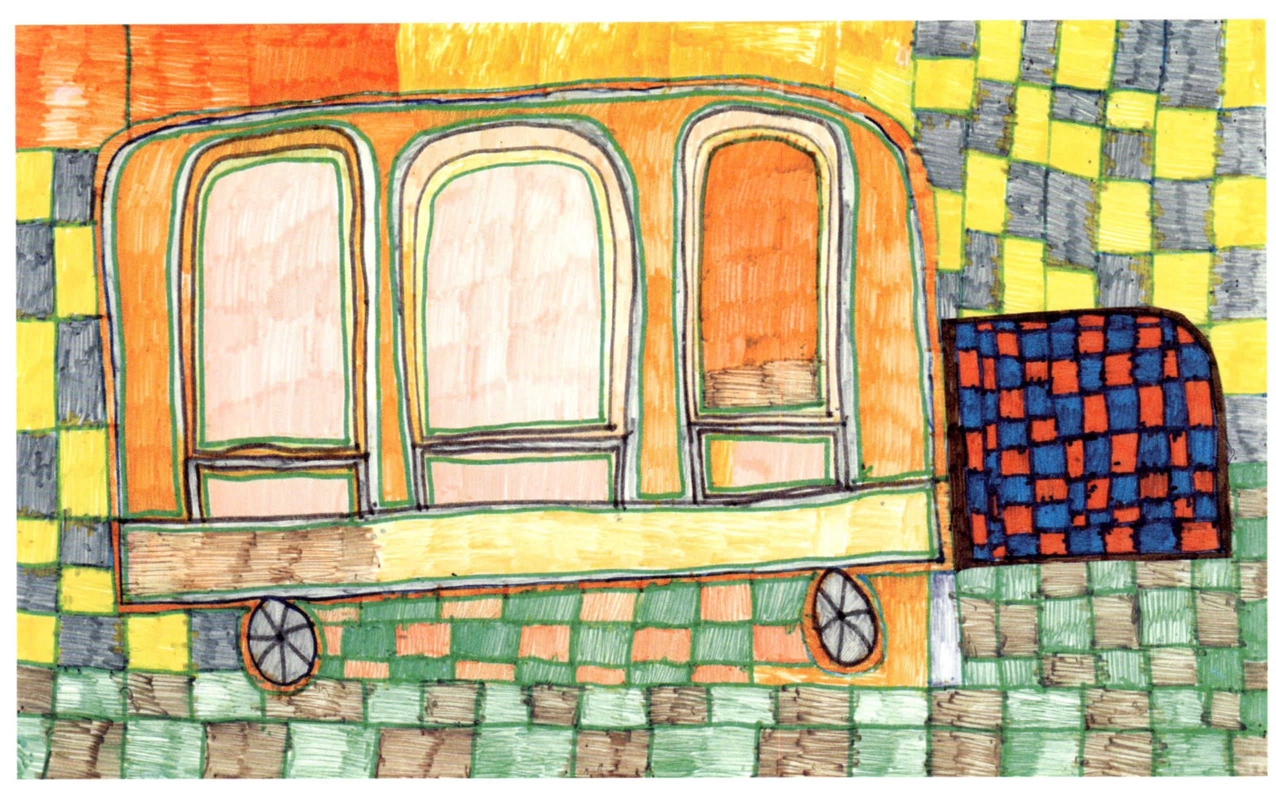

Dominique Bertoliatti
Sans titre untitled, ca. 1990
feutre sur papier
felt pen on paper
26,8 x 44,5 cm

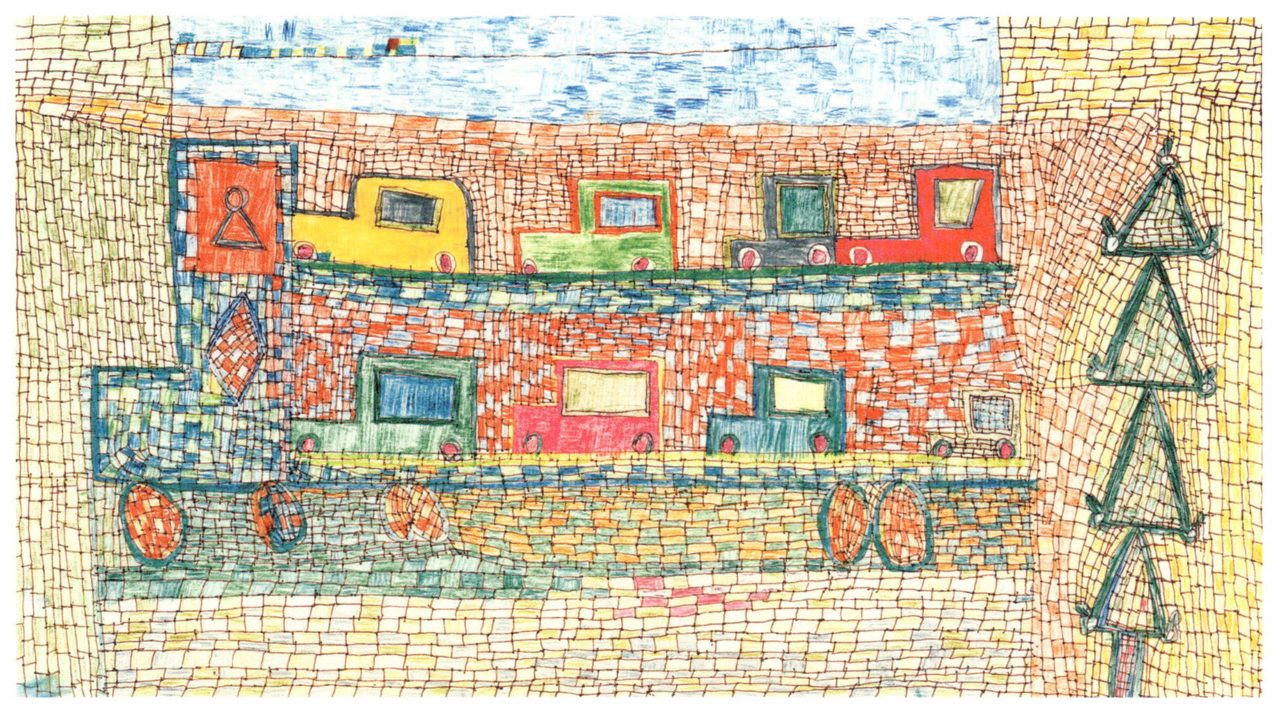

Dominique Bertoliatti
Sans titre untitled, ca. 1990
feutre et crayon de couleur sur papier
felt pen and coloured pencil on paper
27 x 50 cm

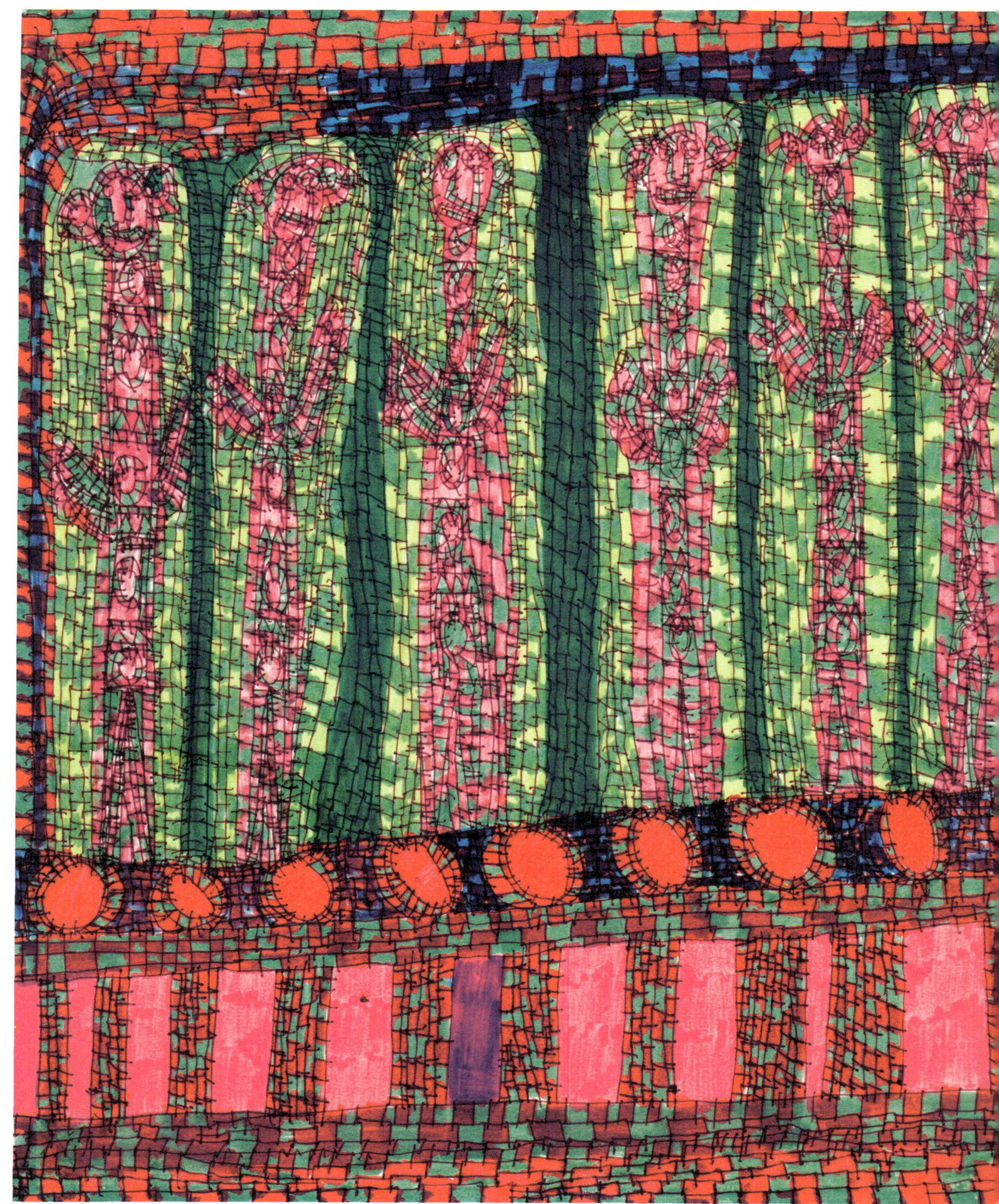

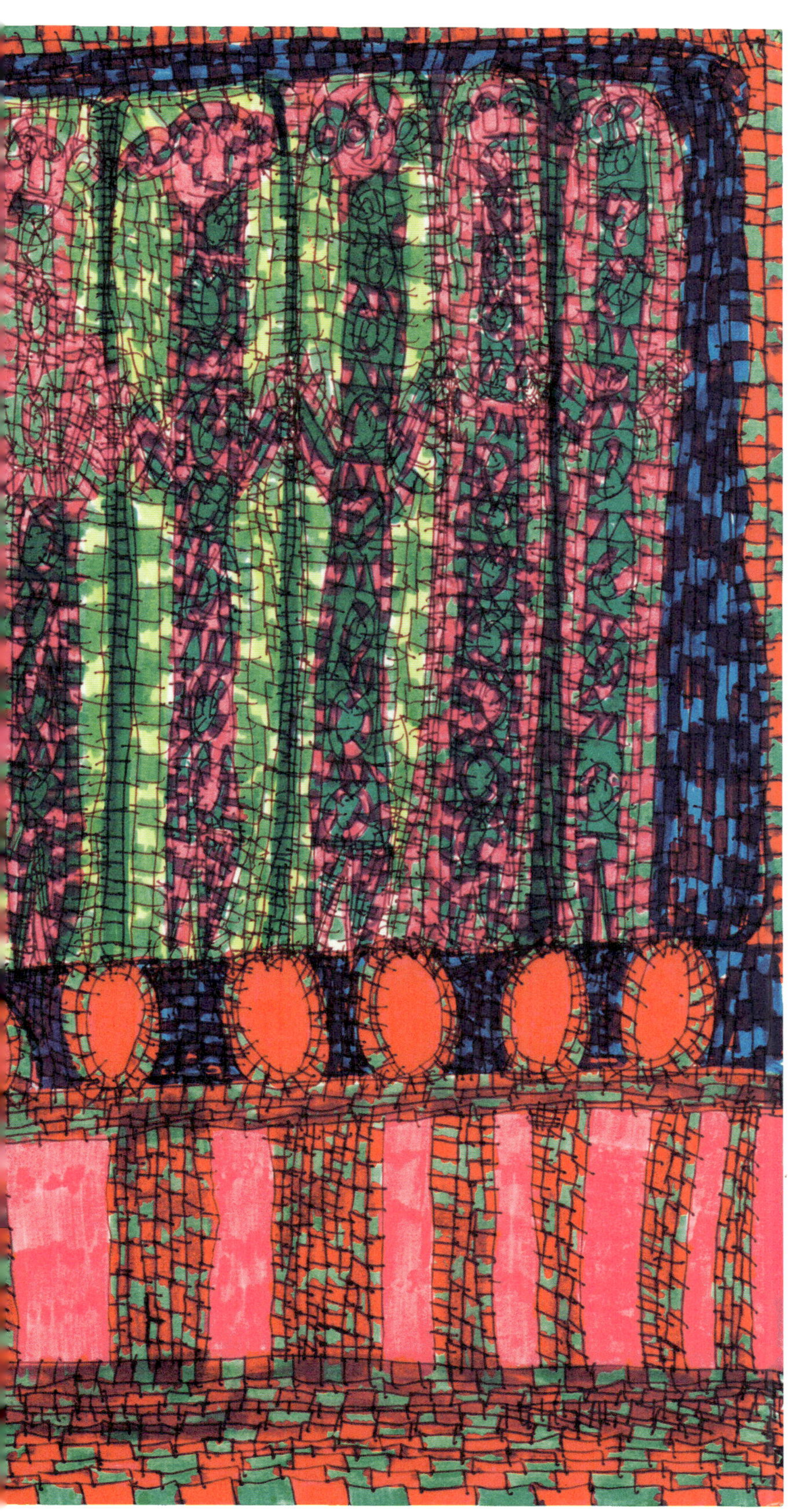

Dominique Bertoliatti
Sans titre untitled, ca. 1990
feutre sur papier
felt pen on paper
35 x 50 cm

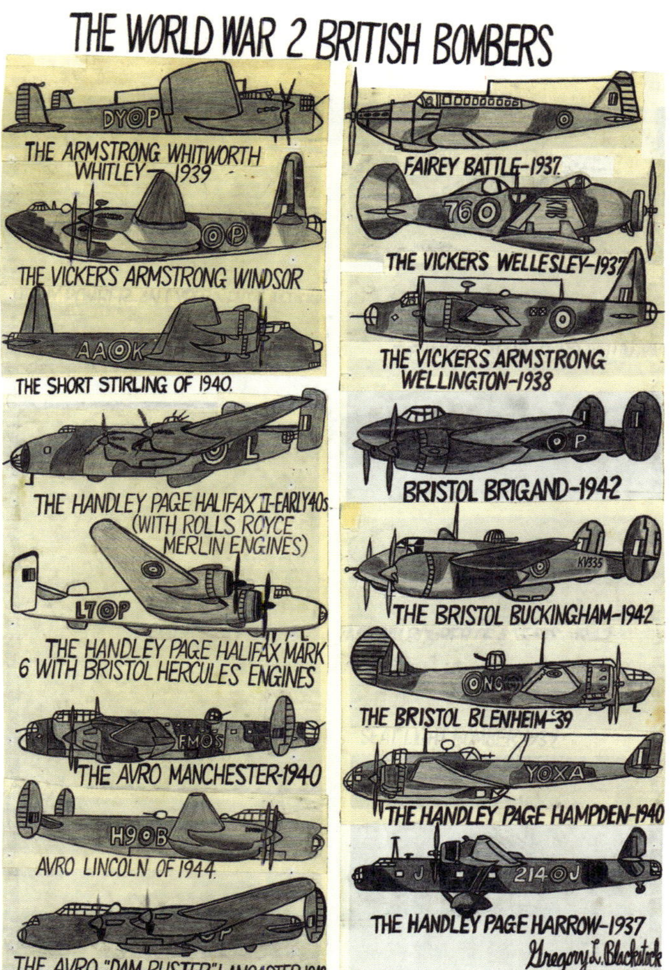

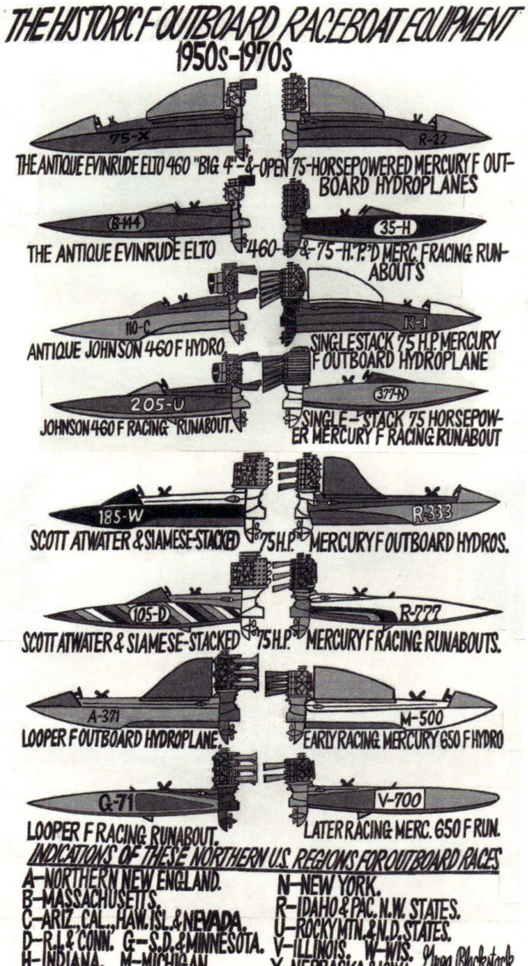

Gregory L. Blackstock
The World War 2 British Bombers, 1998
mine de plomb et feutre sur papier
lead pencil and felt pen on paper
94,5 x 65,5 cm

Gregory L. Blackstock
The Historic F Outboard Raceboat Equipment 1950s-1970s, 2004
mine de plomb, feutre, correcteur blanc et craie grasse sur papier lead pencil, felt pen, white corrector and crayon on paper
112,5 x 61,6 cm

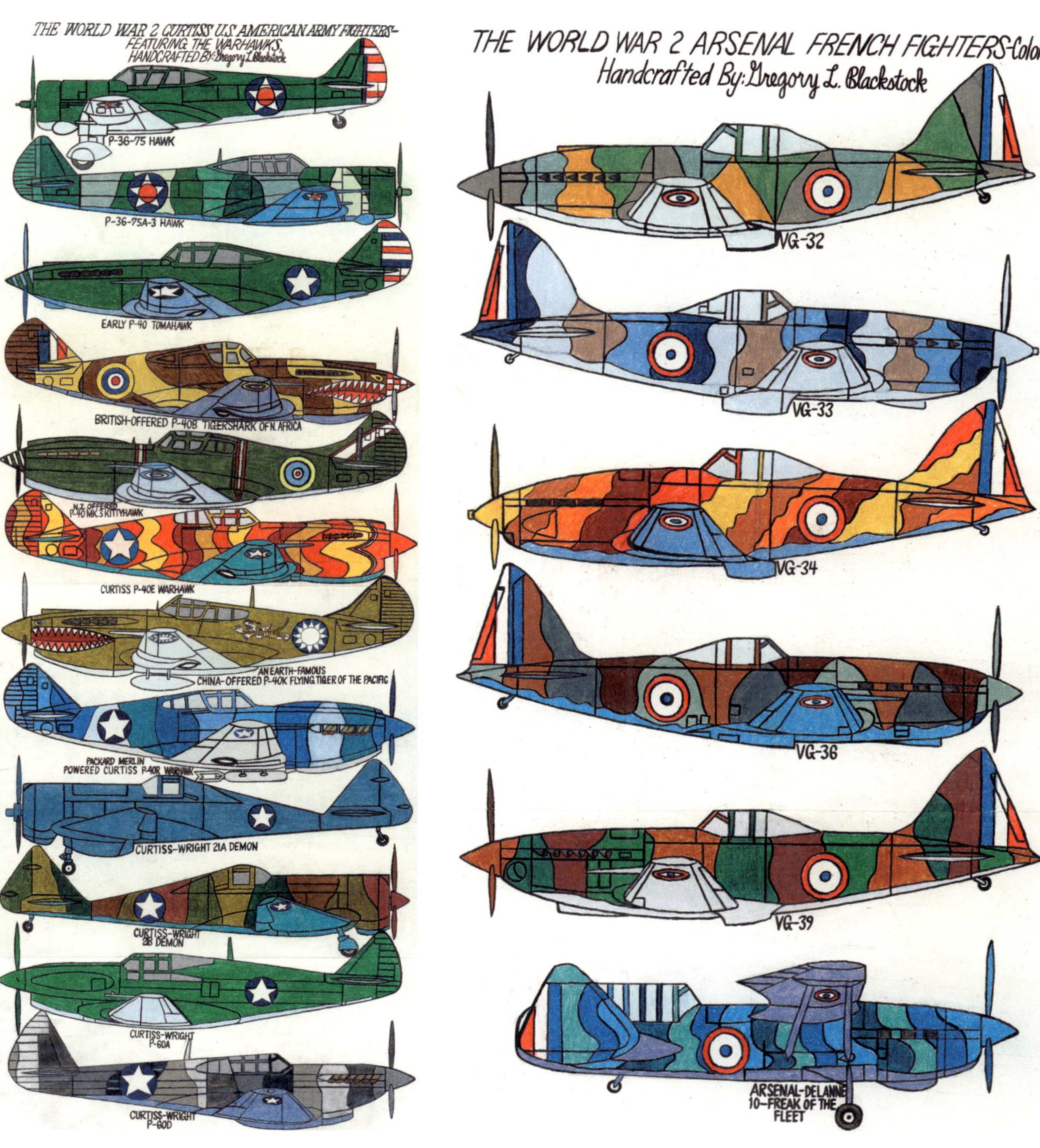

Gregory L. Blackstock
The World War 2 Curtiss U.S. American Army Fighters, ca. 1986-2011
mine de plomb, feutre et craie grasse sur papier lead pencil, felt pen and crayon on paper
119,4 x 45,6 cm

Gregory L. Blackstock
The World War 2 Arsenal French Fighters-Color, 2011
mine de plomb, feutre, craie grasse et crayon de couleur sur papier lead pencil, felt pen, crayon and coloured pencil on paper
84,6 x 45,6 cm

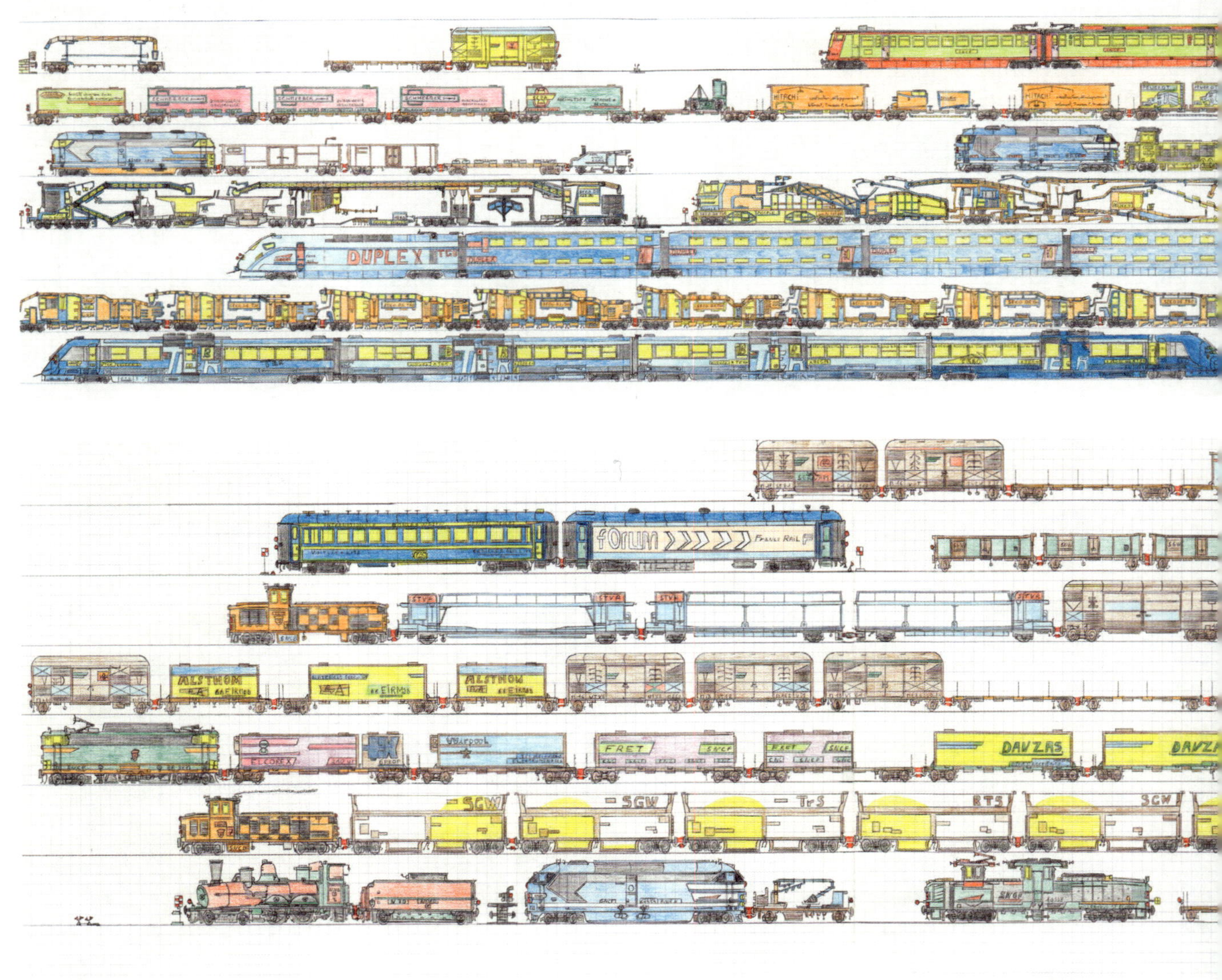

David Braillon
Duplex TGV, 2000
crayon de couleur et stylo-bille sur papier
ballpoint pen and coloured pencil on paper
29,7 x 168 cm

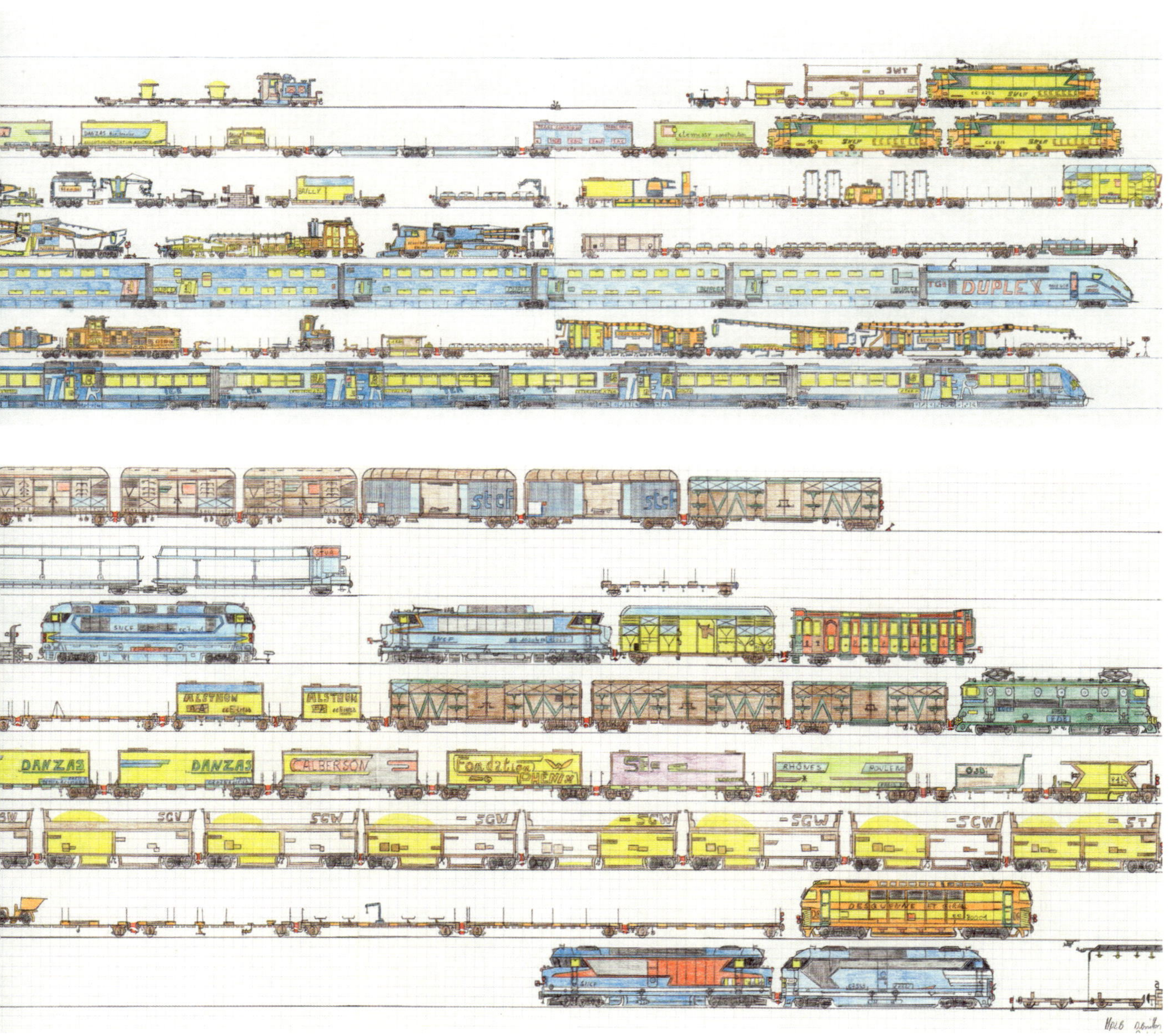

David Braillon
Danzas, 2000
crayon de couleur et stylo-bille sur papier
ballpoint pen and coloured pencil on paper
29,7 x 126 cm

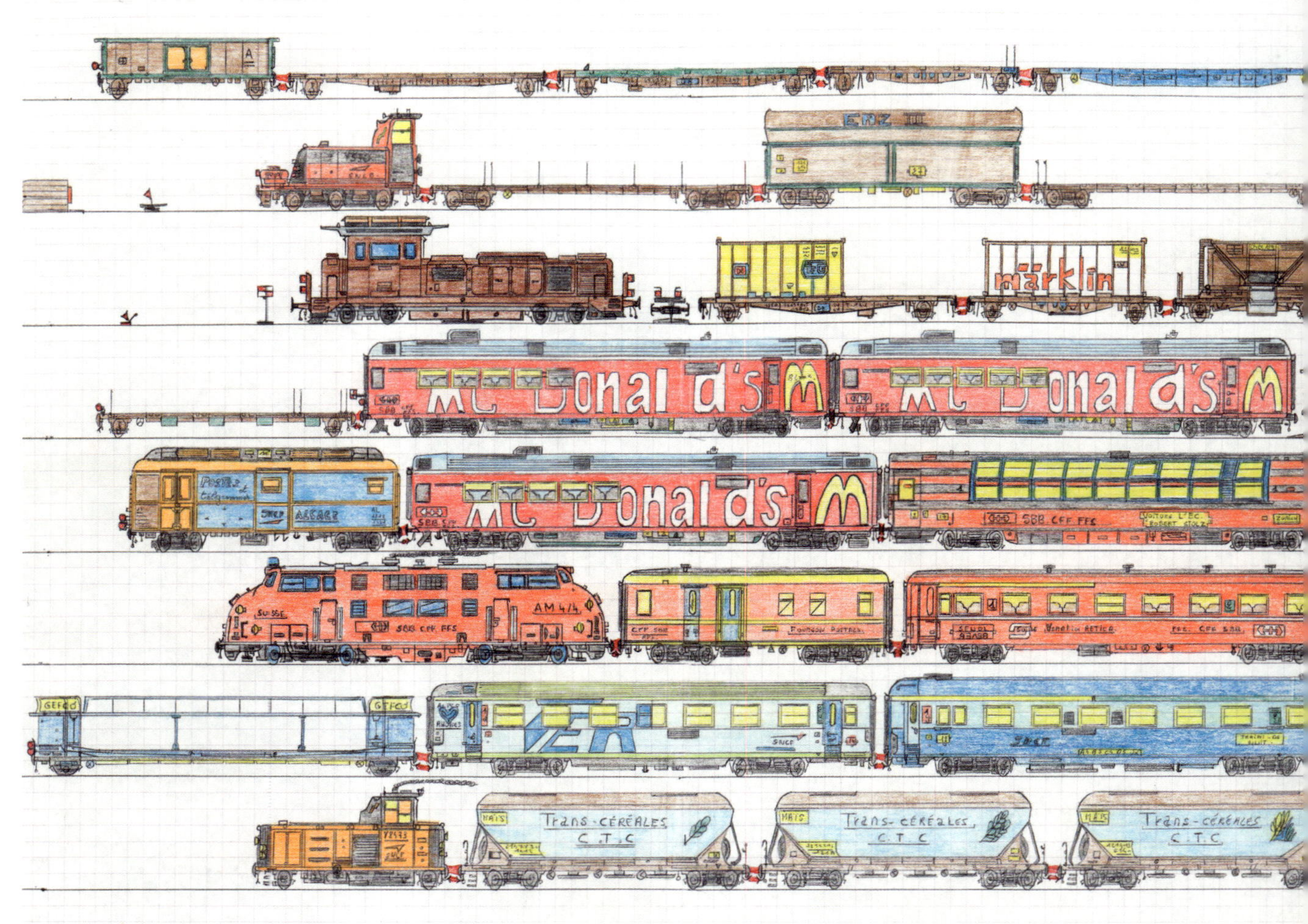

David Braillon
Trans-Cereal C.T.C., 2001
crayon de couleur et stylo-bille sur papier
ballpoint pen and coloured pencil on paper
29,7 x 84,3 cm

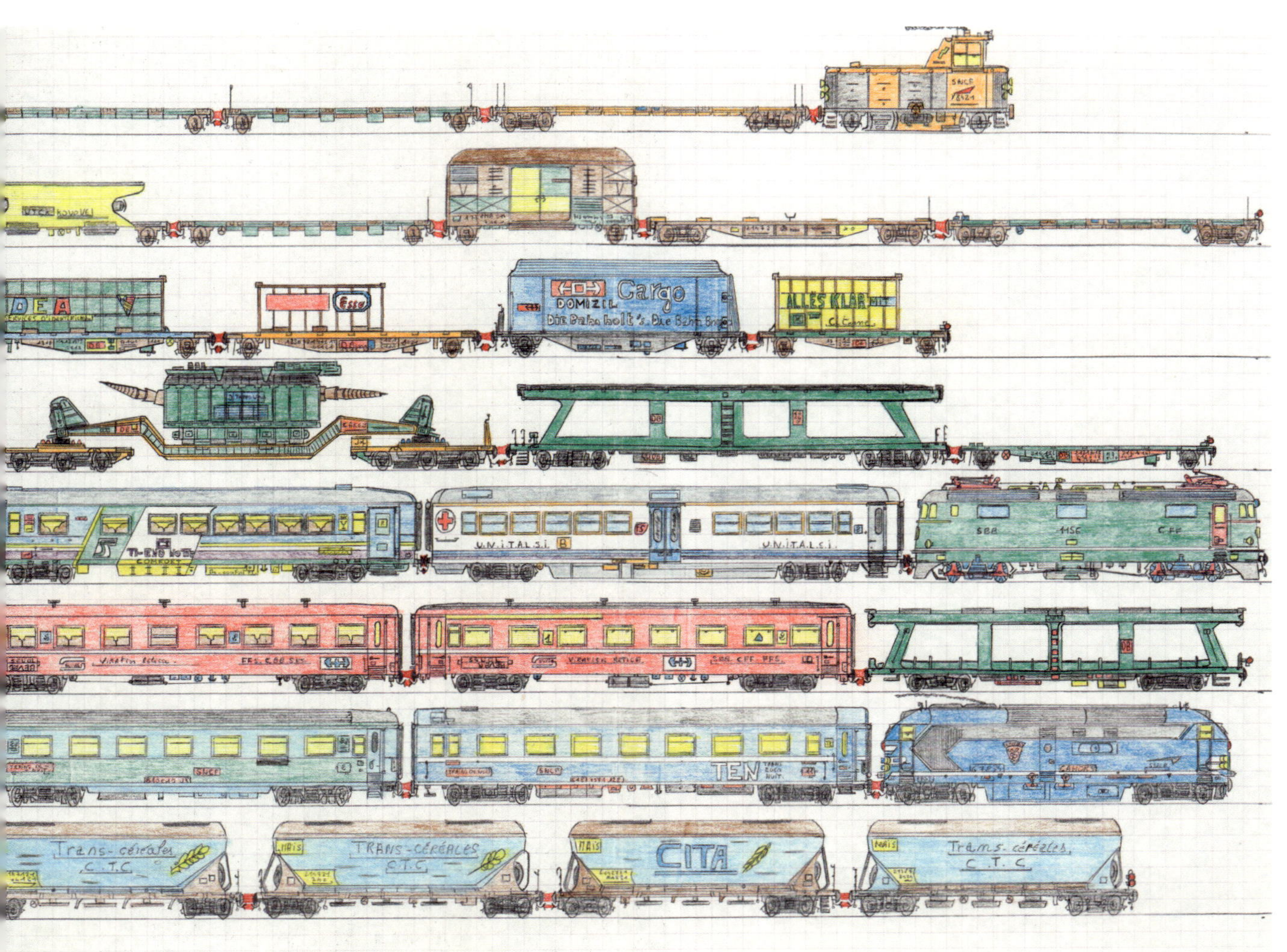
Cargo
DOMIZIL
ALLES KLAR
U.N.I.T.A.L.S.I.
TEN
Trans-céréales
C.T.C
CITA

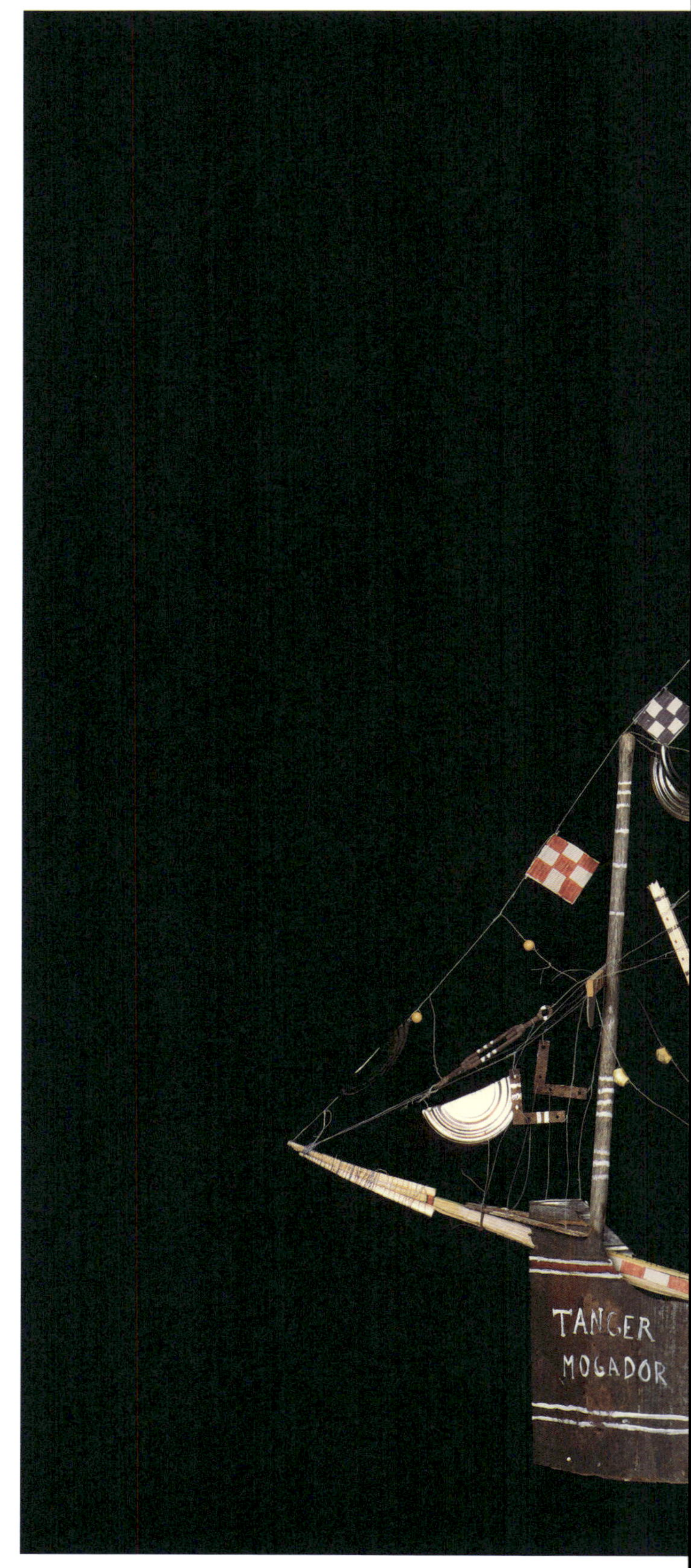

François Burland
Tanger-Mogador, 1998
métal, bois et plastique
metal, wood and plastic
195 x 225 x 107 cm

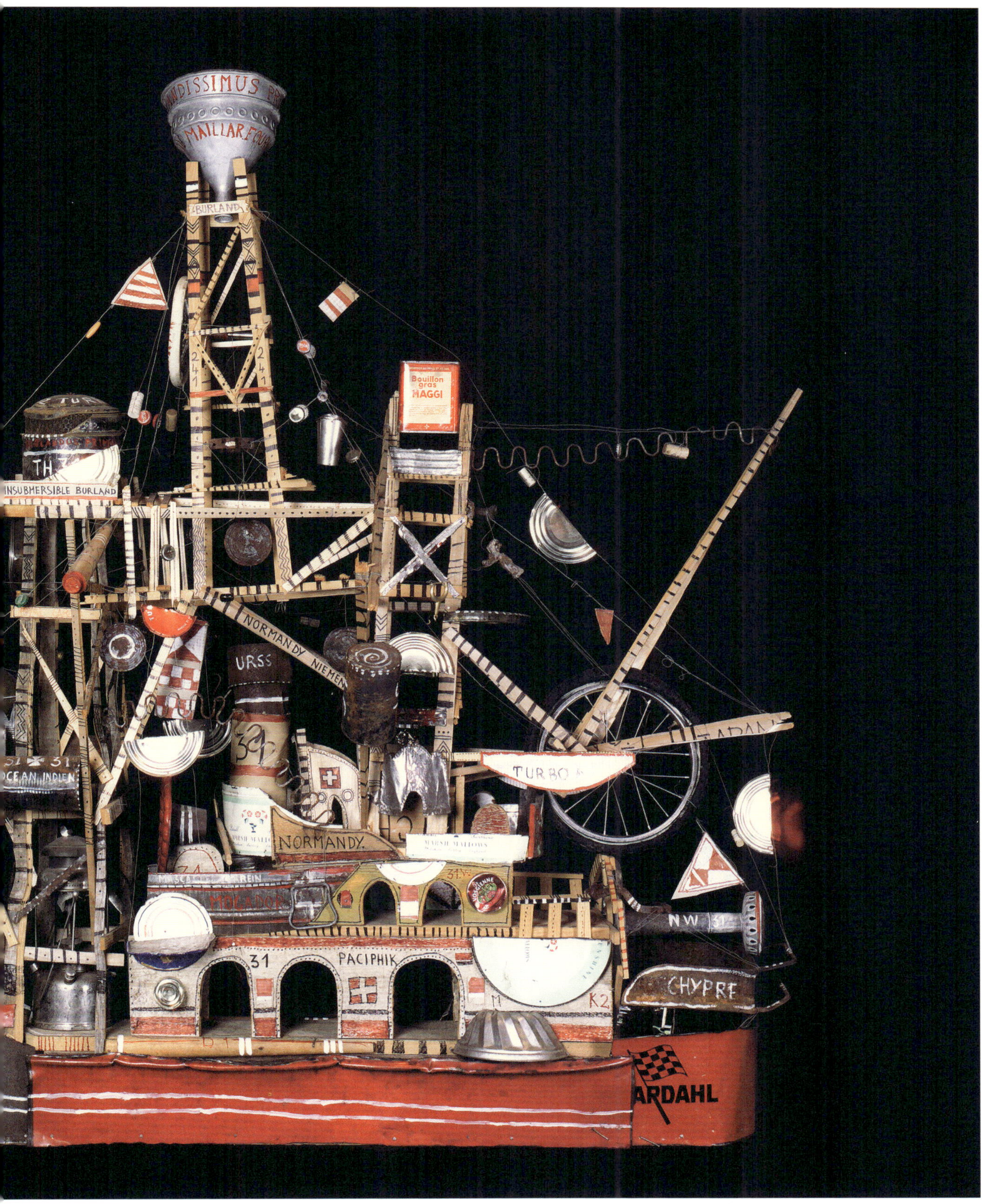
BURLAND
INSUBMERSIBLE BURLAND
Bouillon gras MAGGI
NORMANDY NIEMEN
URSS
OCEAN INDIEN
TURBO
NORMANDY
MOGADOR
31
PACIPHIK
K2
NW 31
CHYPRE
ARDAHL

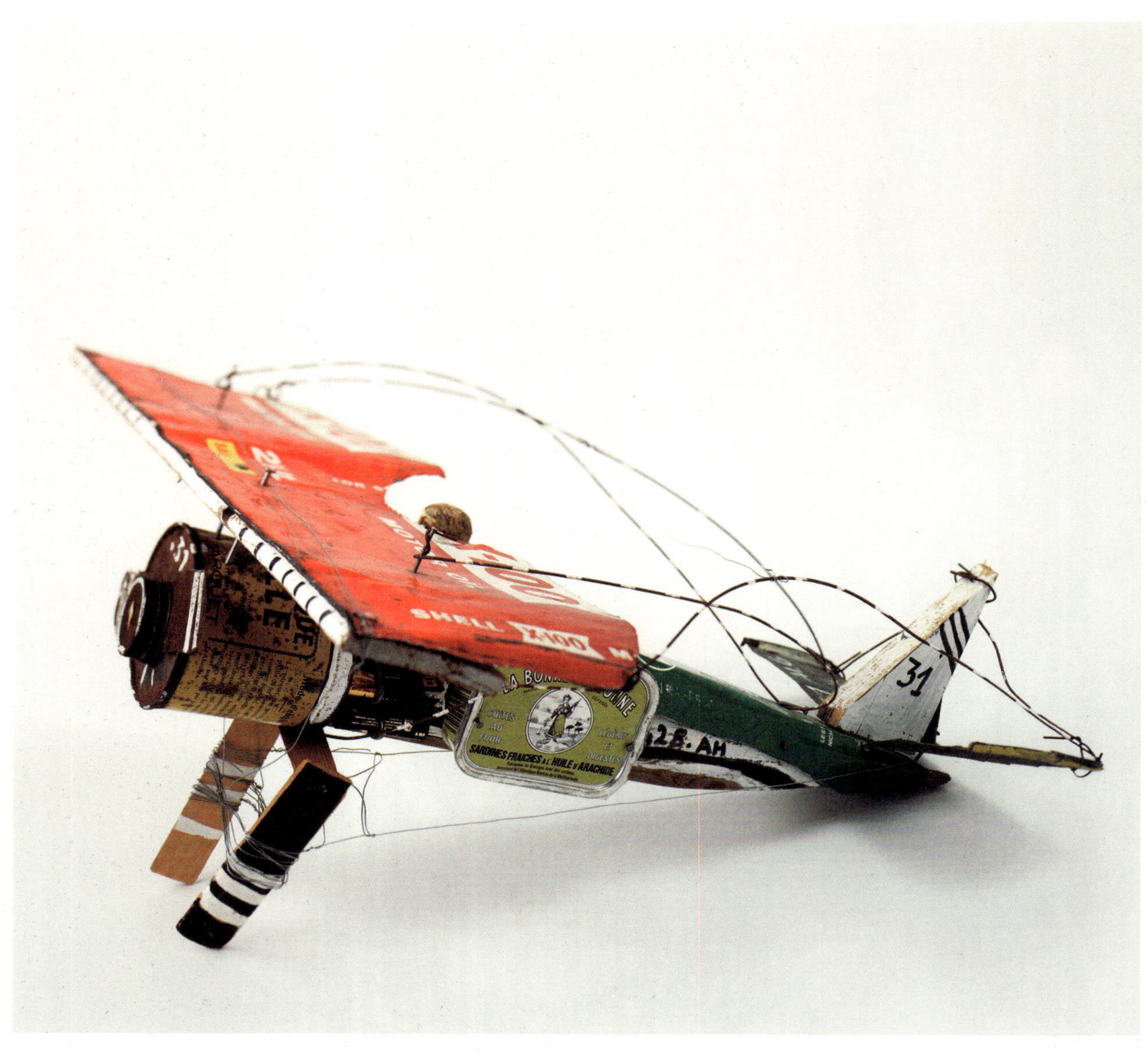

François Burland
Sans titre untitled, 1995
bois, boîtes de conserve et matériaux divers wood, tin cans and miscellaneous materials
30 x 53 x 43 cm

François Burland
Croix du Sud, 1995
bois, boîtes de conserve et matériaux divers wood, tin cans and miscellaneous materials
77 x 70 x 32 cm

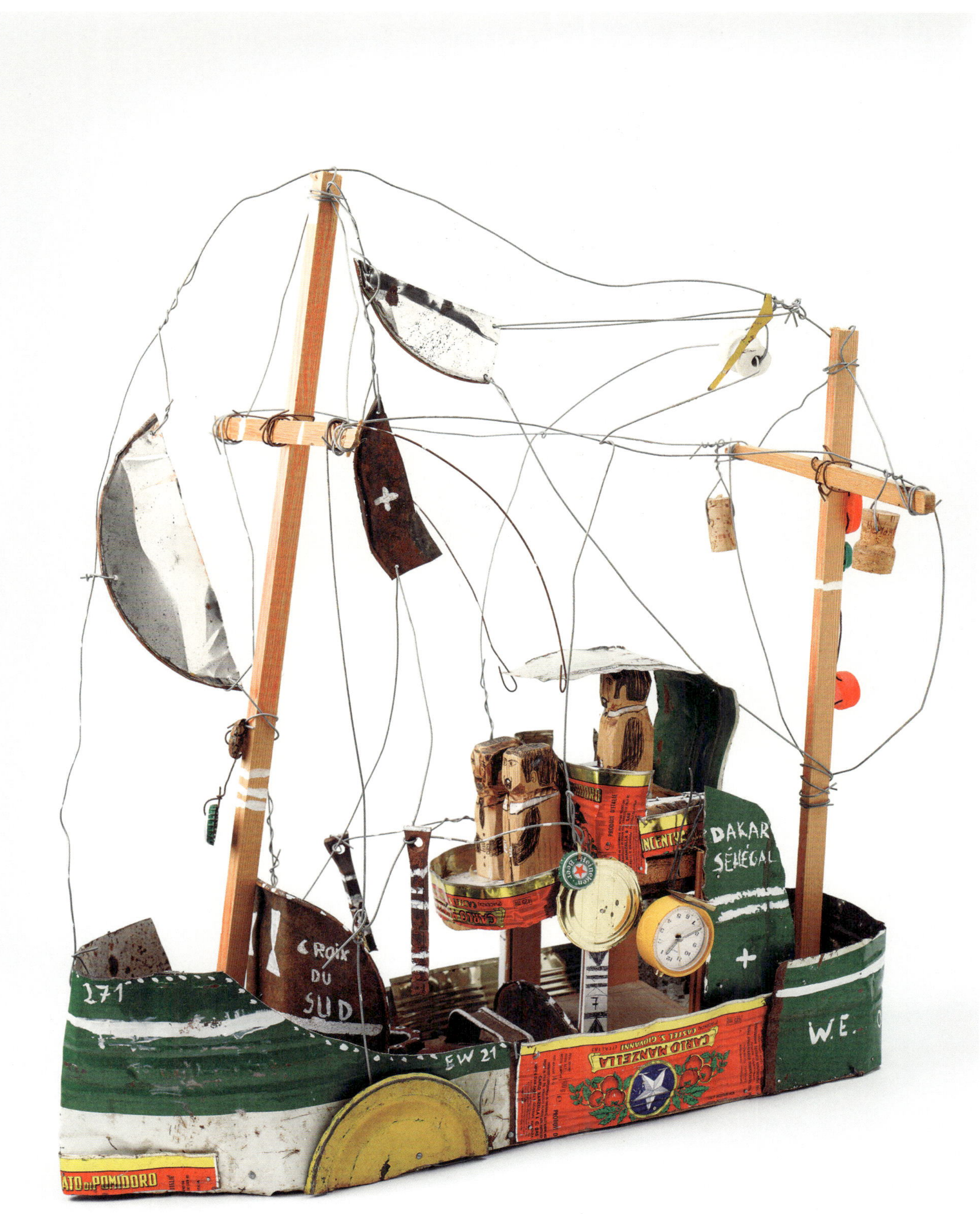

271
CRoix DU SUD
EW 21
DAKAR SÉNÉGAL
W.E.
CARLO MANZELLA
CASTEL S. GIOVANNI

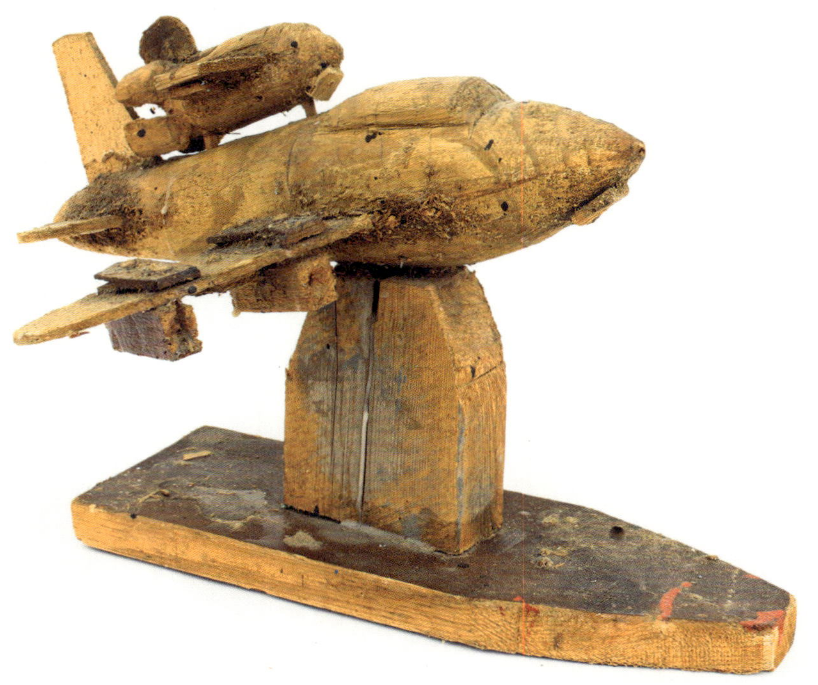

John Byam
Sans titre *untitled*, ca. 1970-1990
bois, sciure et colle
wood, sawdust and glue
22,9 x 29,2 x 10,2 cm

John Byam
Sans titre *untitled*, ca. 1970-1990
bois, sciure et colle
wood, sawdust and glue
5,1 x 12,7 x 5,1 cm

John Byam
Sans titre *untitled*, ca. 1970-1990
bois, sciure et colle
wood, sawdust and glue
15,2 x 33 x 10,2 cm

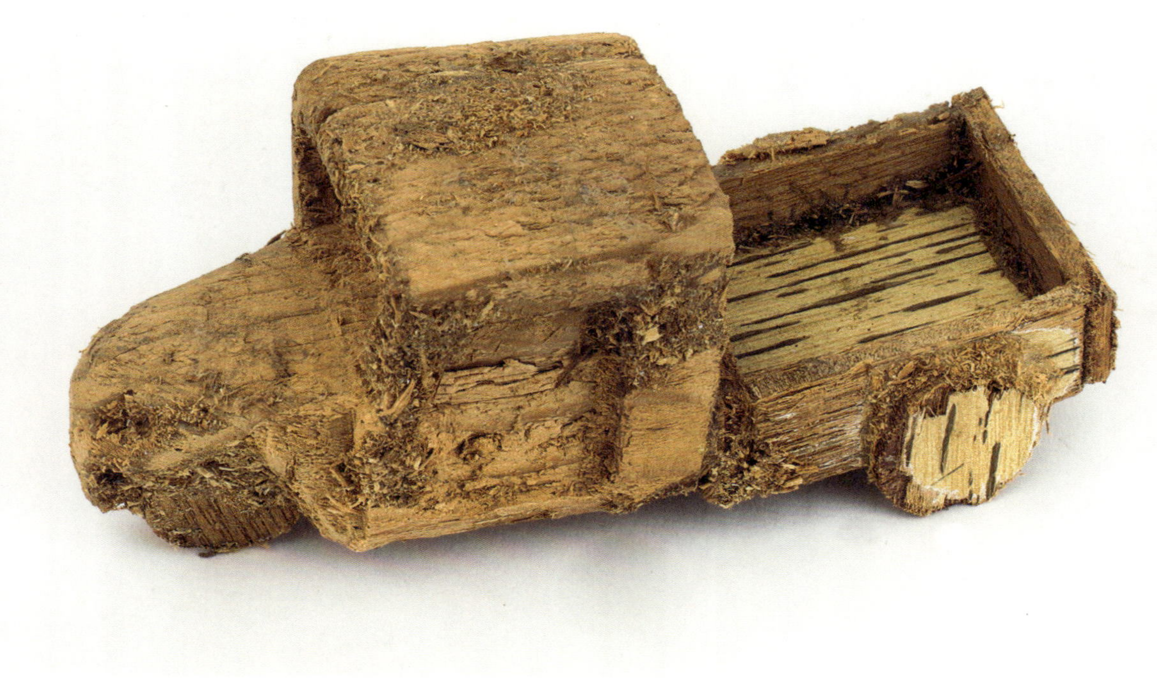

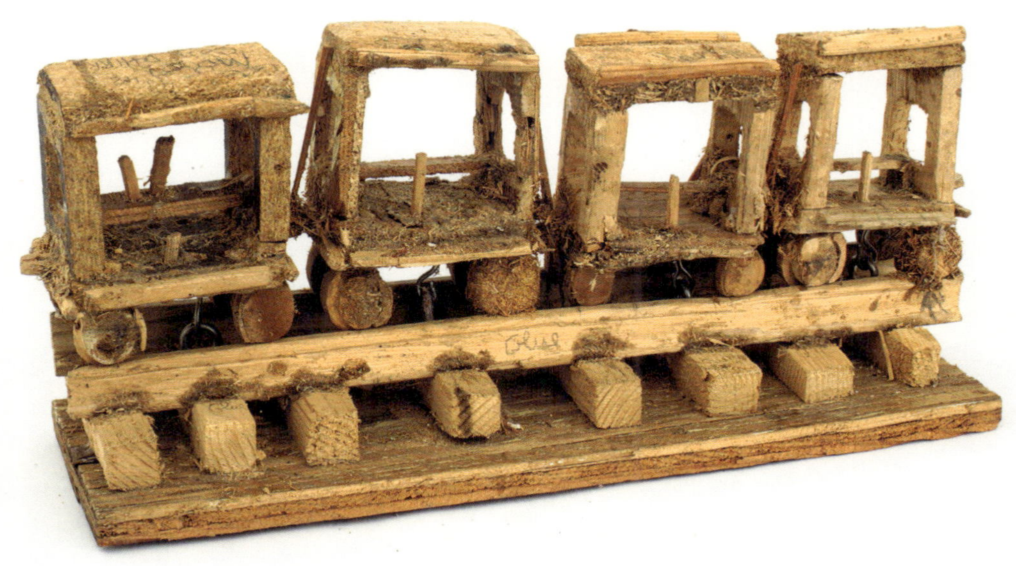

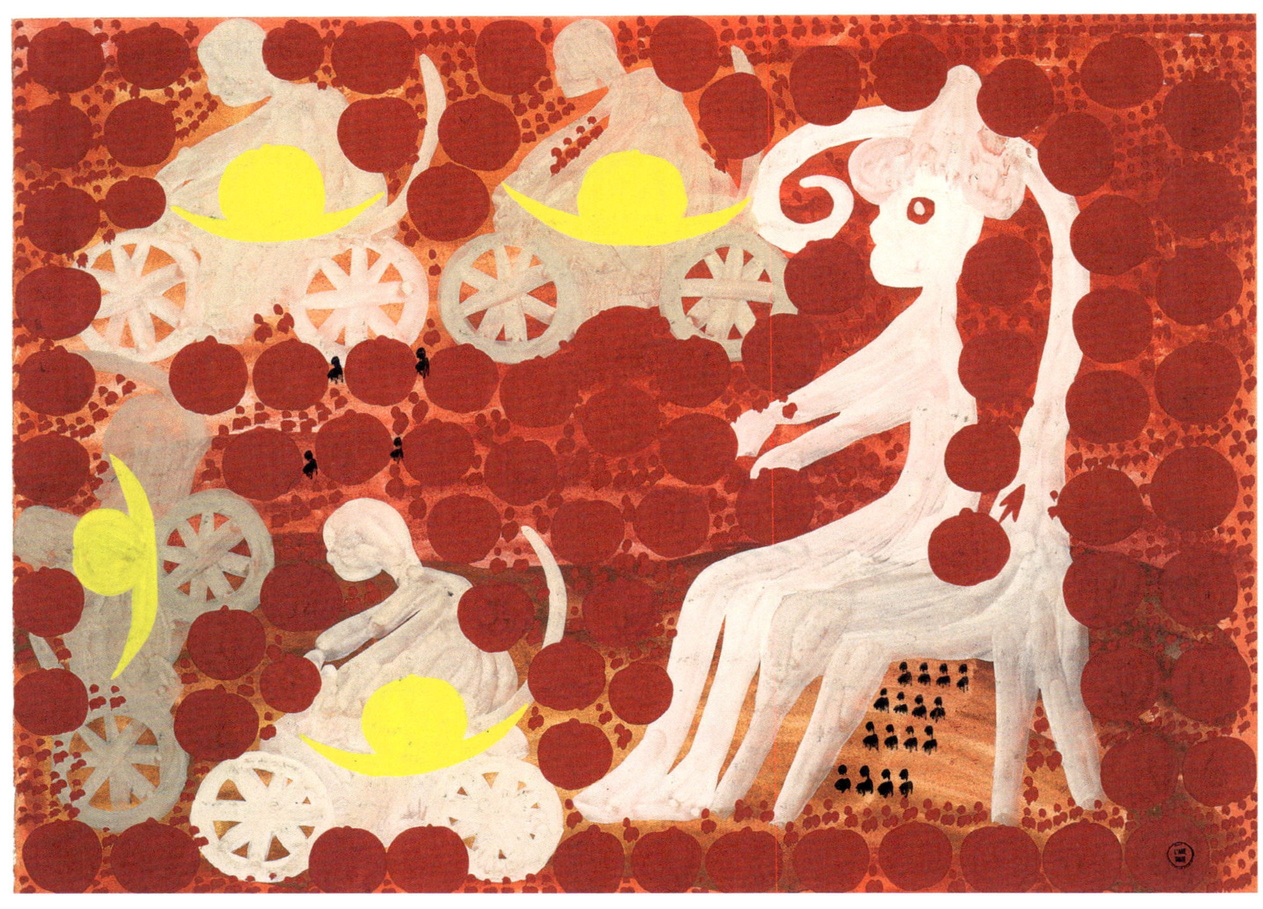

Carlo
Sans titre untitled, 1962
gouache sur papier
gouache on paper
35 x 50 cm

Carlo
Sans titre untitled, 1965
gouache sur papier
gouache on paper
70 x 50 cm

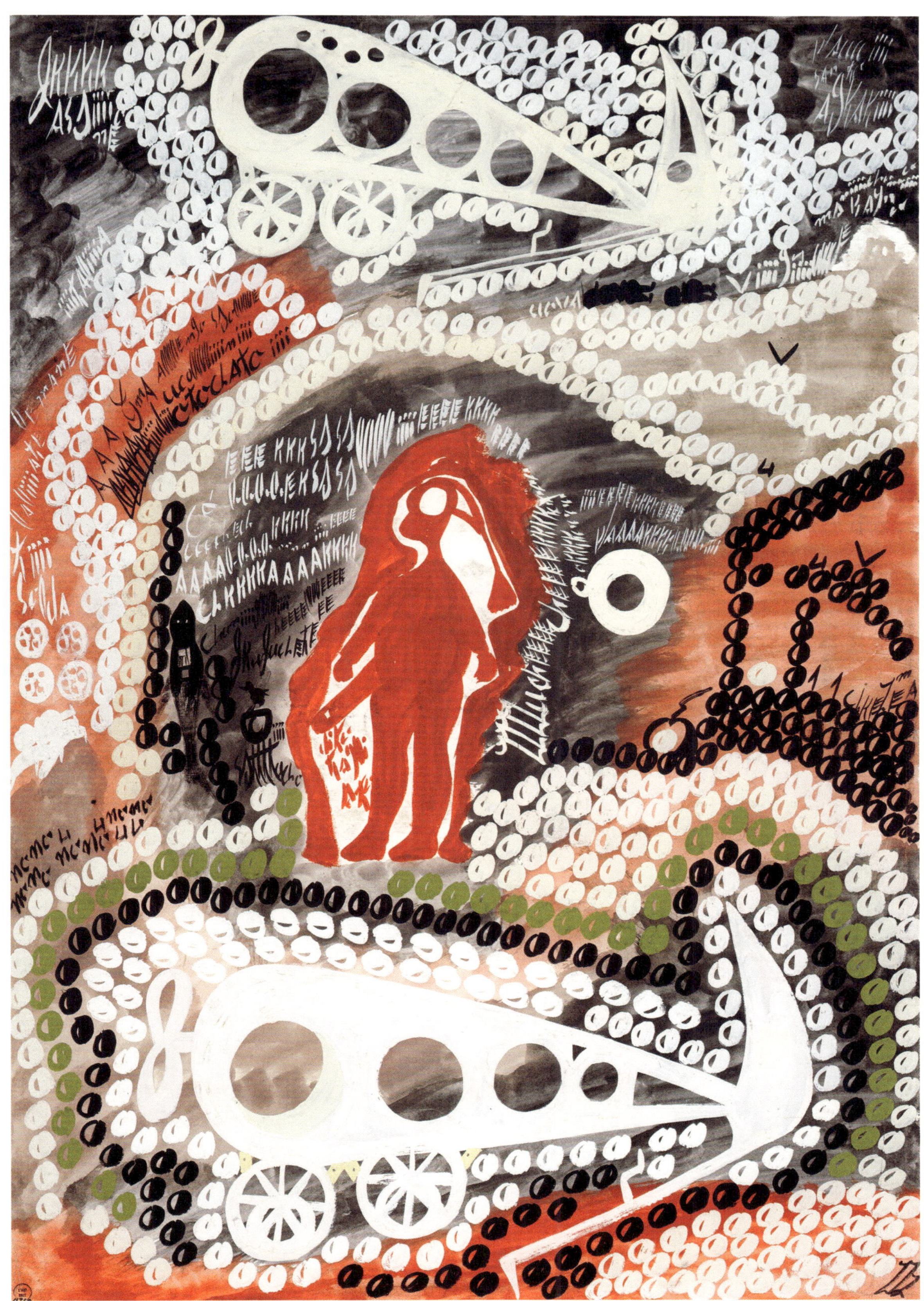

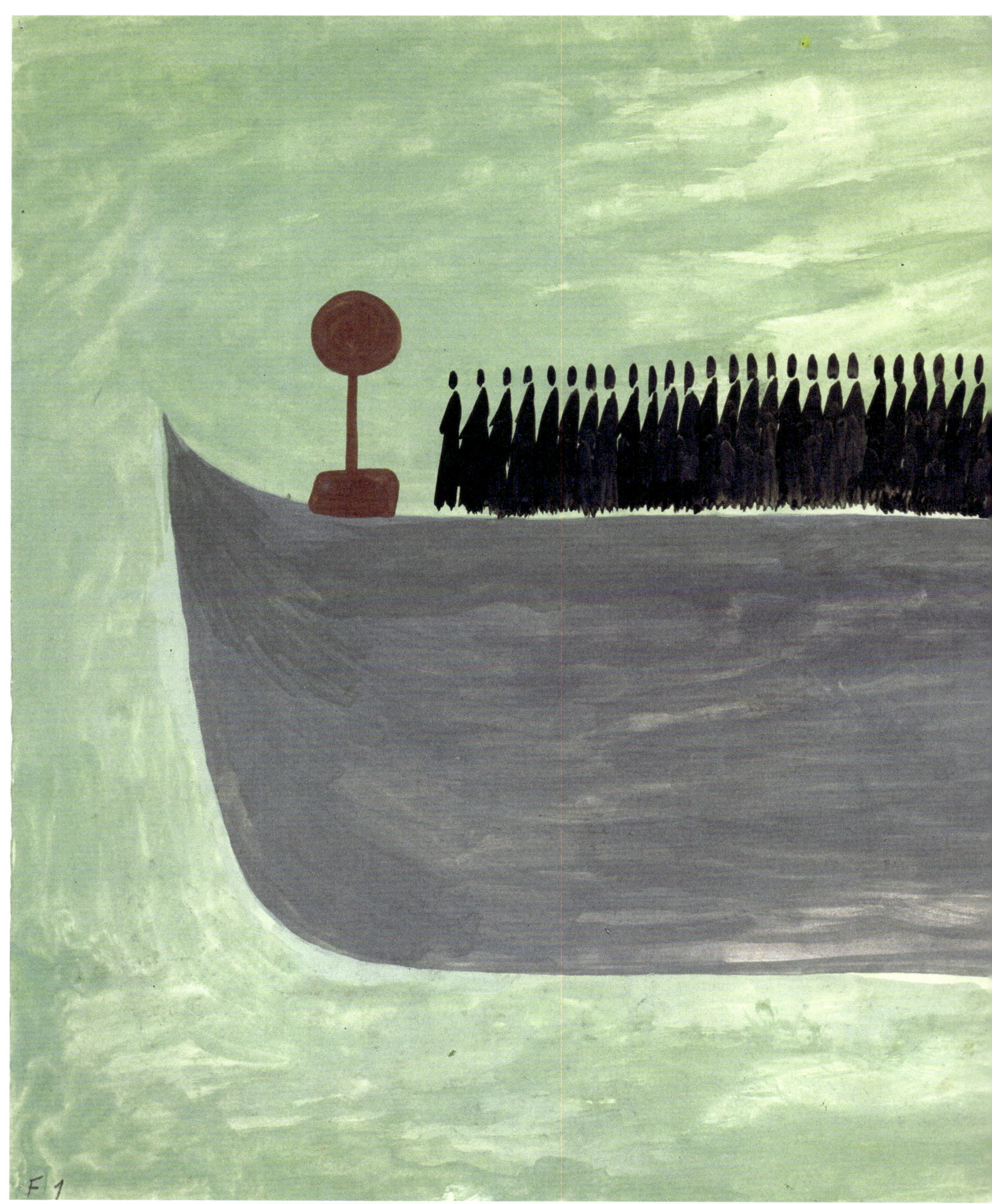

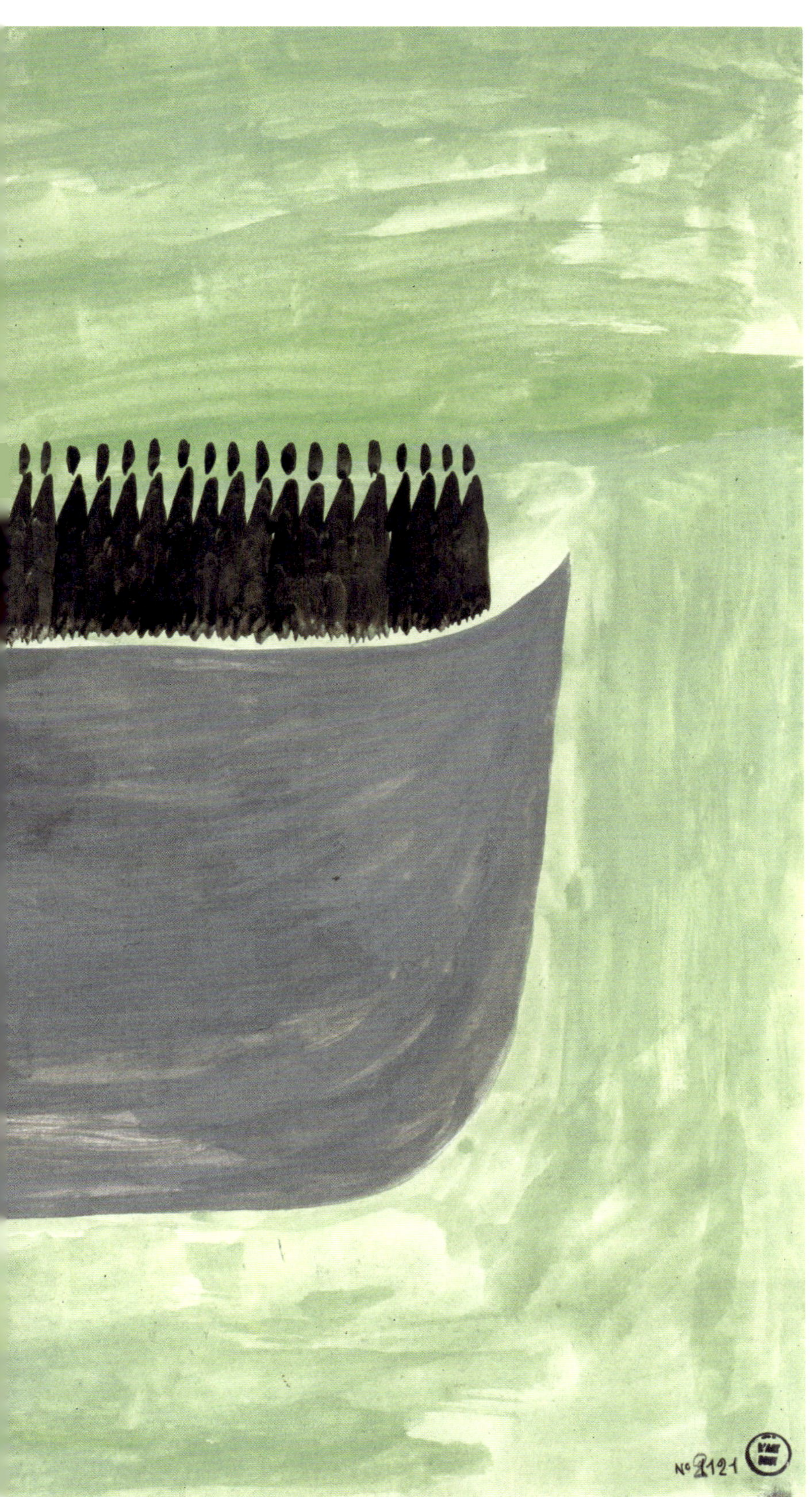

Carlo
Sans titre untitled, 1963
gouache sur papier
gouache on paper
35 x 50 cm

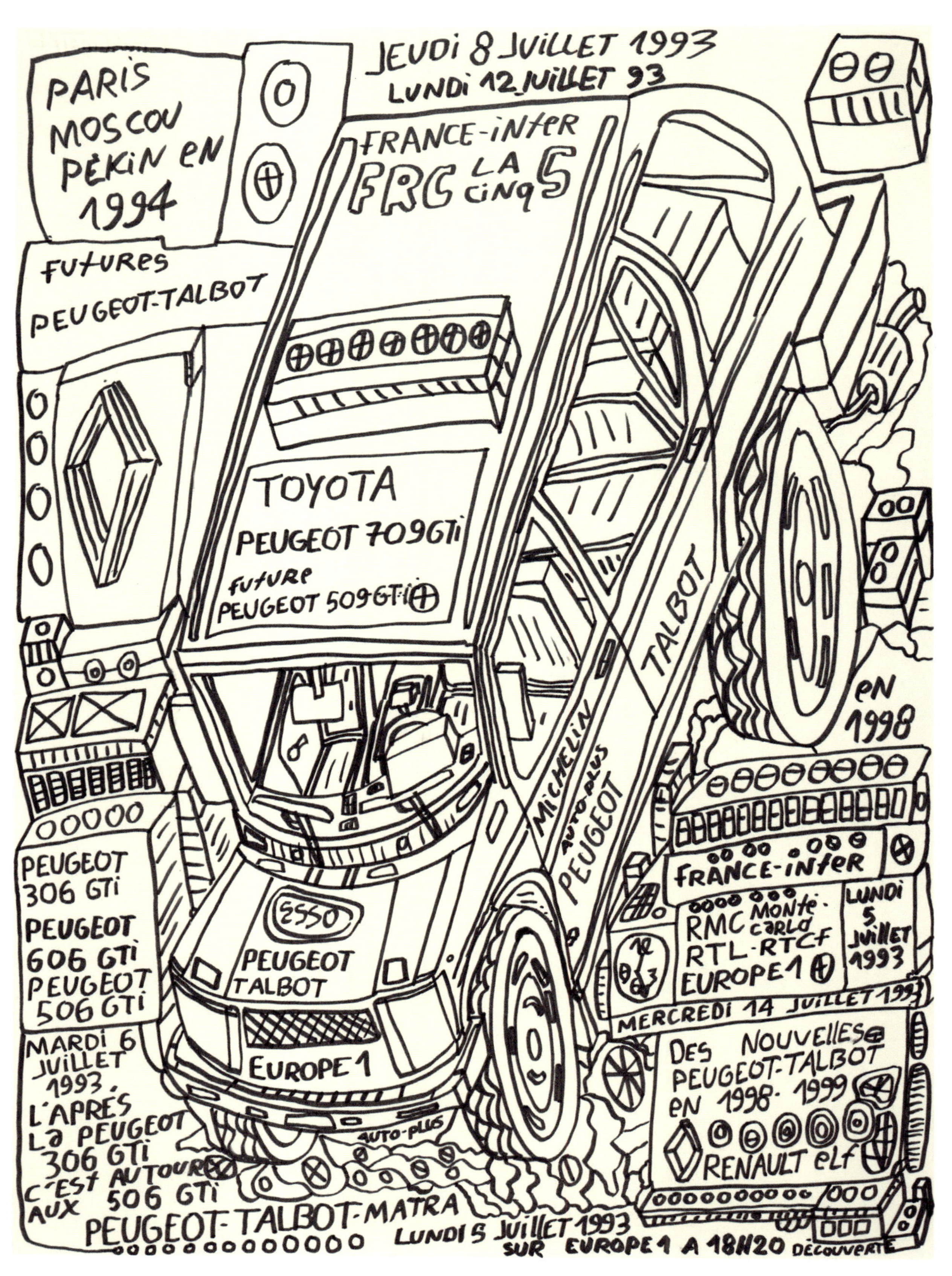
PARIS MOSCOU PÉKIN EN 1994
JEUDI 8 JUILLET 1993
LUNDI 12 JUILLET 93
FRANCE-INTER
FRC LA CINQ 5
FUTURES PEUGEOT-TALBOT
TOYOTA
PEUGEOT 709 GTi
FUTURE PEUGEOT 509 GTi
TALBOT
MICHELIN
AUTO-PLUS
PEUGEOT
EN 1998
ESSO
PEUGEOT TALBOT
EUROPE 1
PEUGEOT 306 GTi
PEUGEOT 606 GTi
PEUGEOT 506 GTi
FRANCE-INTER
RMC MONTE-CARLO
RTL-RTCF
EUROPE 1
LUNDI 5 JUILLET 1993
MERCREDI 14 JUILLET 1993
DES NOUVELLES PEUGEOT-TALBOT EN 1998-1999
RENAULT ELF
MARDI 6 JUILLET 1993, L'APRÈS LA PEUGEOT 306 GTi C'EST AUTOUR AUX 506 GTi
AUTO-PLUS
PEUGEOT-TALBOT-MATRA
LUNDI 5 JUILLET 1993 SUR EUROPE 1 A 18H20 DÉCOUVERTE

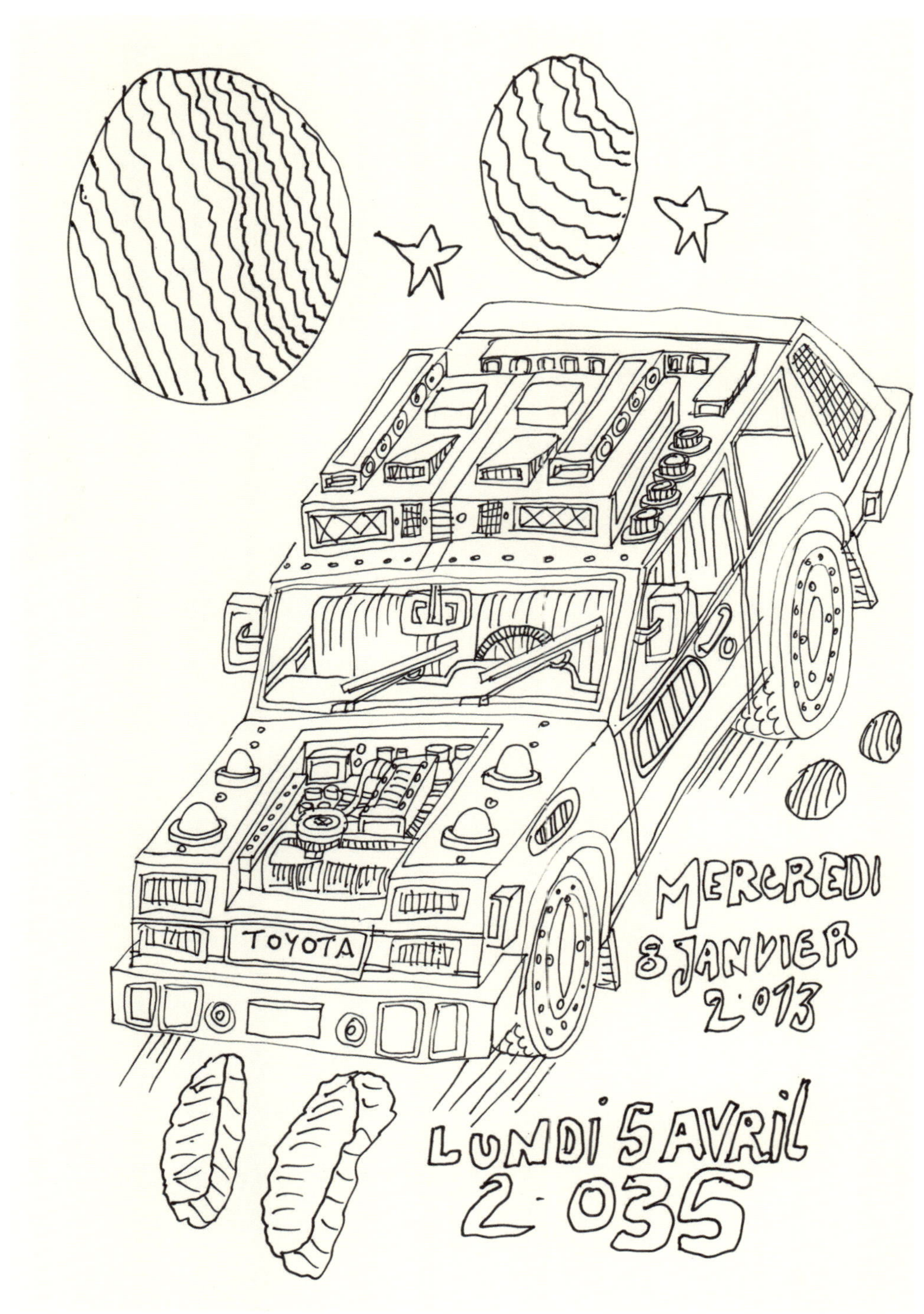

Serge Delaunay
Paris-Moscou-Pékin 1994, 1993
feutre sur papier
felt pen on paper
73 x 55 cm

Serge Delaunay
Toyota, 2013
feutre sur papier
felt pen on paper
42 x 29,8 cm

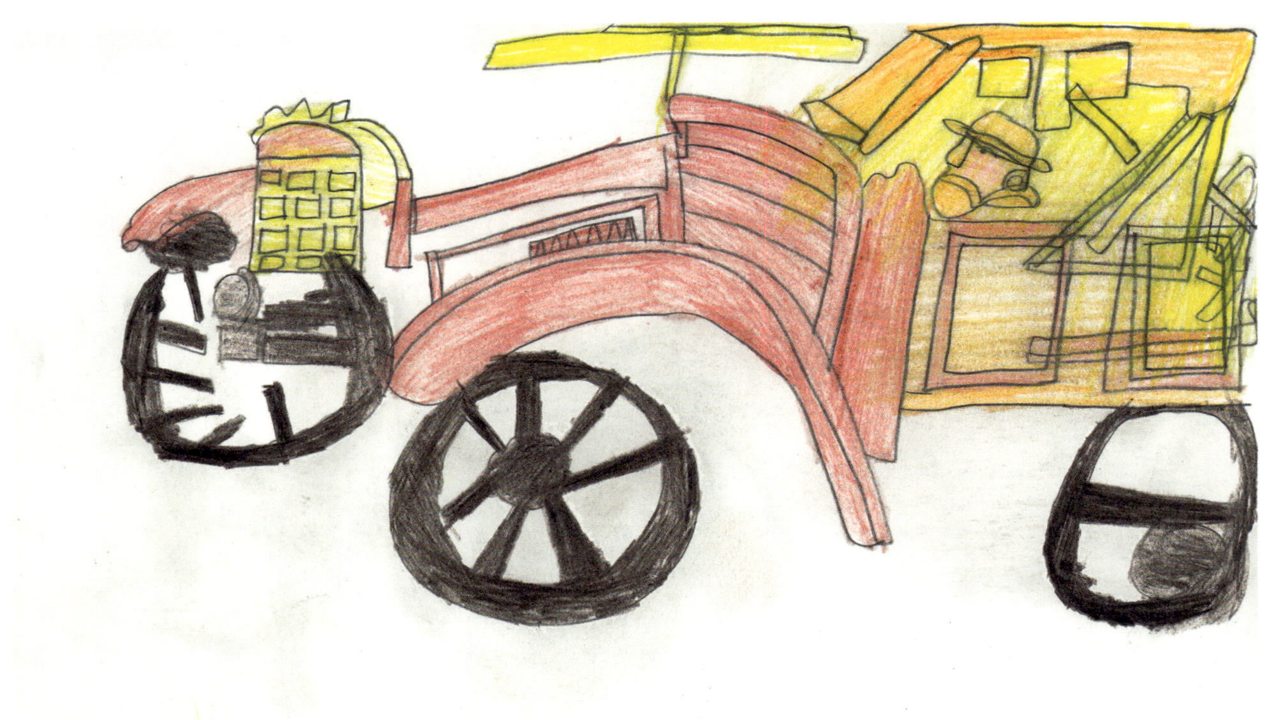

Curzio Di Giovanni
La macchinnaa anntticca, 2002
mine de plomb et crayon de couleur sur papier lead pencil and coloured pencil on paper
24 x 33 cm

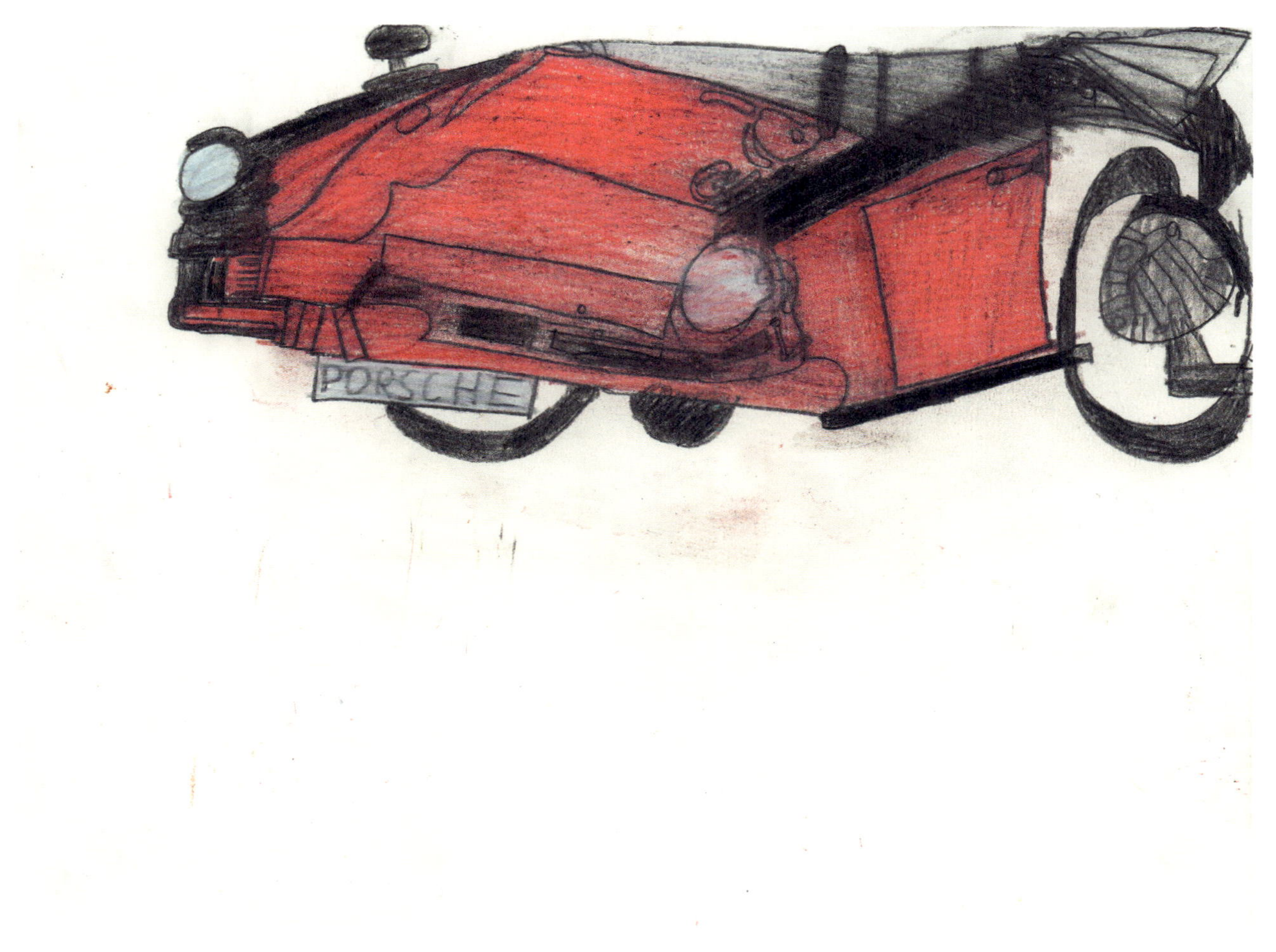

Curzio Di Giovanni
Unnaa Posc rossa scurra rossa rossa, 2002
mine de plomb et crayon de couleur
sur papier lead pencil and coloured
pencil on paper
24 x 33 cm

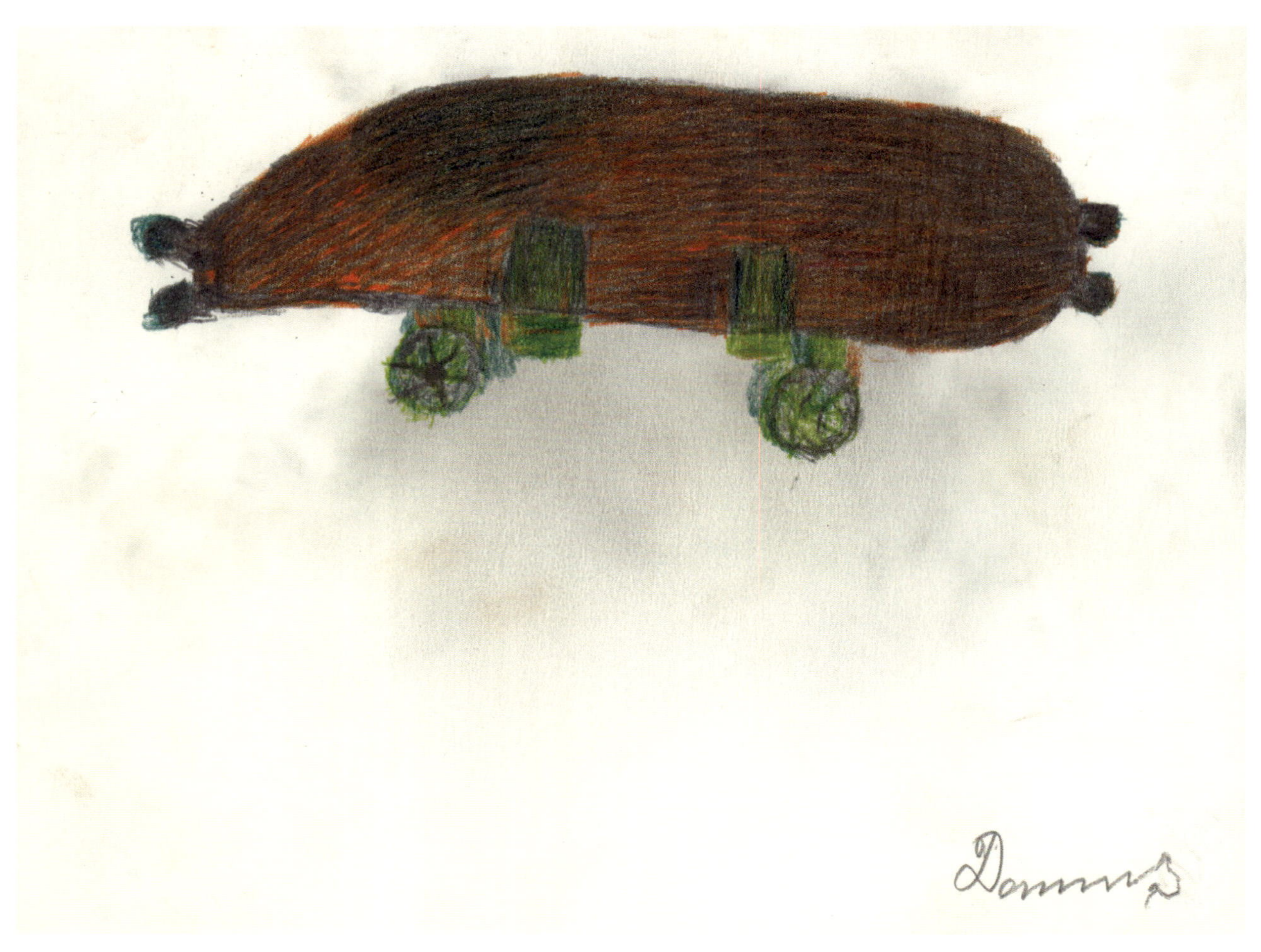

Anton Dobay
Sans titre untitled, 1977
crayon de couleur sur papier
coloured pencil on paper
22 x 30 cm

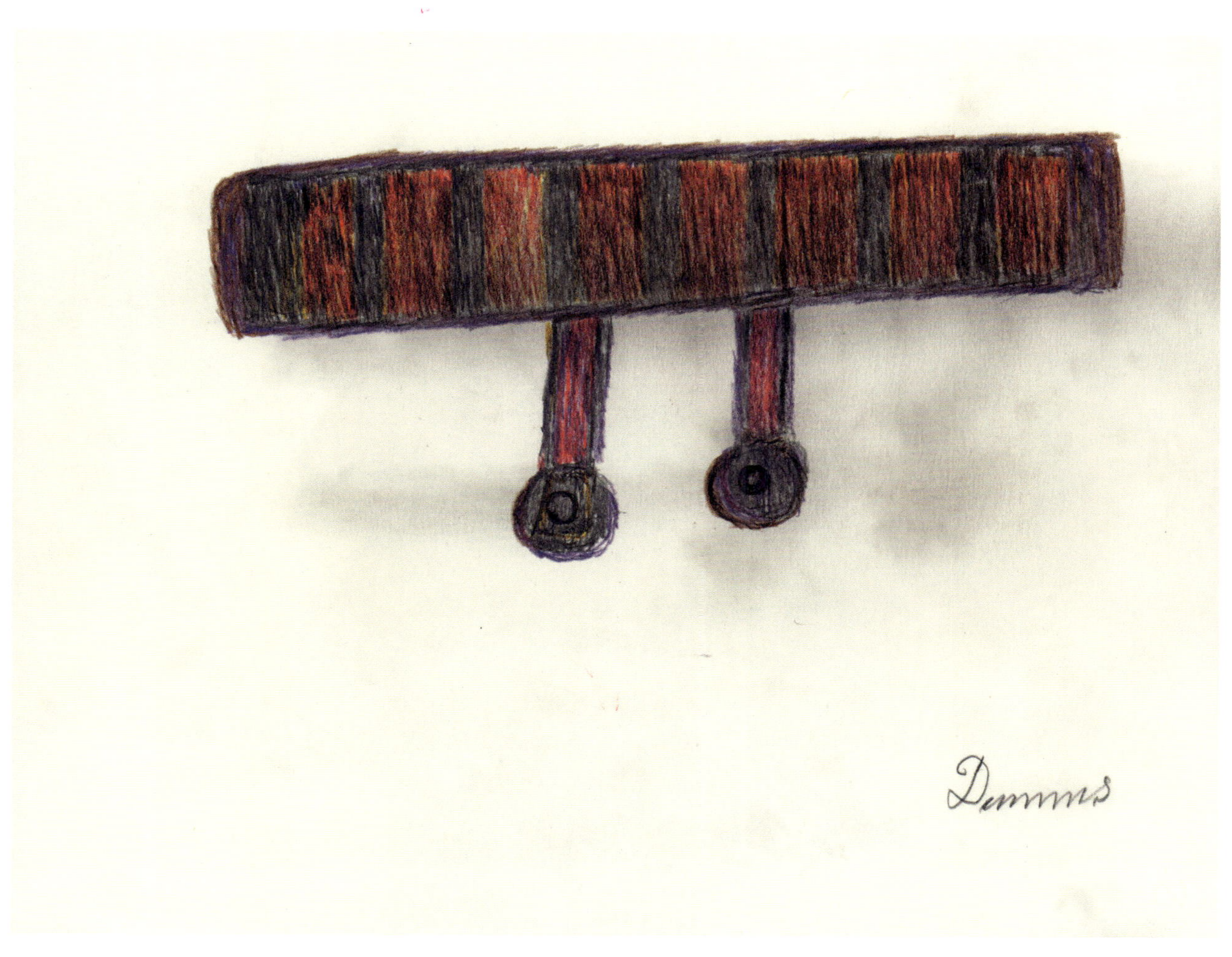

Anton Dobay
Sans titre untitled, 1977
crayon de couleur et craie grasse sur papier
coloured pencil and crayon on paper
30 x 40 cm

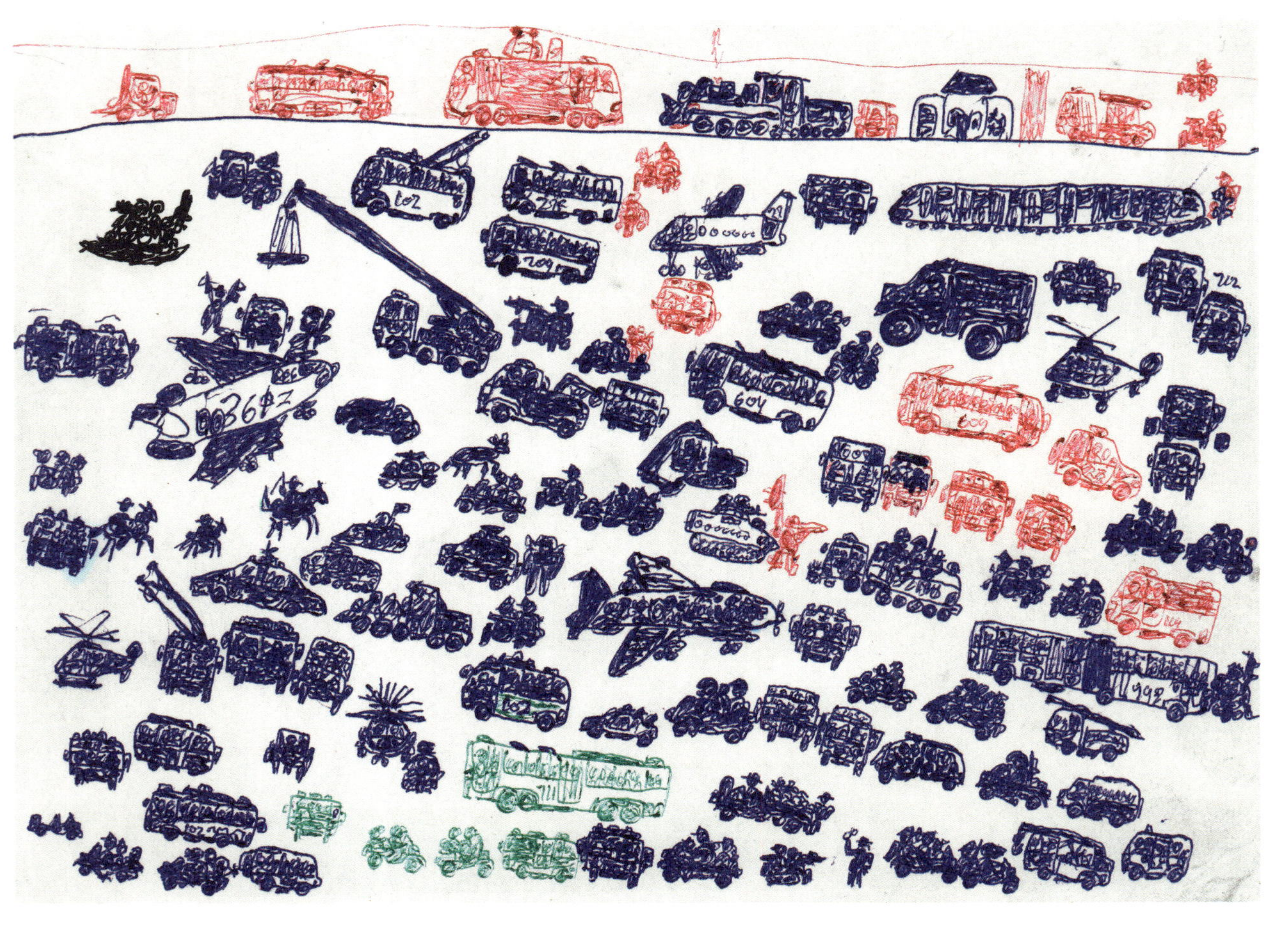

Feng Shi Yi
Sans titre untitled, ca. 2006-2008
stylo-bille sur papier
ballpoint pen on paper
12,4 x 17,1 cm

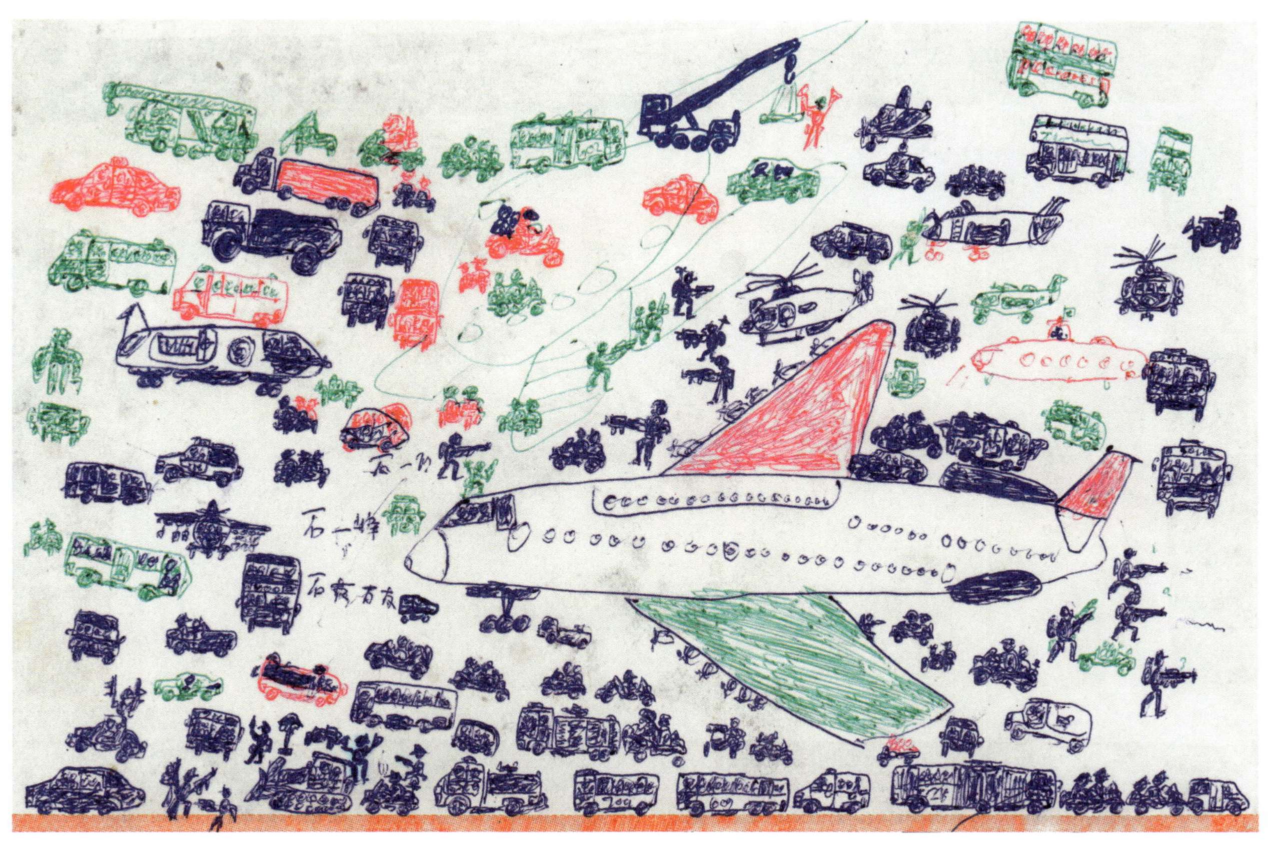

Feng Shi Yi
Sans titre untitled, ca. 2006-2008
stylo-bille sur papier
ballpoint pen on paper
12,1 x 18,5 cm

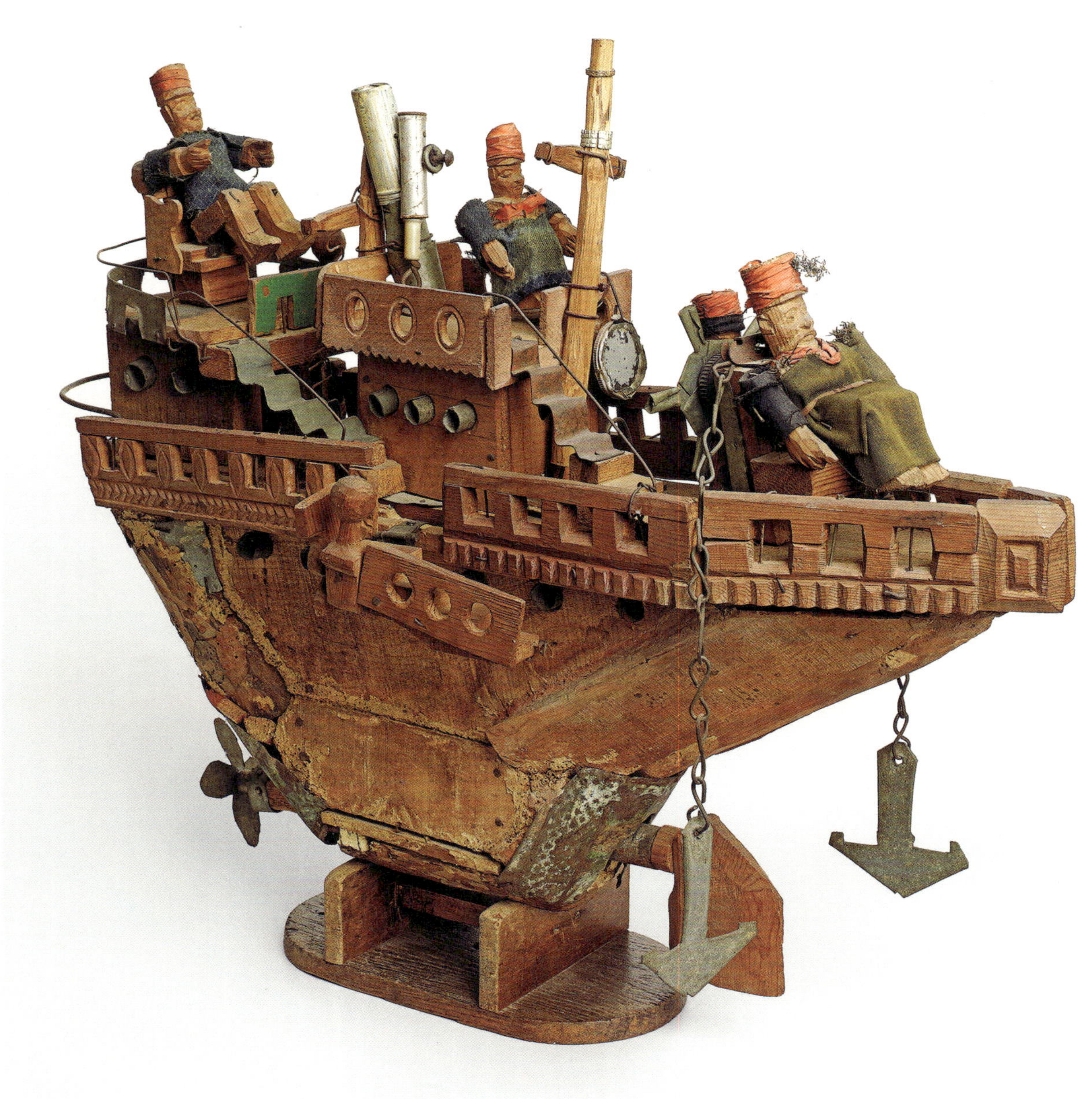

Auguste Forestier
Sans titre untitled, ca. 1935-1949
bois et matériaux divers
wood and miscellaneous materials
68 x 82 x 29 cm

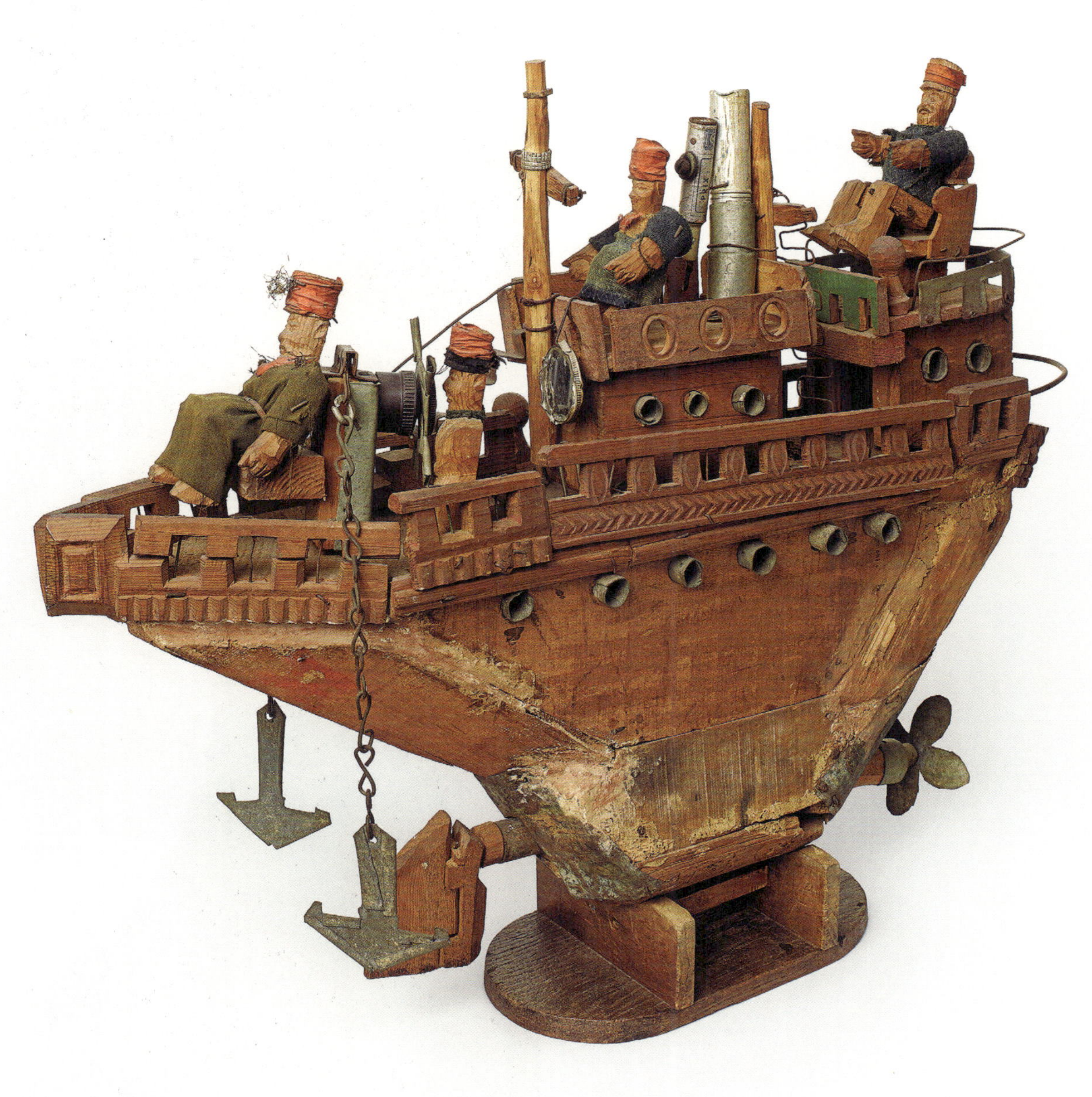

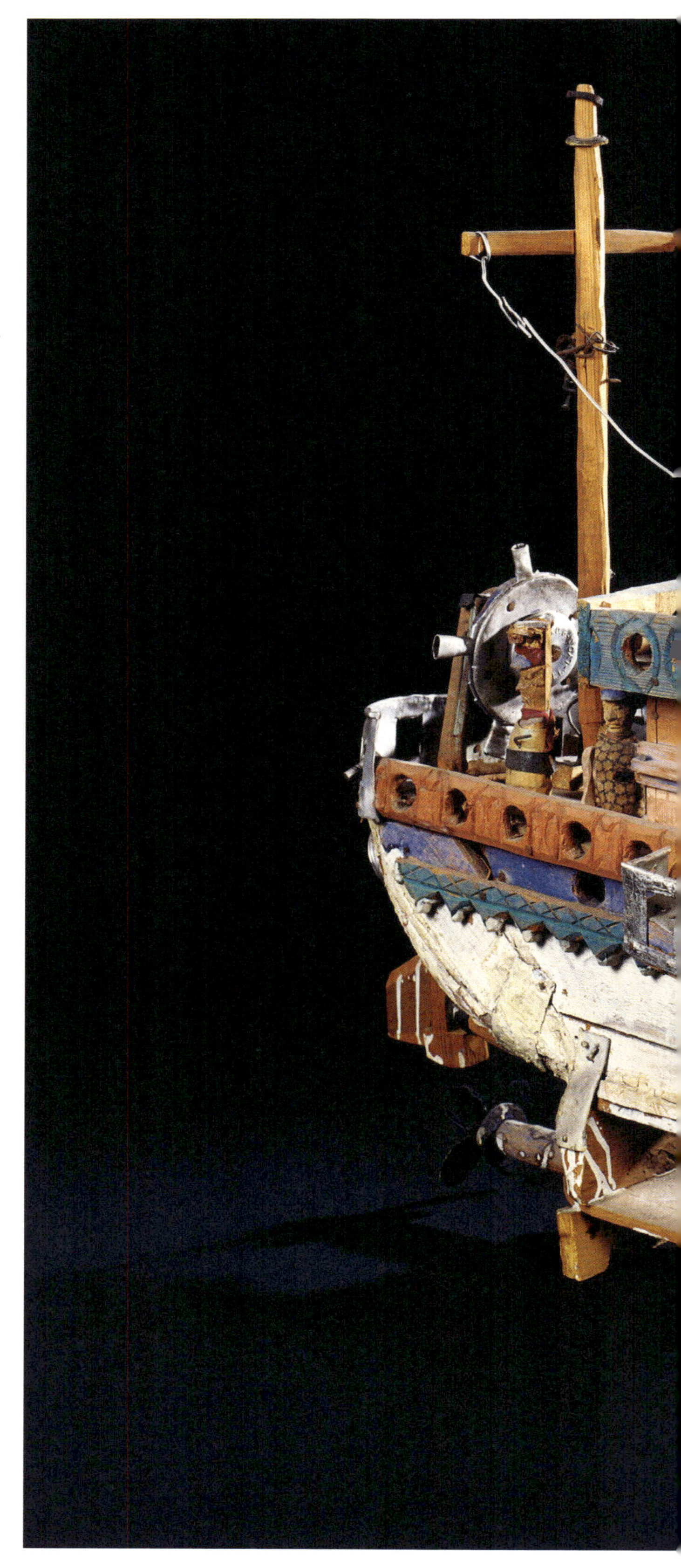

Auguste Forestier
Sans titre untitled, ca. 1935-1949
bois et matériaux divers
wood and miscellaneous materials
71 x 98 x 23 cm

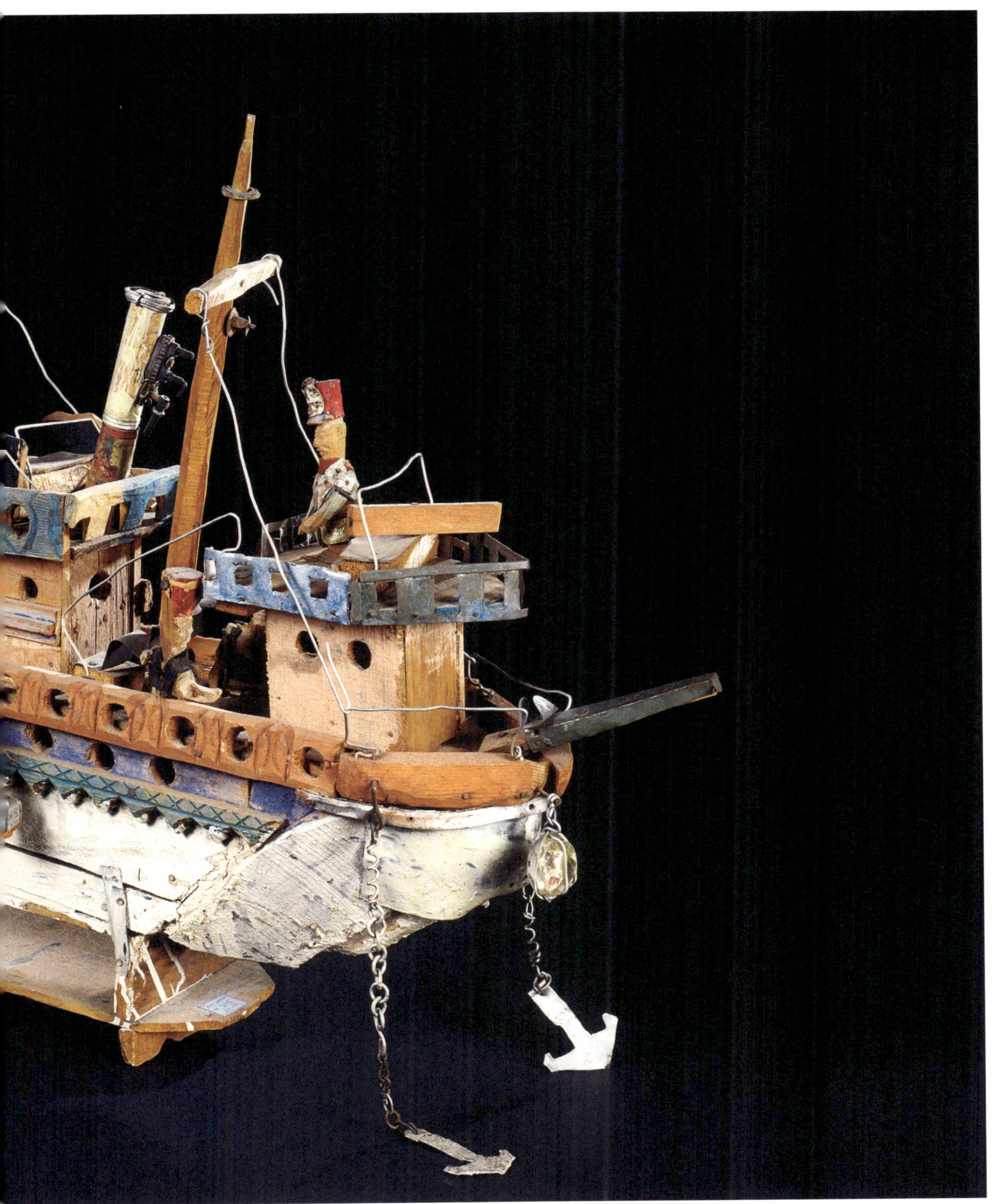

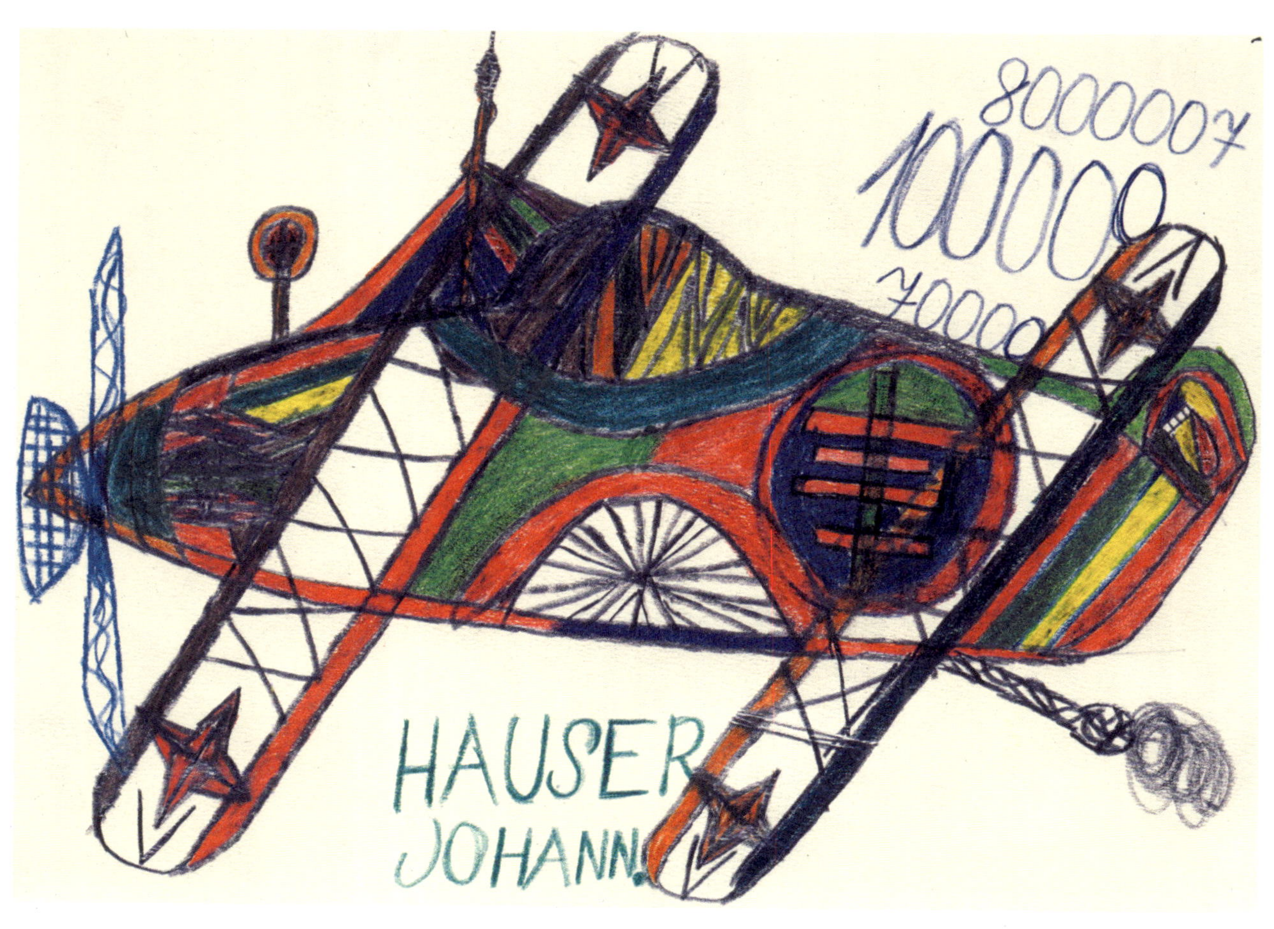

Johann Hauser
Sans titre untitled, ca. 1958-1978
craie grasse sur papier
crayon on paper
31 x 45 cm

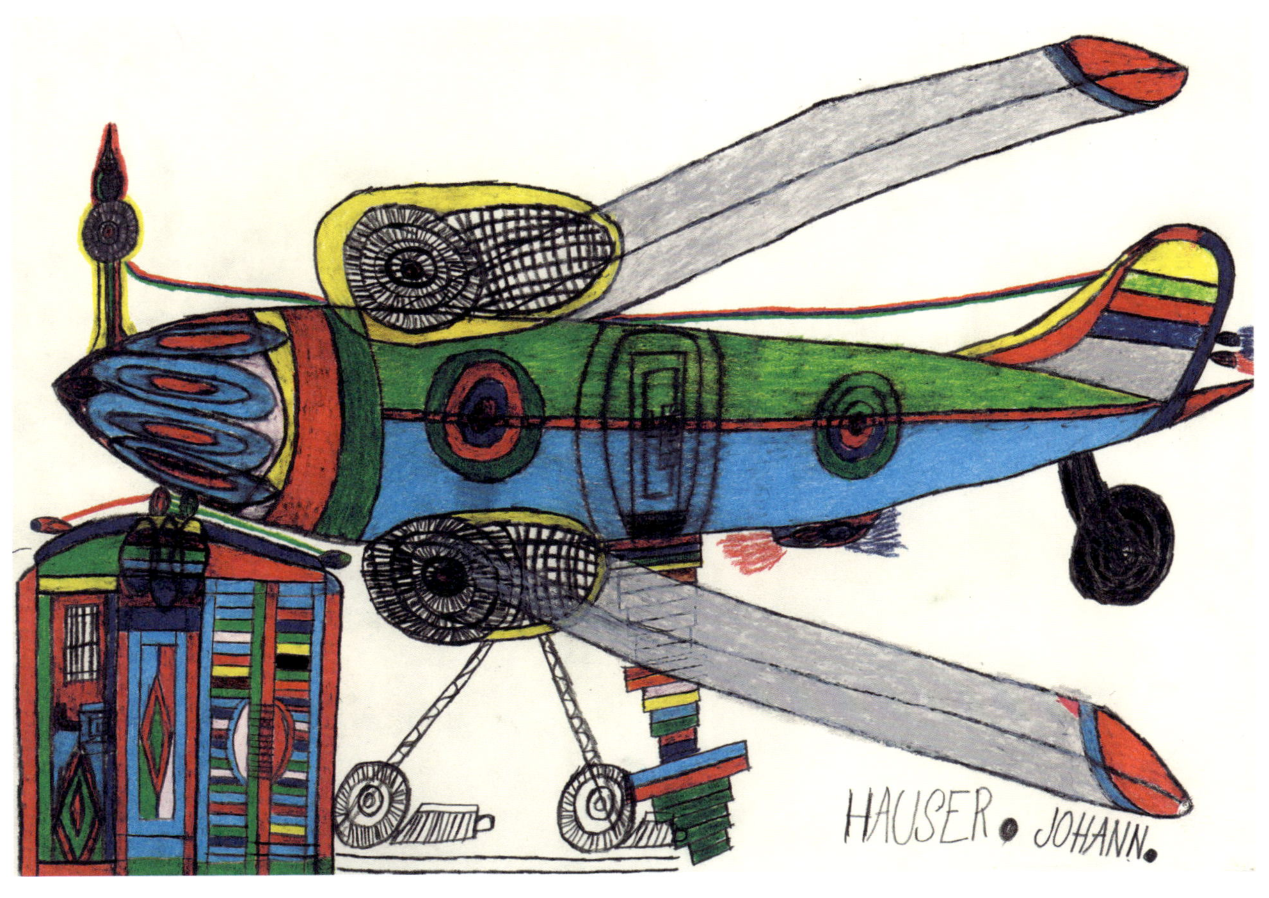

Johann Hauser
Sans titre untitled, ca. 1958-1964
mine de plomb et crayon de couleur sur papier lead pencil and coloured pencil on paper
20,7 x 29,6 cm

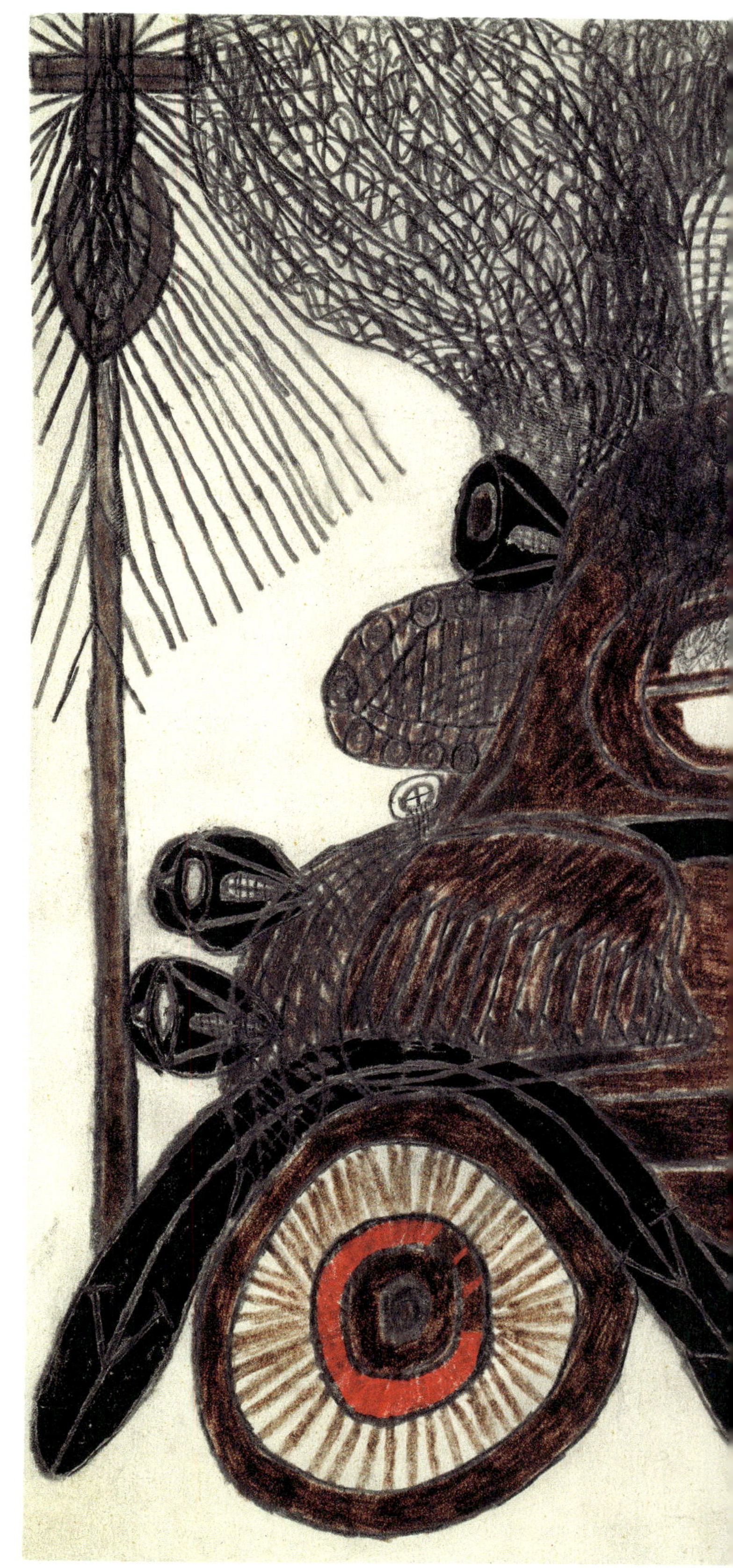

Johann Hauser
Sans titre untitled, 1966
mine de plomb et feutre indélébile sur papier lead pencil and indelible felt pen on paper
29,8 x 40,2 cm

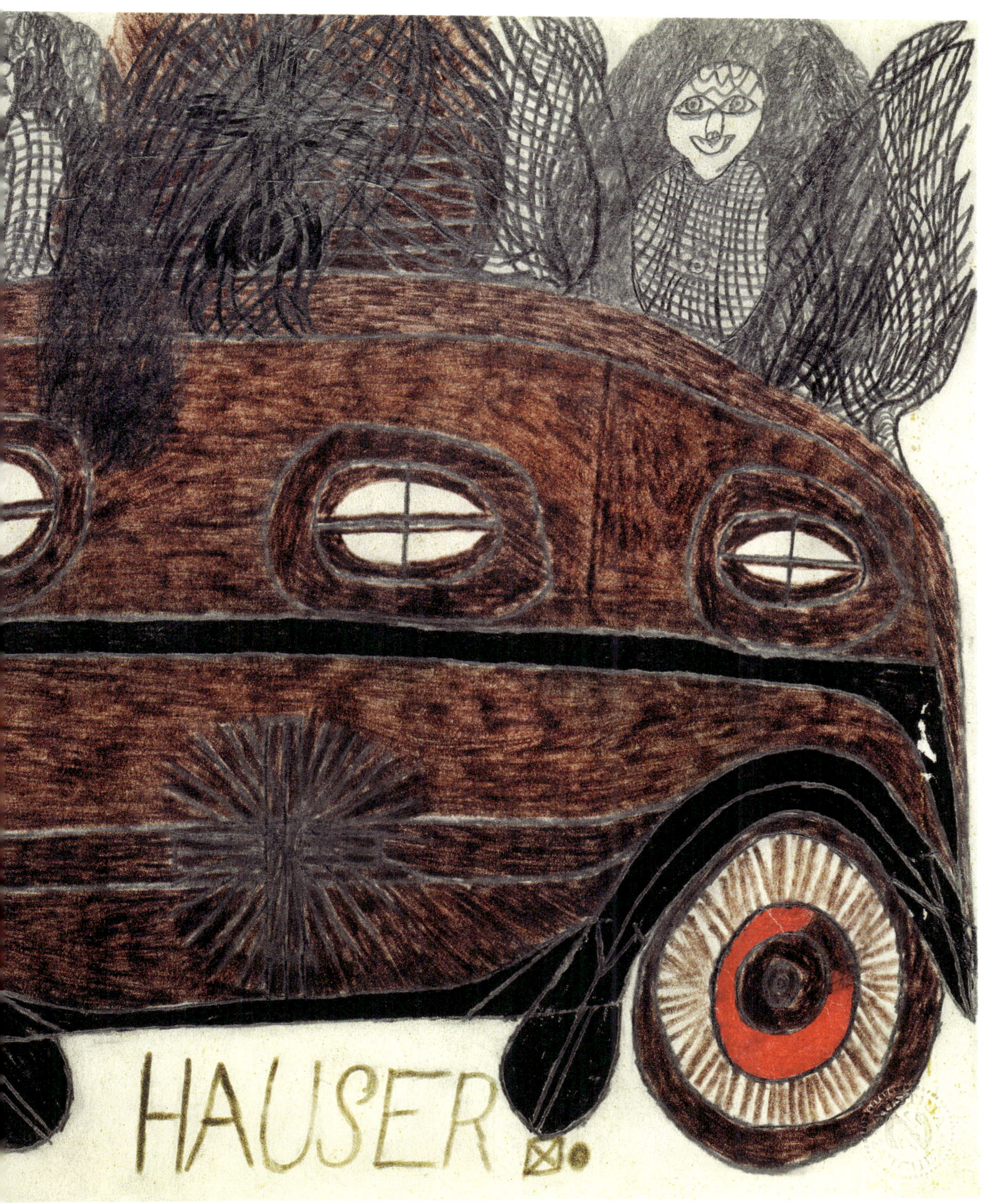
HAUSER

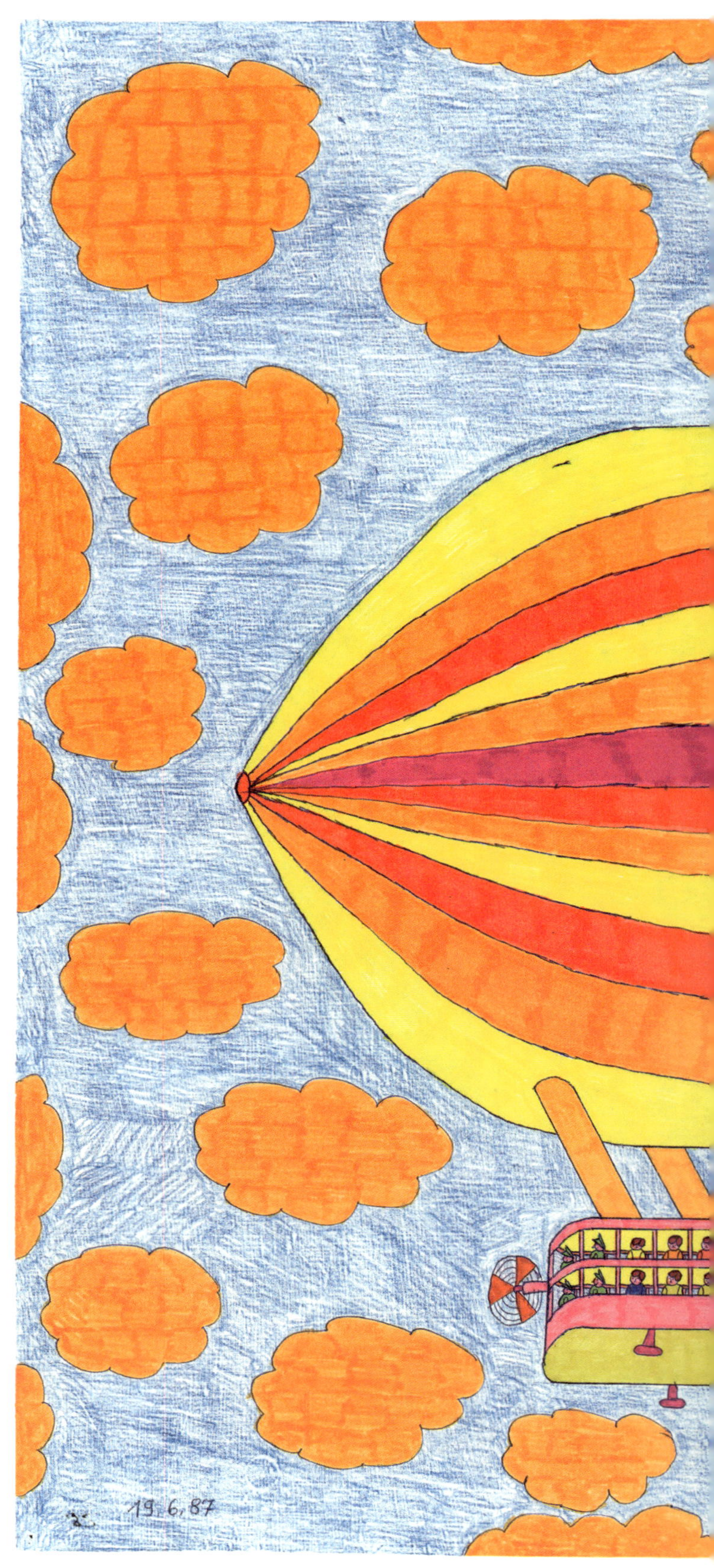

Helmut
Sans titre untitled, 1987
stylo-bille, feutre et crayon de couleur sur papier ballpoint pen, felt pen and coloured pencil on paper
42 x 56,5 cm

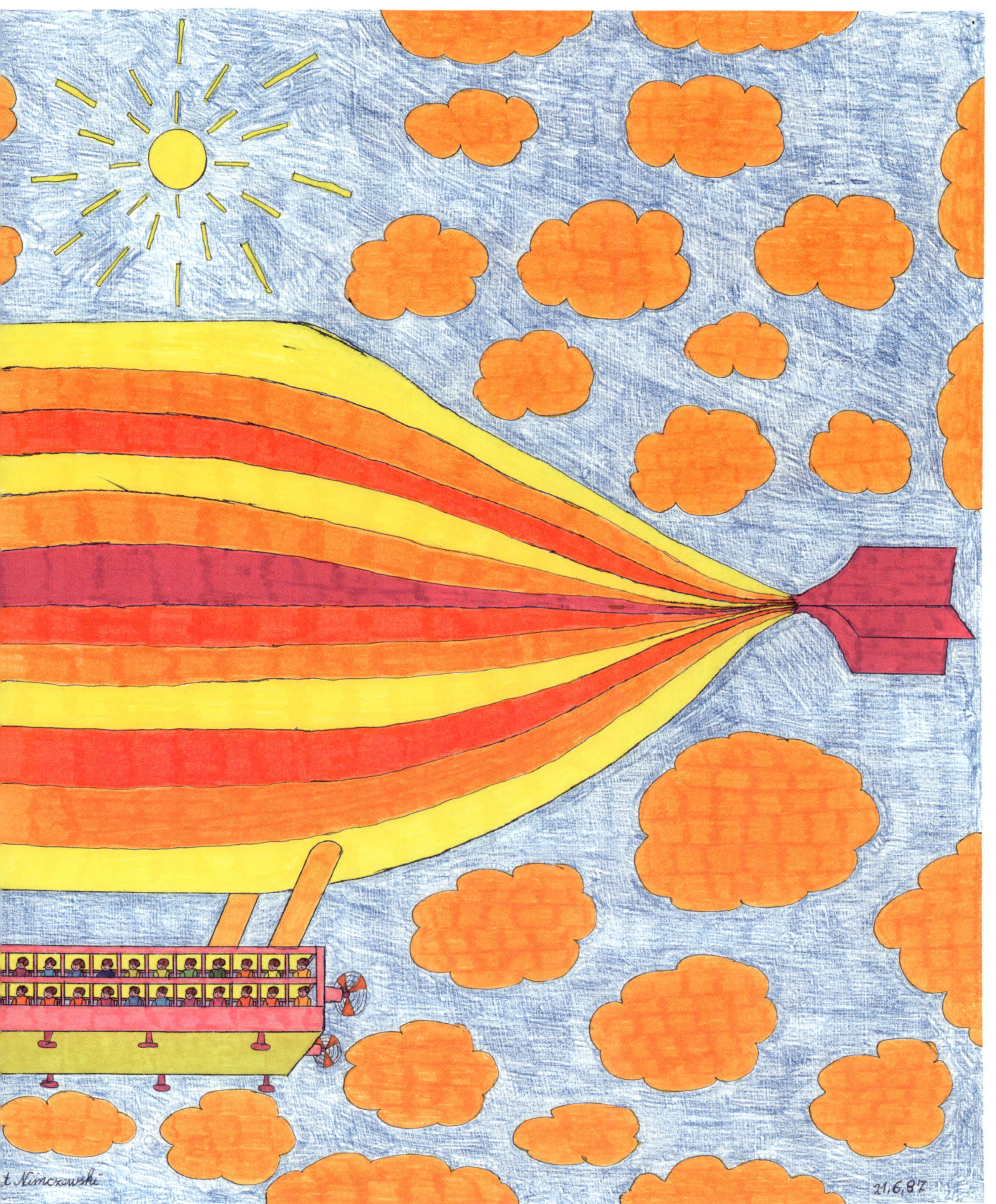
t. Nimczewski
21,6,87

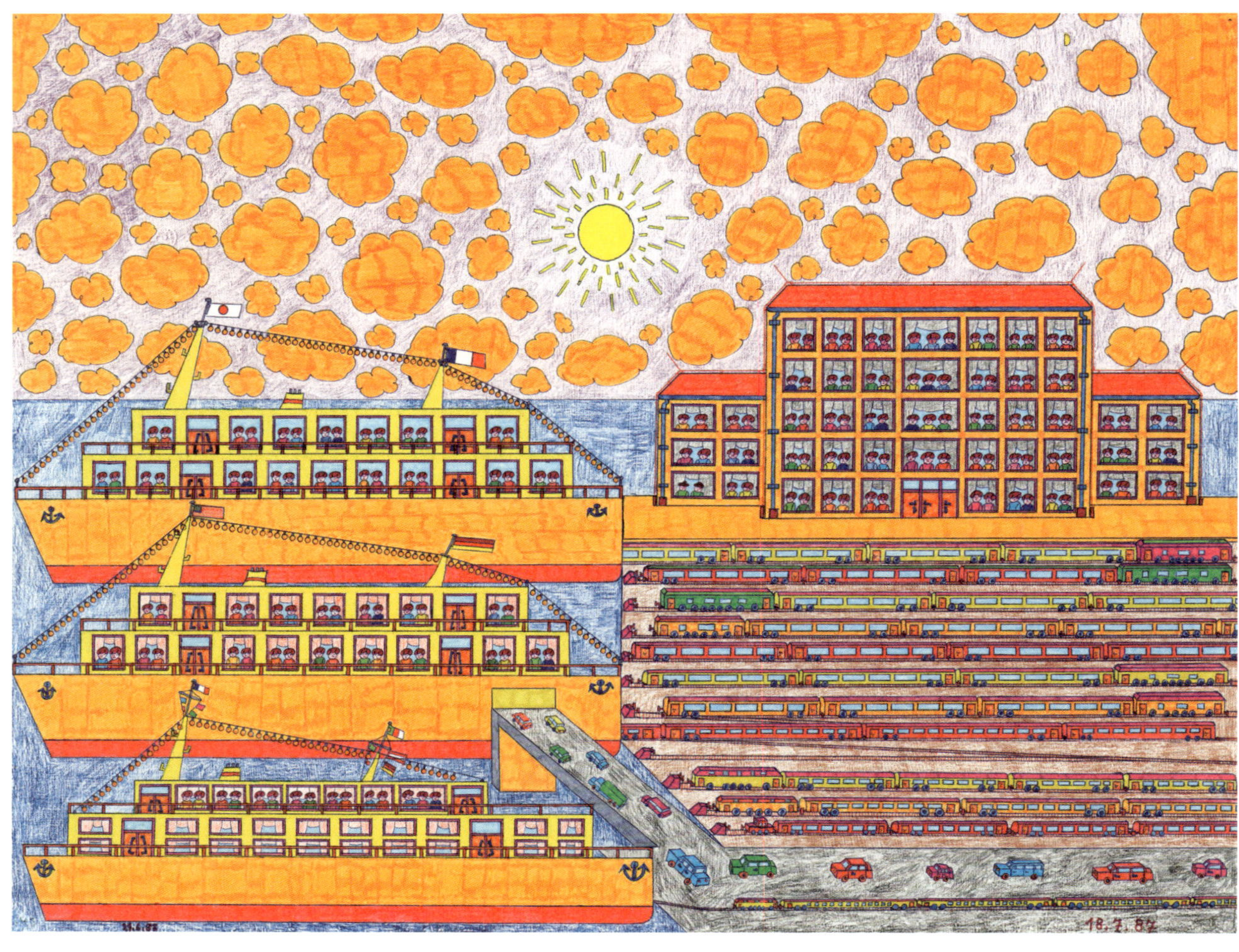

Helmut
Sans titre untitled, 1987
stylo-bille, feutre et crayon de couleur
sur papier ballpoint pen, felt pen
and coloured pencil on paper
42 x 56,5 cm

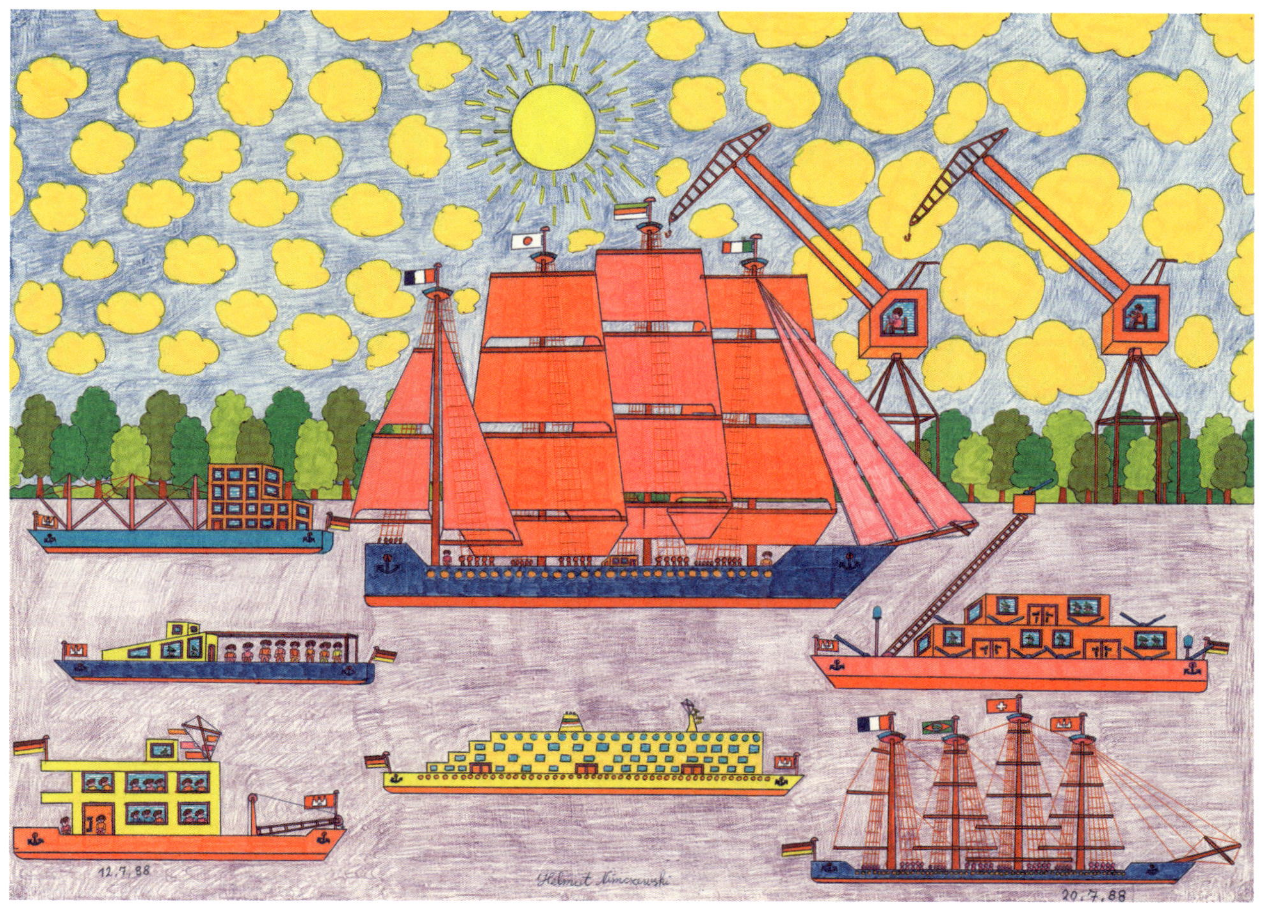

Helmut
Sans titre *untitled*, 1988
stylo-bille, feutre et crayon de couleur sur papier ballpoint pen, felt pen and coloured pencil on paper
42 x 59,3 cm

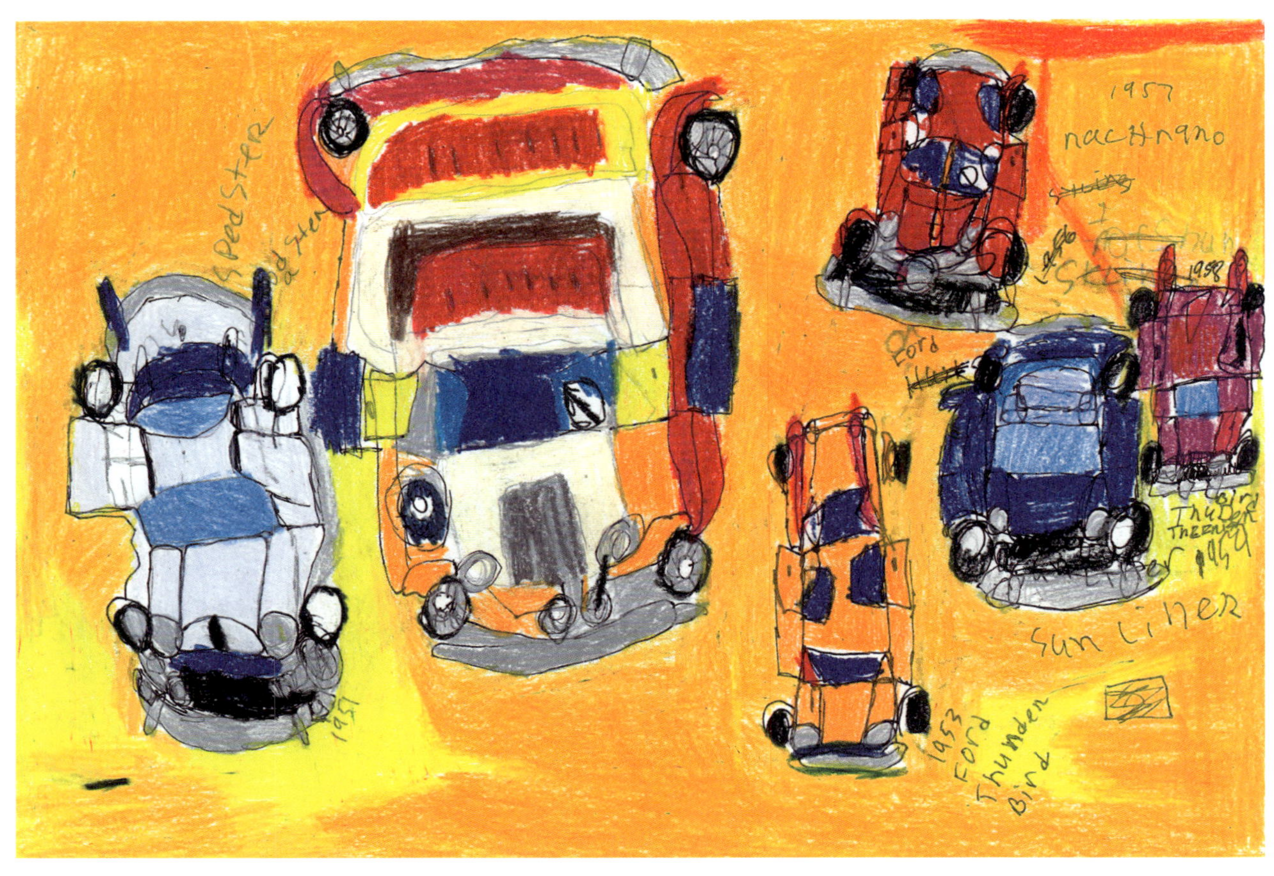

Lorna Hylton
Sans titre untitled, ca. 1991-2005
craie grasse et feutre sur papier
crayon and felt pen on paper
30,6 x 45,5 cm

Lorna Hylton
Sans titre untitled, ca. 1991-2005
craie grasse et feutre sur papier
crayon and felt pen on paper
61 x 48 cm

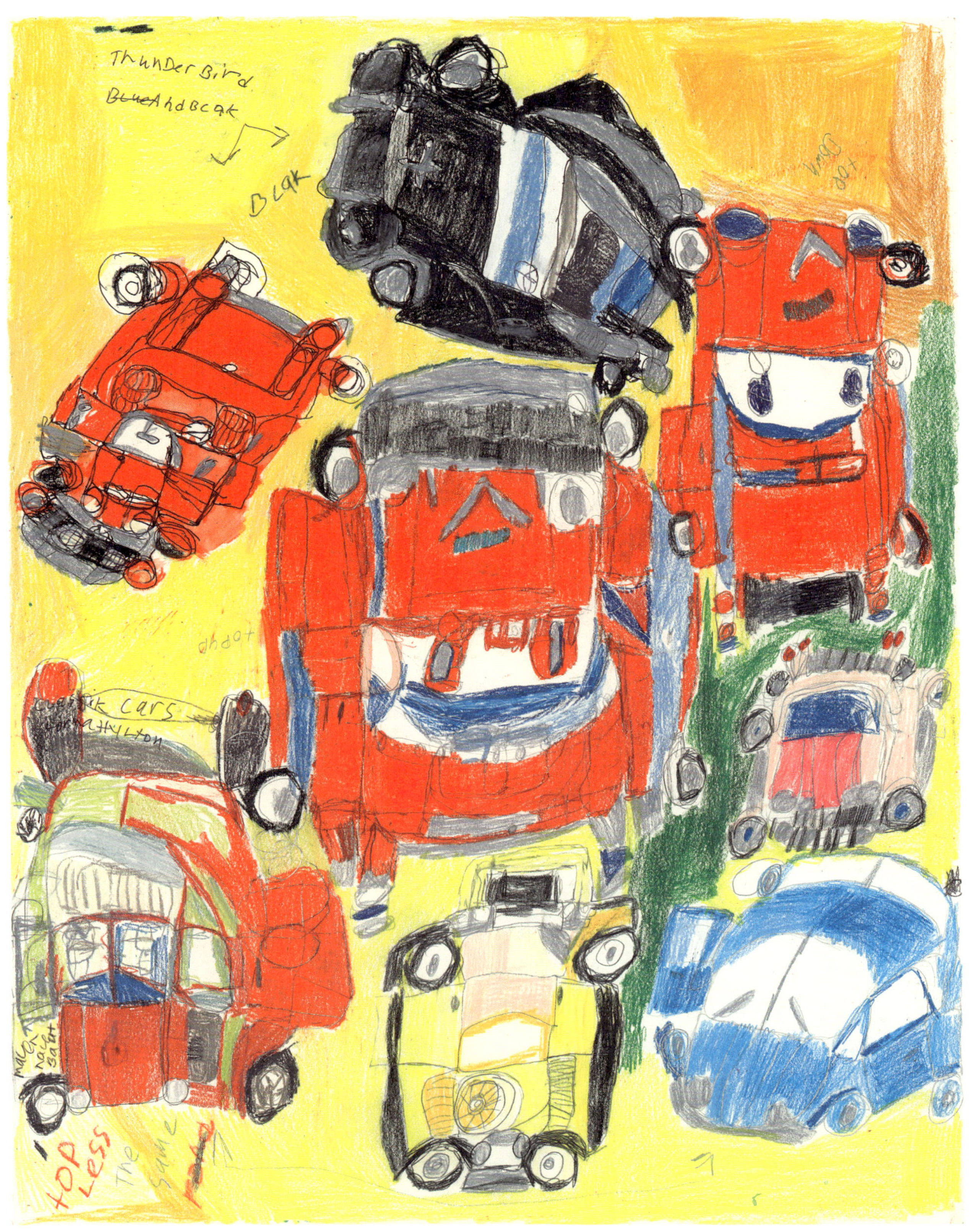
ThunDer Bird
Blak
TOP Less
The same

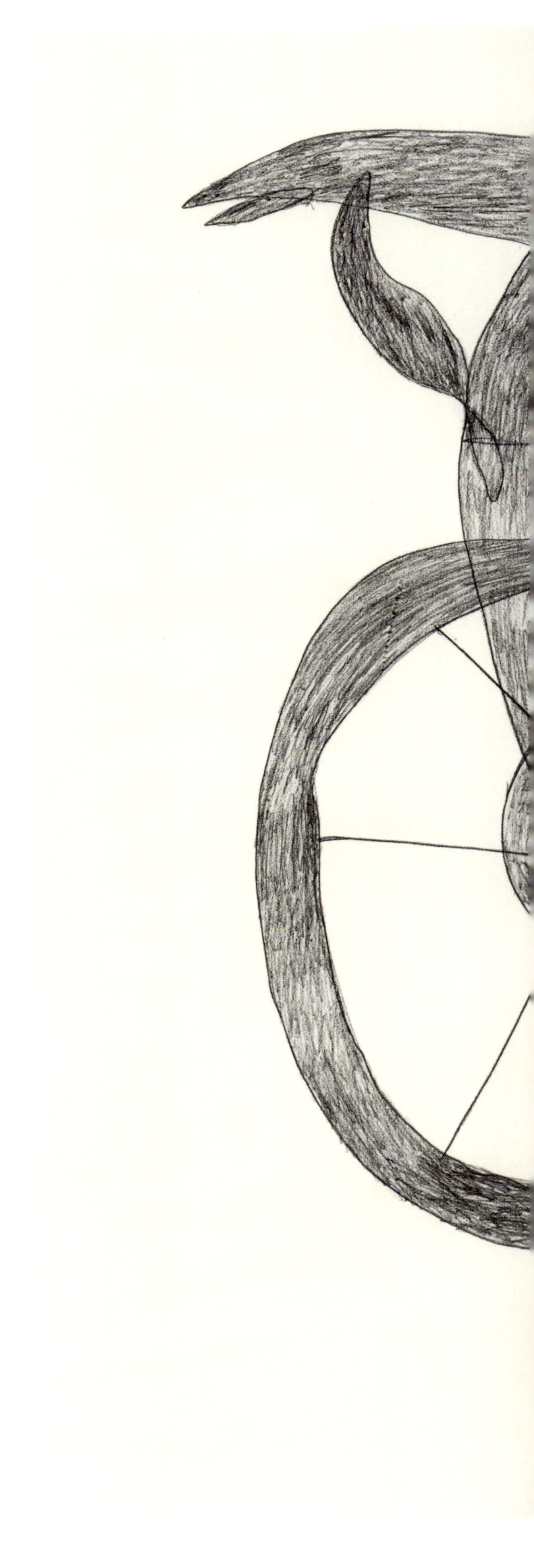

Franz Kernbeis
Sans titre untitled, 1990
crayon de couleur sur papier
coloured pencil on paper
150 x 180 cm

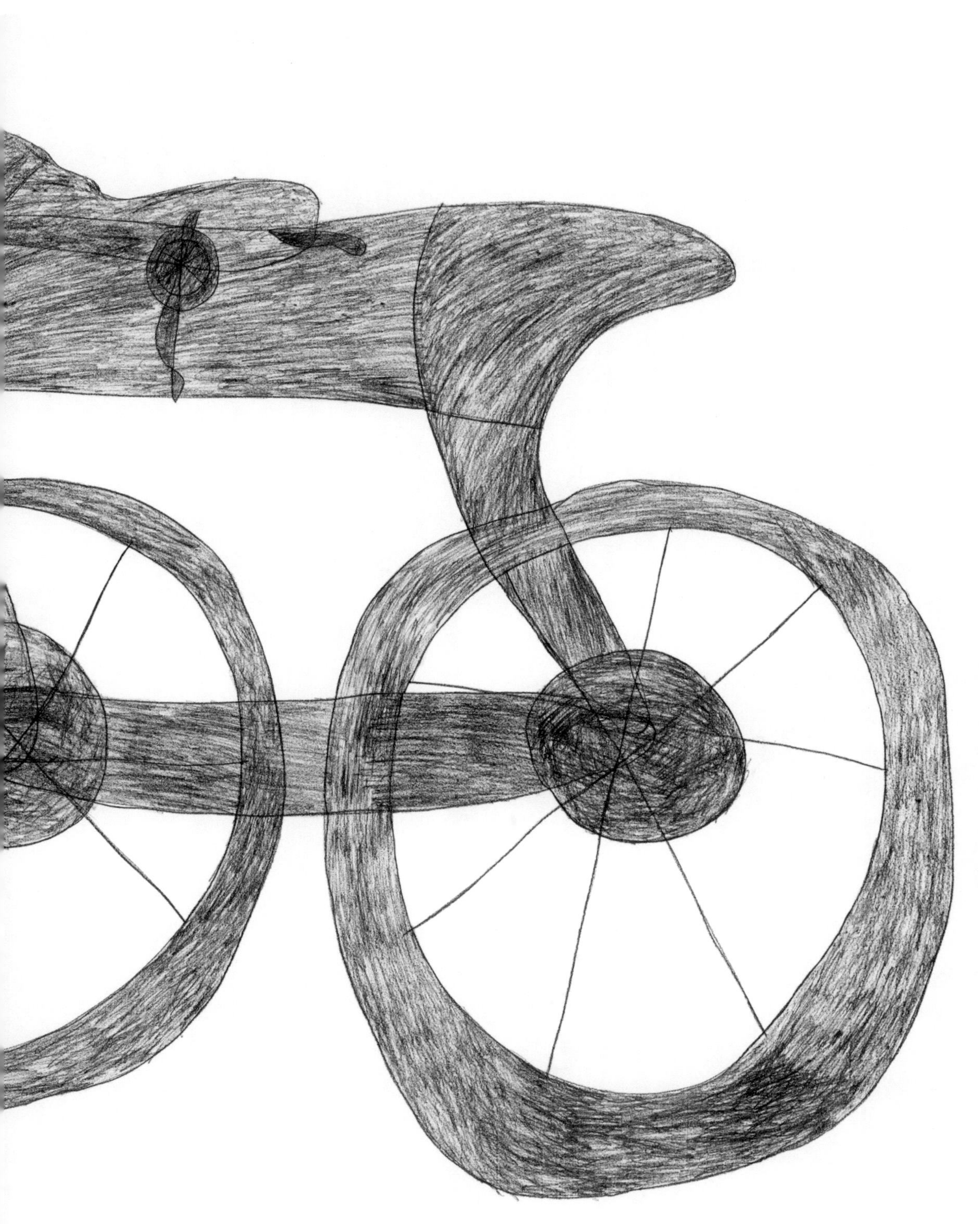
1990. Franz Kernbeis

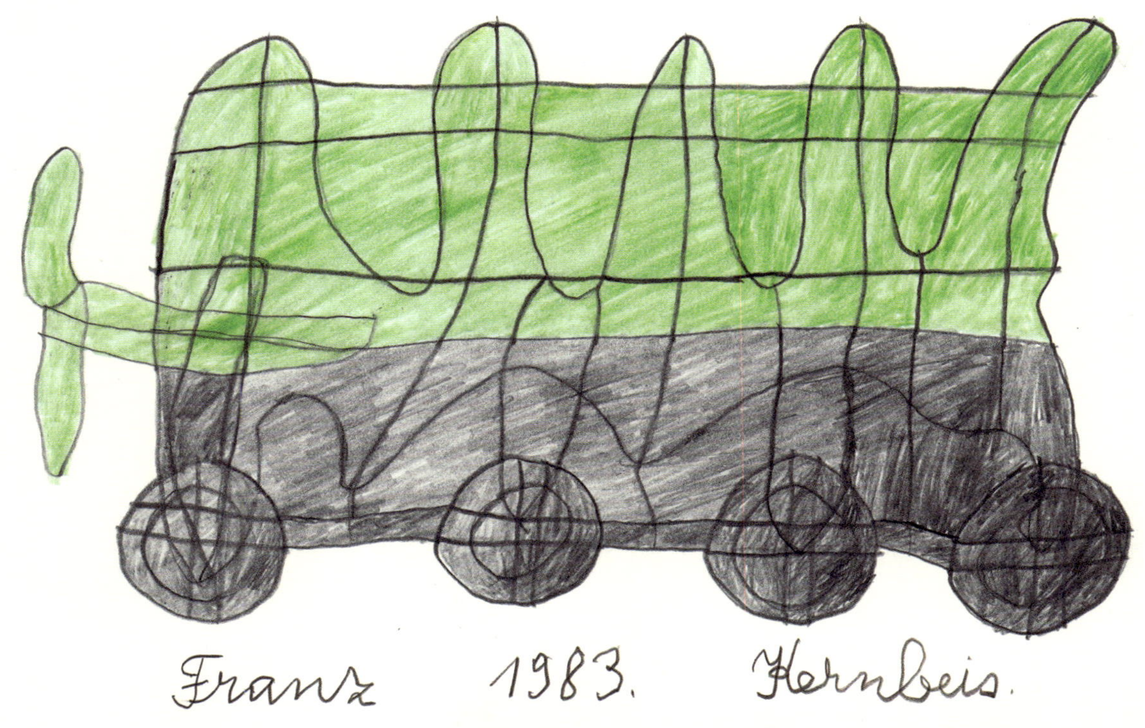

Franz Kernbeis
Heuwagen, 1983
crayon de couleur sur papier
coloured pencil on paper
21 x 29,5 cm

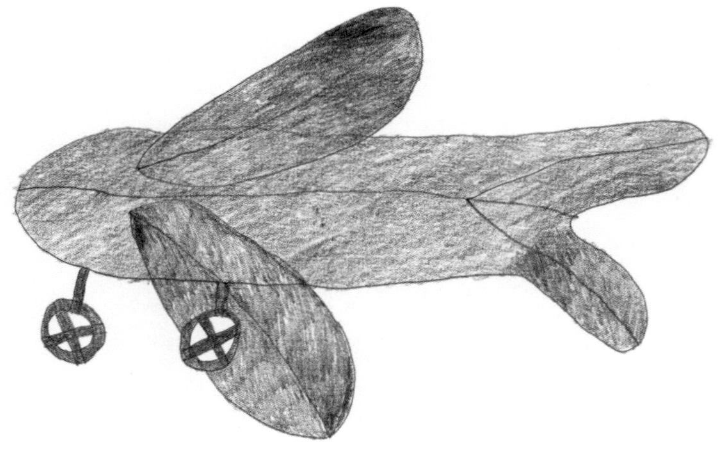

Franz Kernbeis
Sans titre untitled, 1981
mine de plomb sur papier
lead pencil on paper
30 x 40 cm

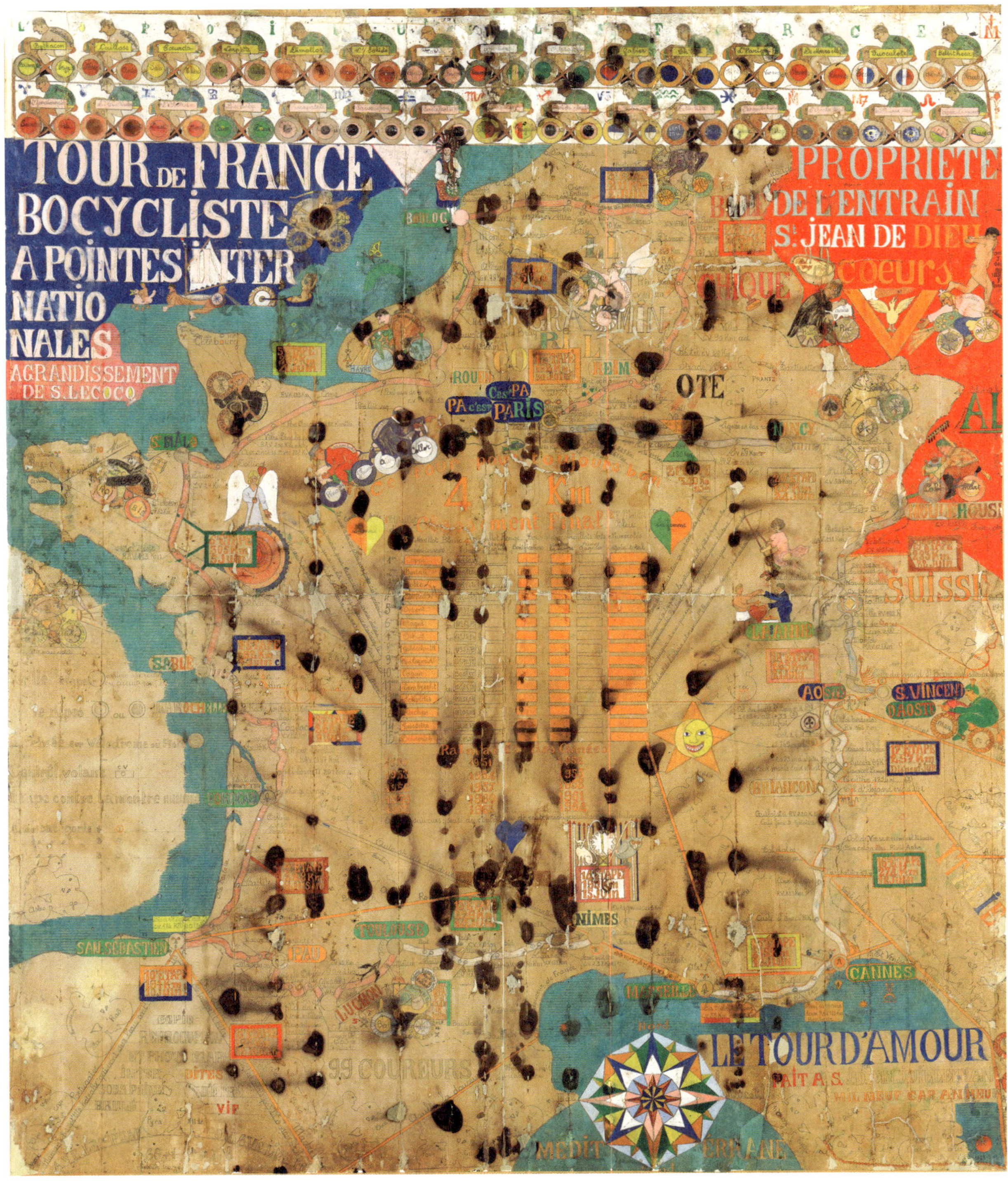

Sylvain Lecocq
Tour de France bocycliste.
Le Tour d'amour, 1949
mine de plomb et gouache
sur papier d'emballage
lead pencil and gouache
on wrapping paper
142 x 117 cm

Sylvain Lecocq
Tour de France bocycliste.
Le Tour d'amour, 1949
(détail detail)

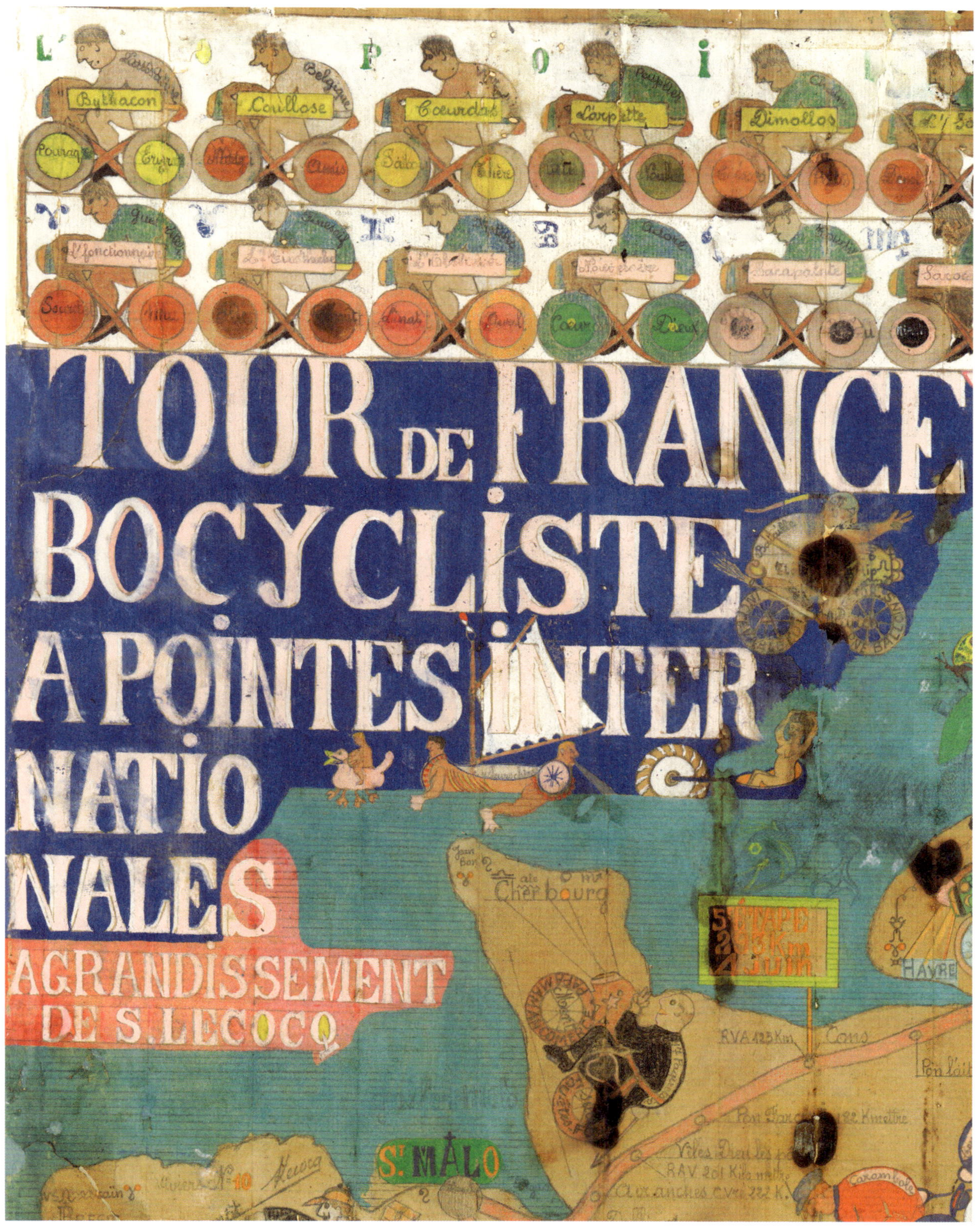
TOUR DE FRANCE
BOCYCLISTE
A POINTES INTER
NATIO
NALES
AGRANDISSEMENT
DE S. LECOCQ
Cherbourg
5e ETAPE
93 Km
4 JUIN
HAVRE
St MALO

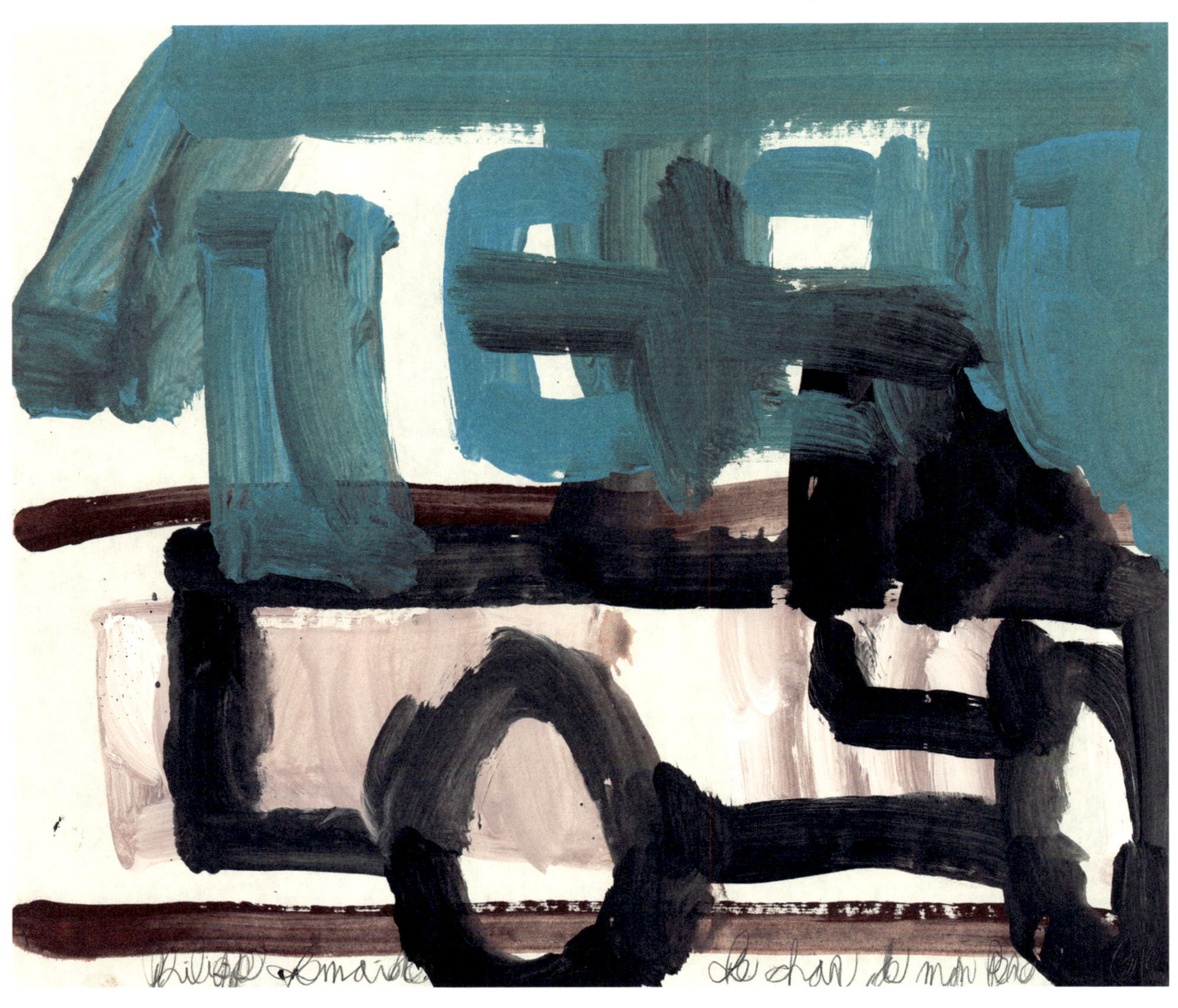

Philippe Lemaire
Le Char de mon père, ca. 2000
gouache sur papier
gouache on paper
35,5 x 43 cm

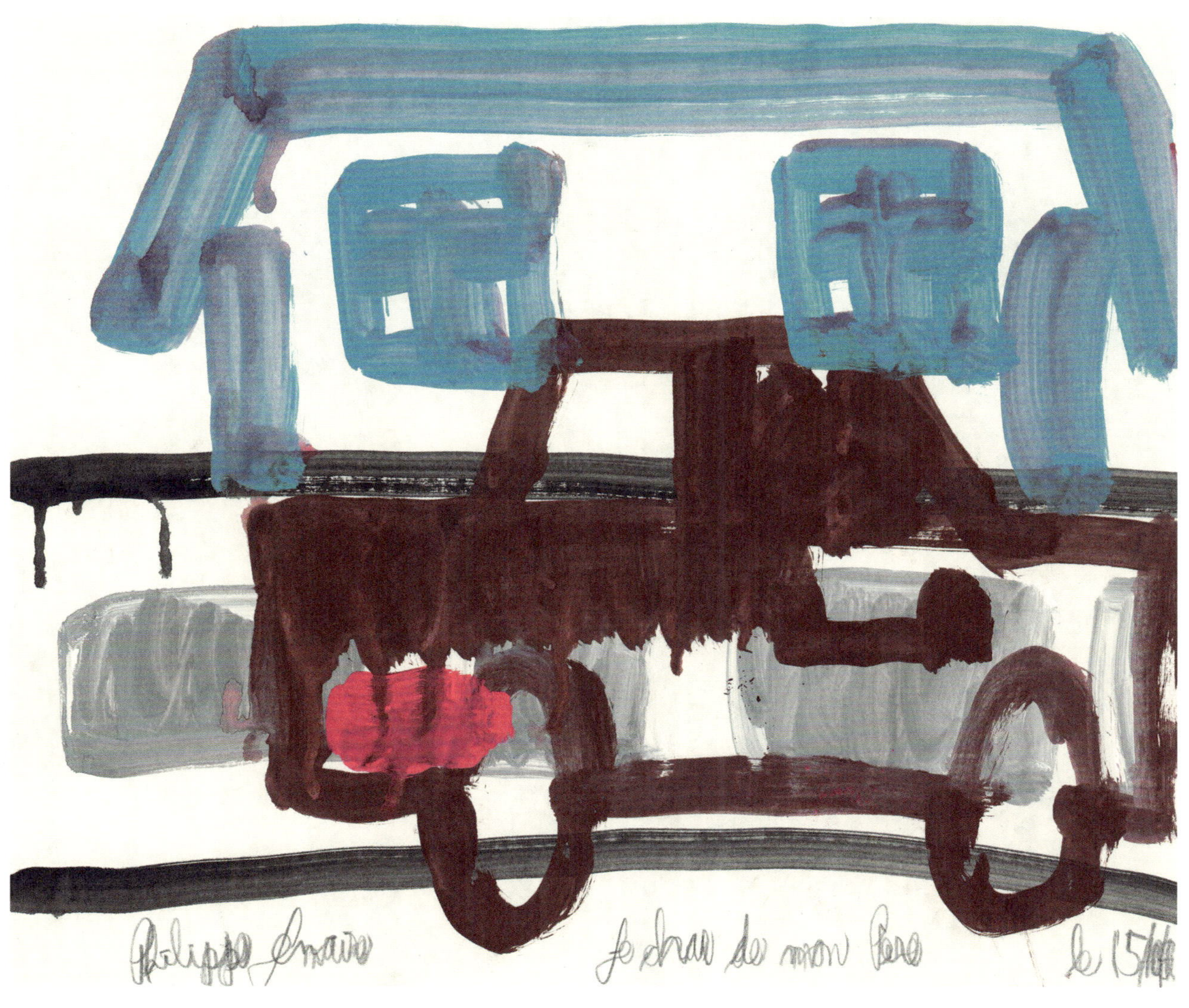

Philippe Lemaire
Le Char de mon père, ca. 2000
gouache sur papier
gouache on paper
35,5 x 43 cm

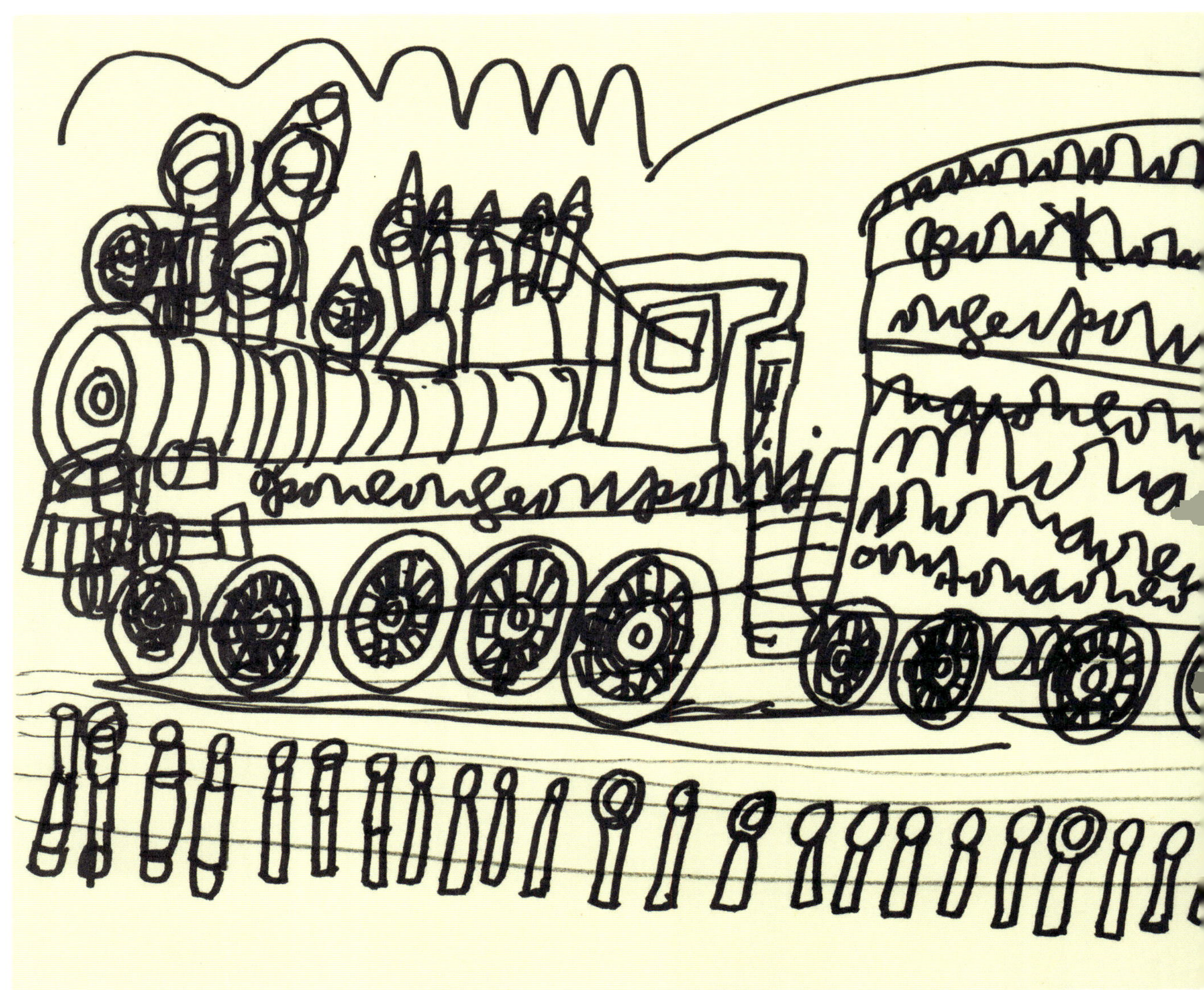

Dwight Mackintosh
Sans titre untitled, 1986
feutre sur papier
felt pen on paper
28,5 x 72,5 cm

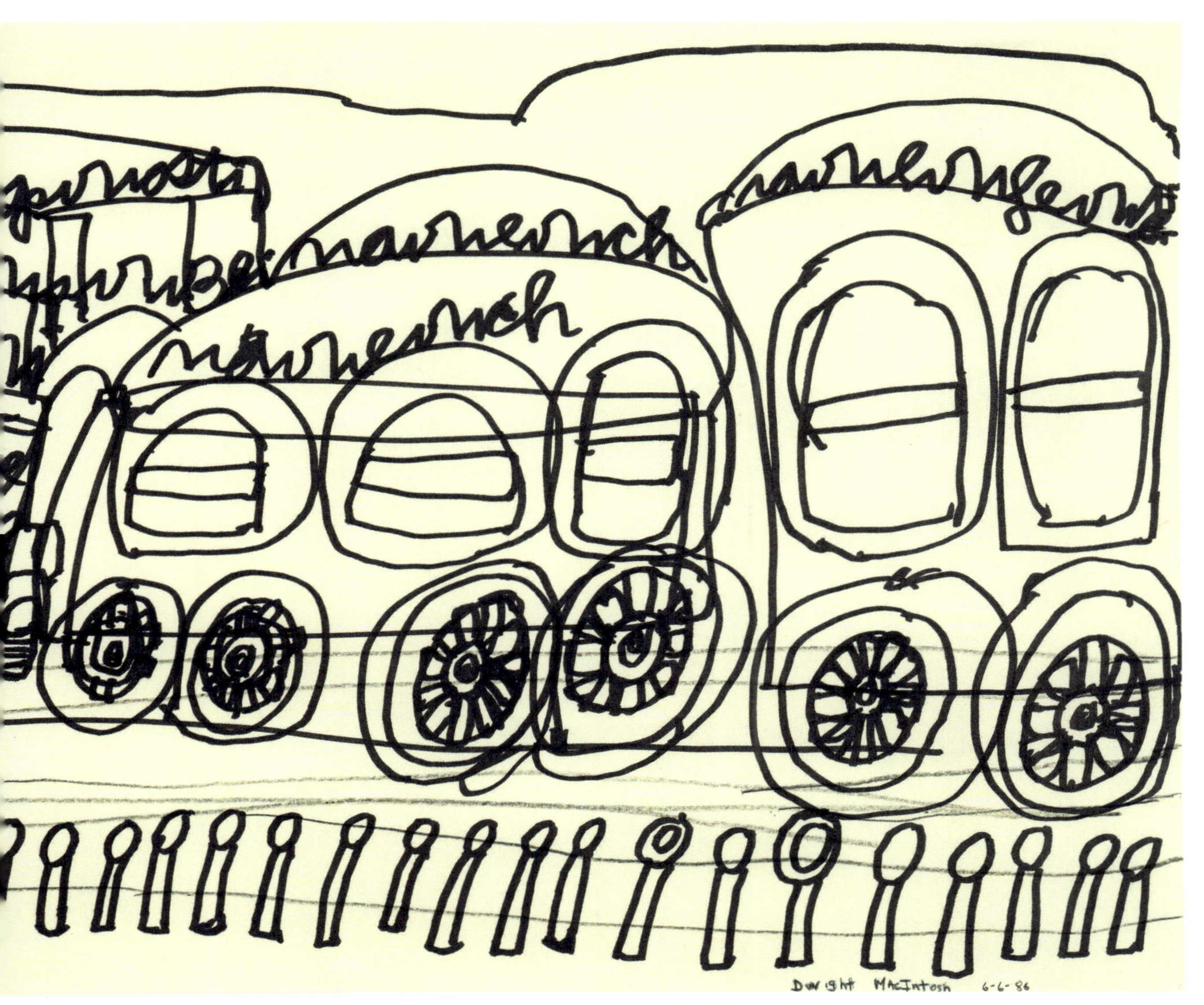
Dwight MAcIntosh 6-6-86

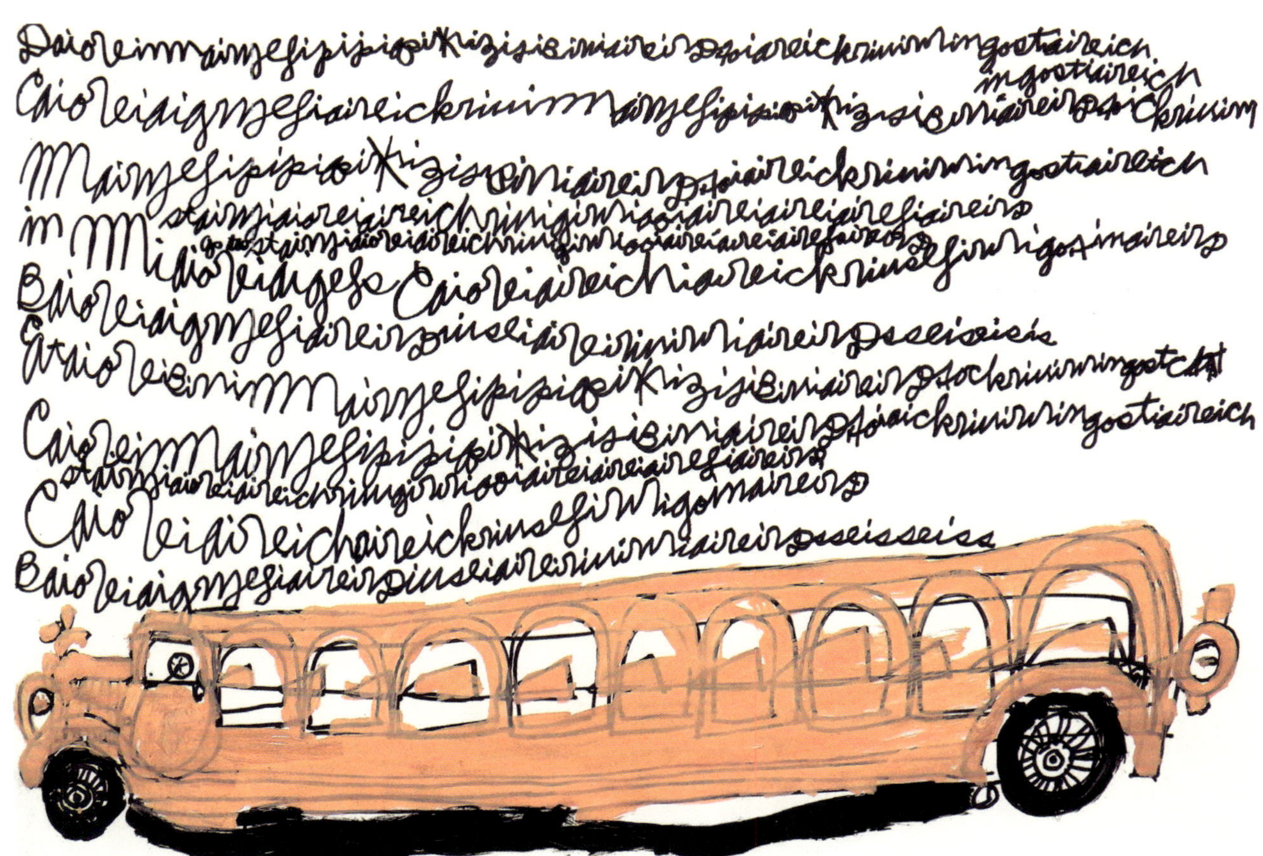

Dwight Mackintosh
Sans titre untitled, 1981
feutre et gouache sur pap er
felt pen and gouache on paper
37 x 75 cm

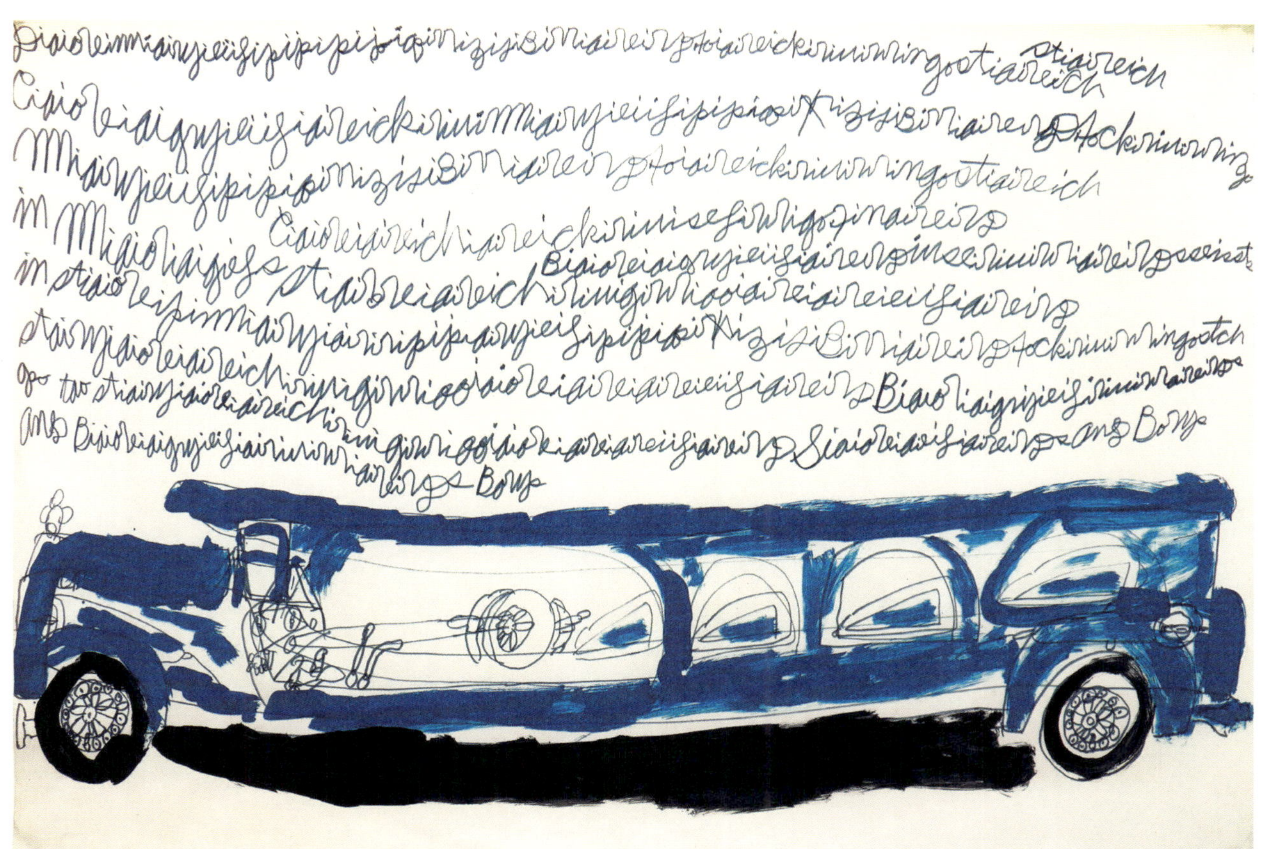

Dwight Mackintosh
Sans titre untitled, 1981
feutre et gouache sur papier
felt pen and gouache on paper
37 x 75 cm

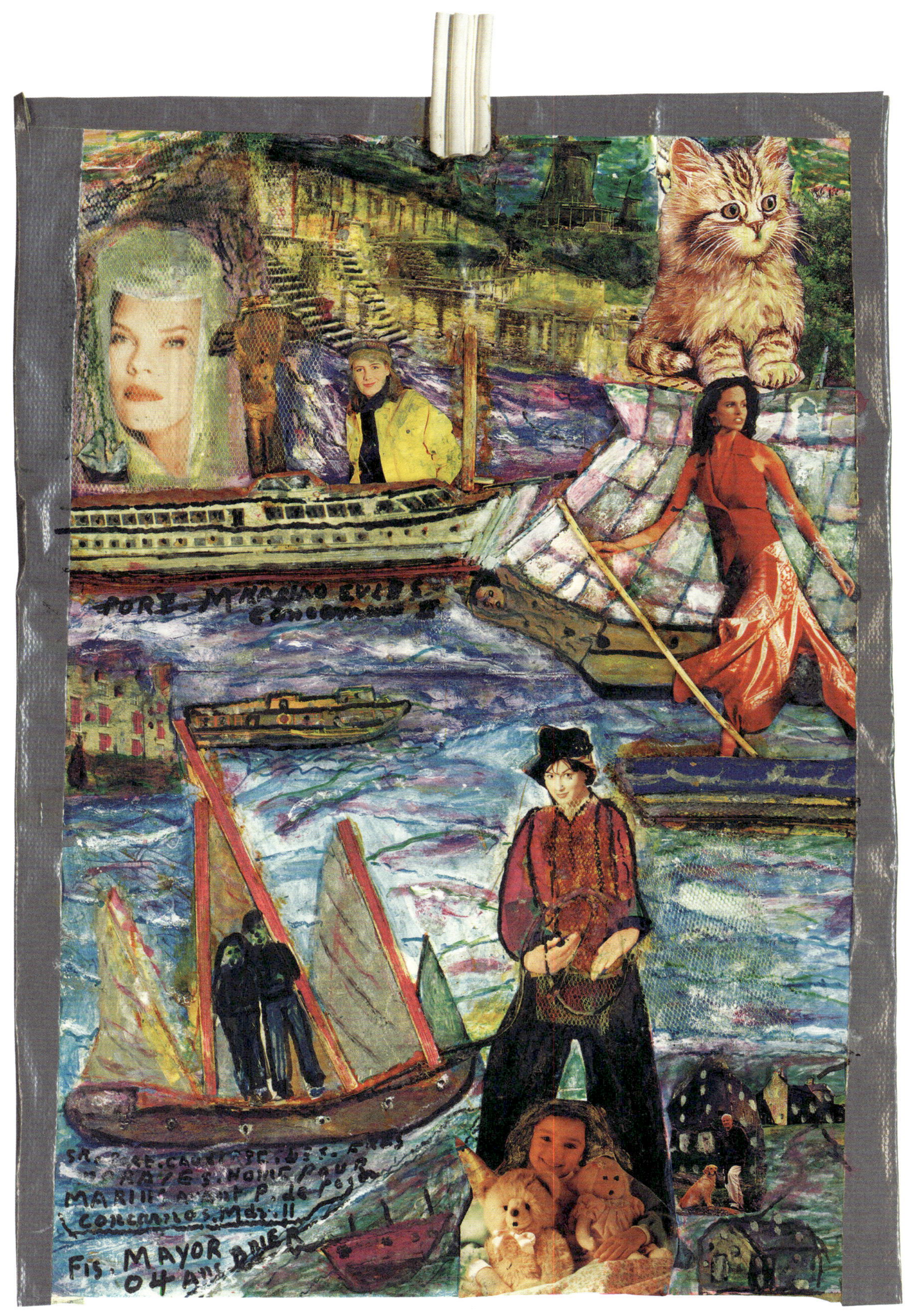
Fis. MAYOR
04 Ans

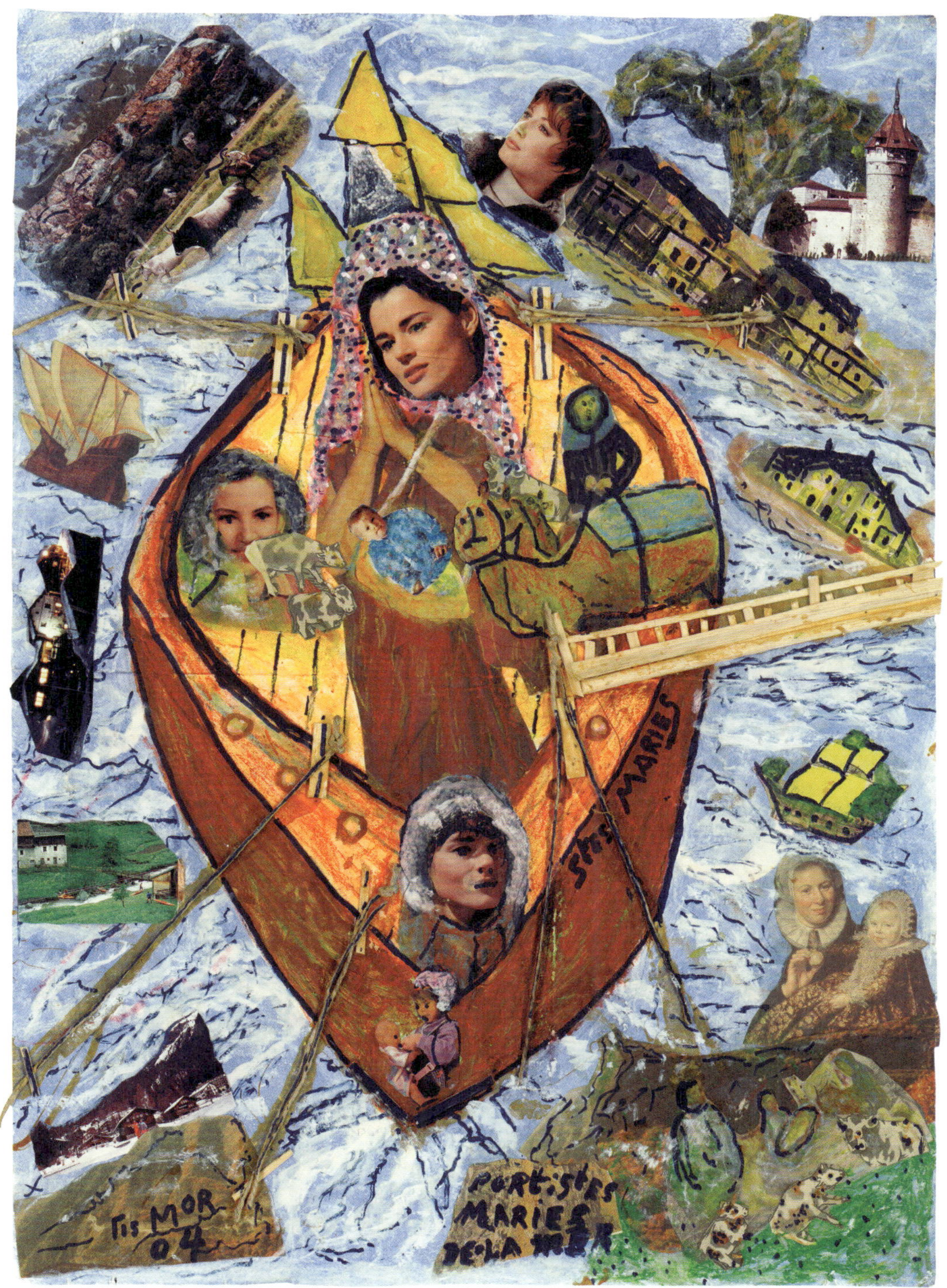

Francis Mayor
Port Marino, pour les marins de Concarneau, ca. 1993-1994
peinture et collage sur papier
paint and collage on paper
57 x 42 cm

Francis Mayor
Port Stes-Maries-de-la-Mer,
ca. 1993-1994
peinture et collage sur papier
paint and collage on paper
56 x 42 cm

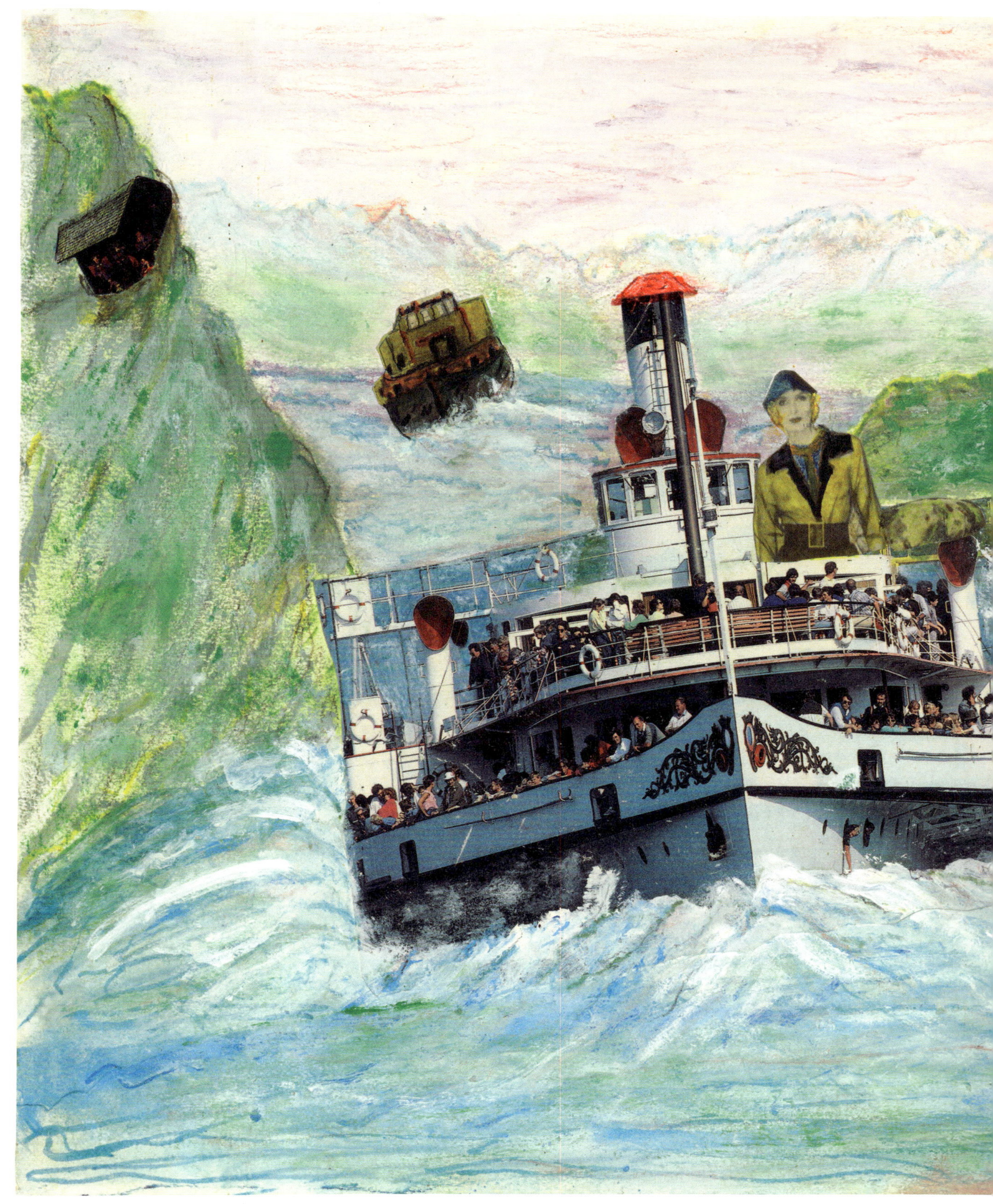

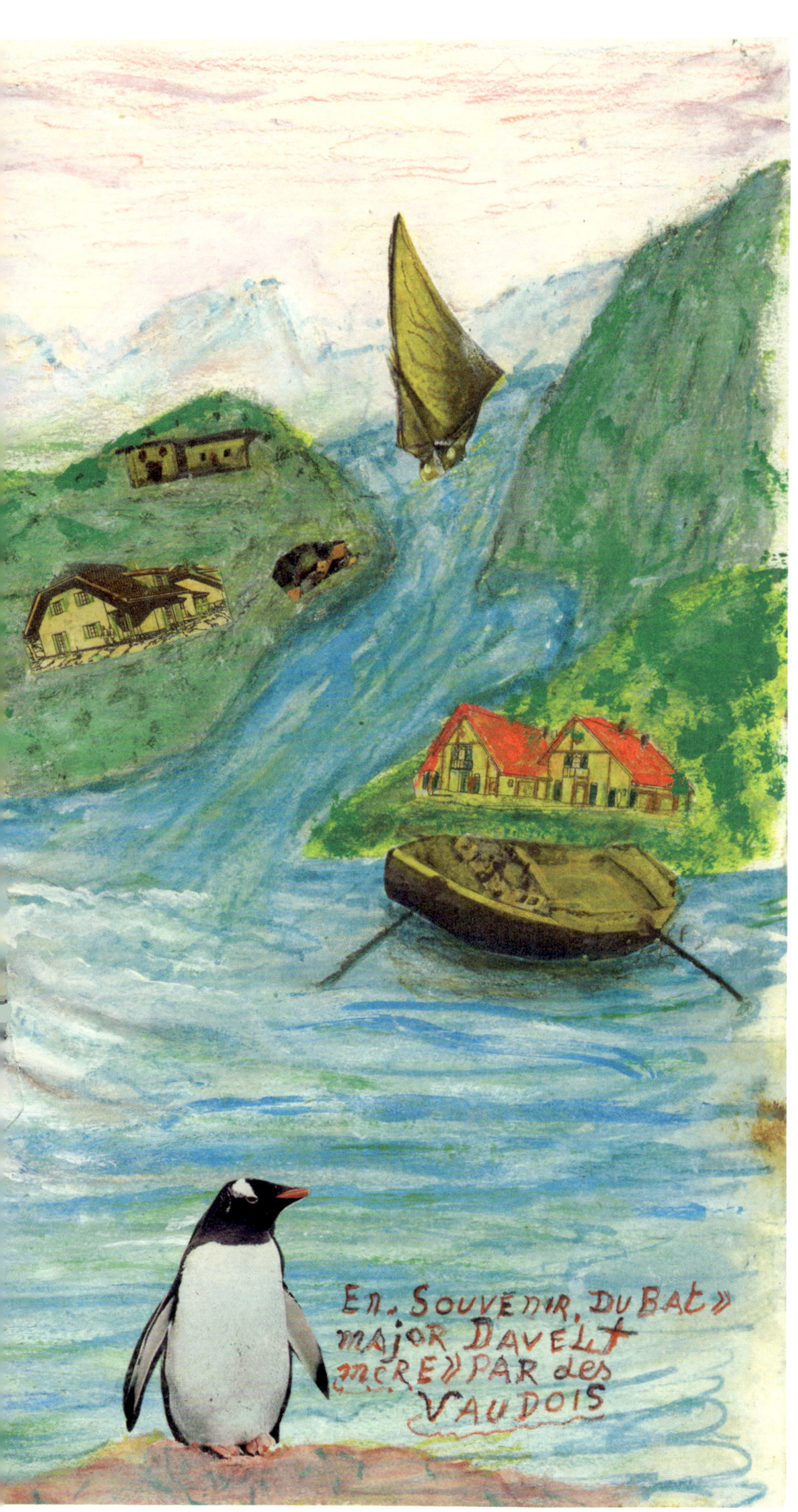

Francis Mayor
En souvenir du «Major Davel», ca. 1990
peinture et collage sur papier
paint and collage on paper
33,5 x 48 cm

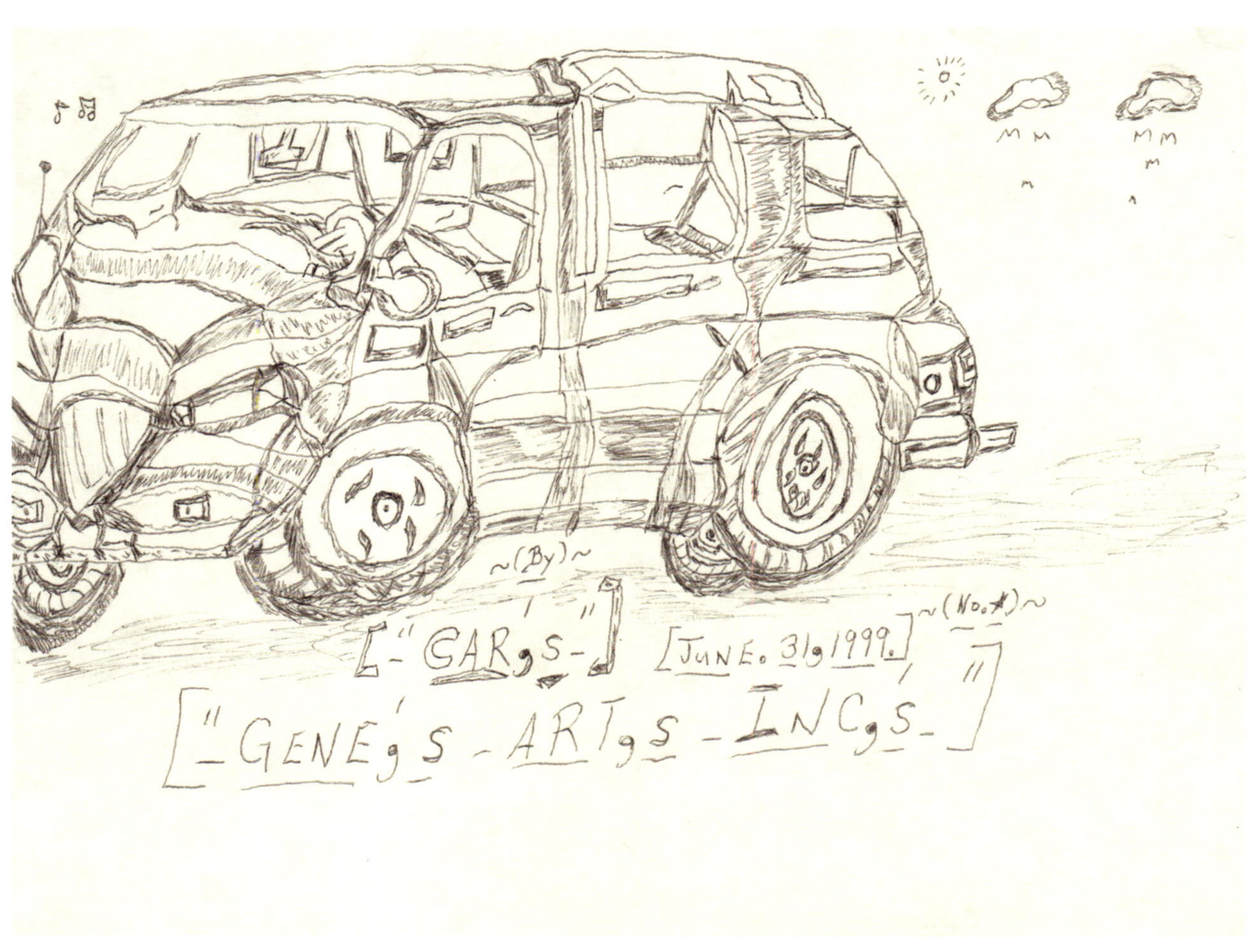

Gene Merritt
CAR,s, 1999
stylo-bille sur papier
ballpoint pen on paper
20,7 x 28 cm

Gene Merritt
A Marathon Runner, 1996
stylo-bille sur papier
ballpoint pen on paper
21,7 x 13,5 cm

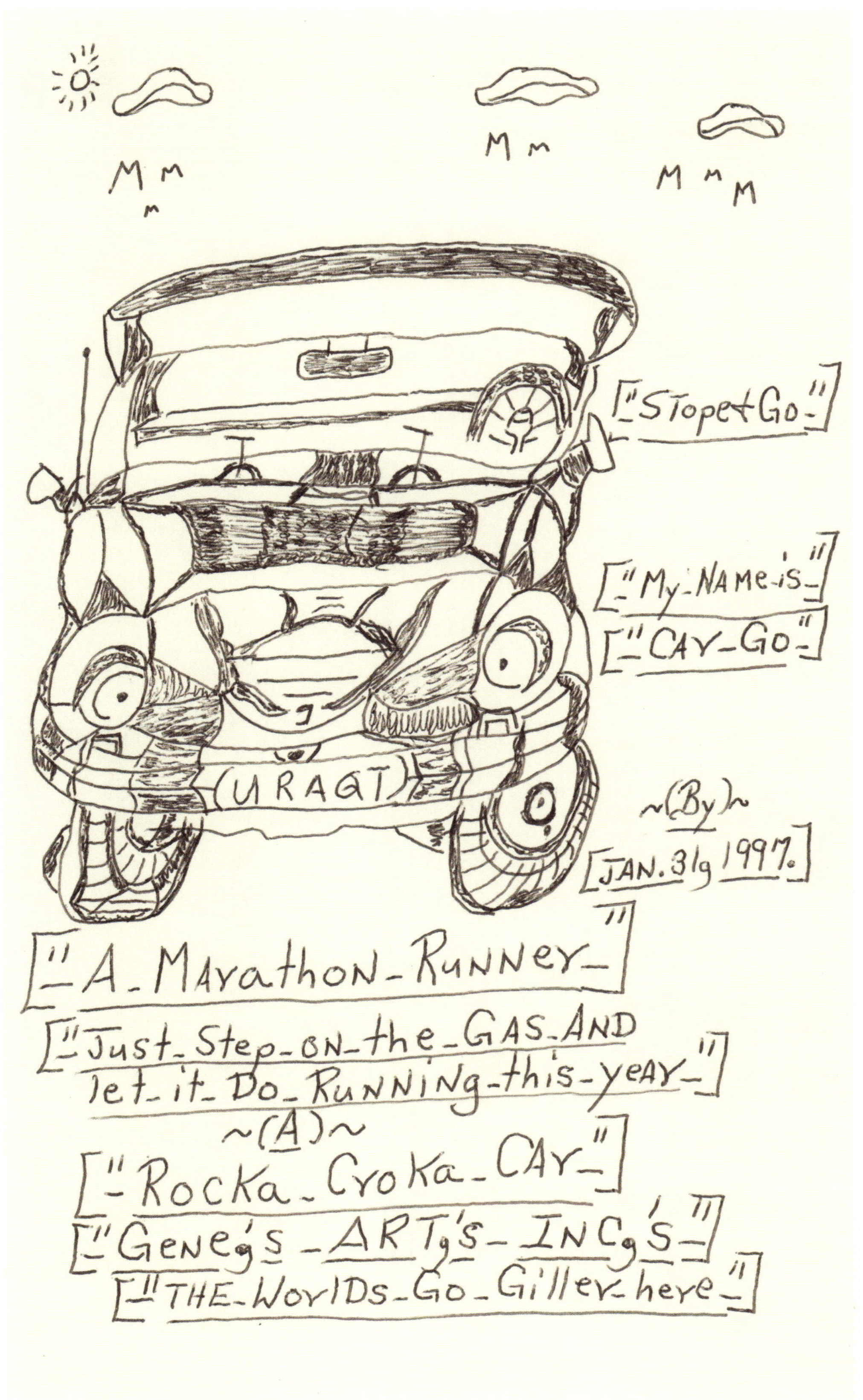
["StopetGo"]
["My-NAME-is"]
["CAr-Go"]
(URAGT)
~(By)~
[JAN. 31g 1997.]
["A-Marathon-Runner"]
["Just-Step-ON-the-GAS-AND
let-it-Do-RuNNiNg-this-year"]
~(A)~
["Rocka-Croka-CAr"]
["Genegs-ARTgs-INCgS"]
["THE-WorlDs-Go-Giller-here"]

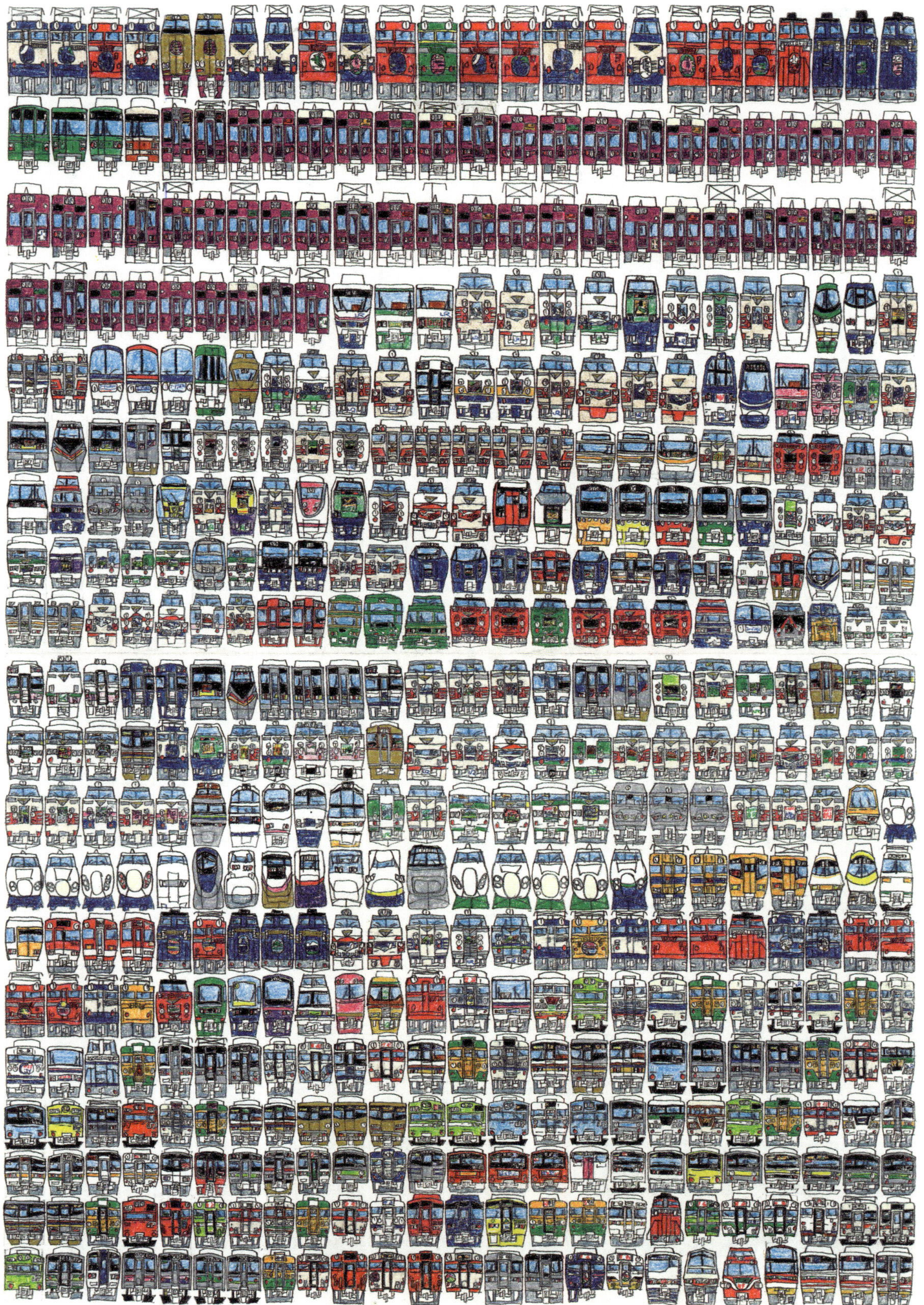

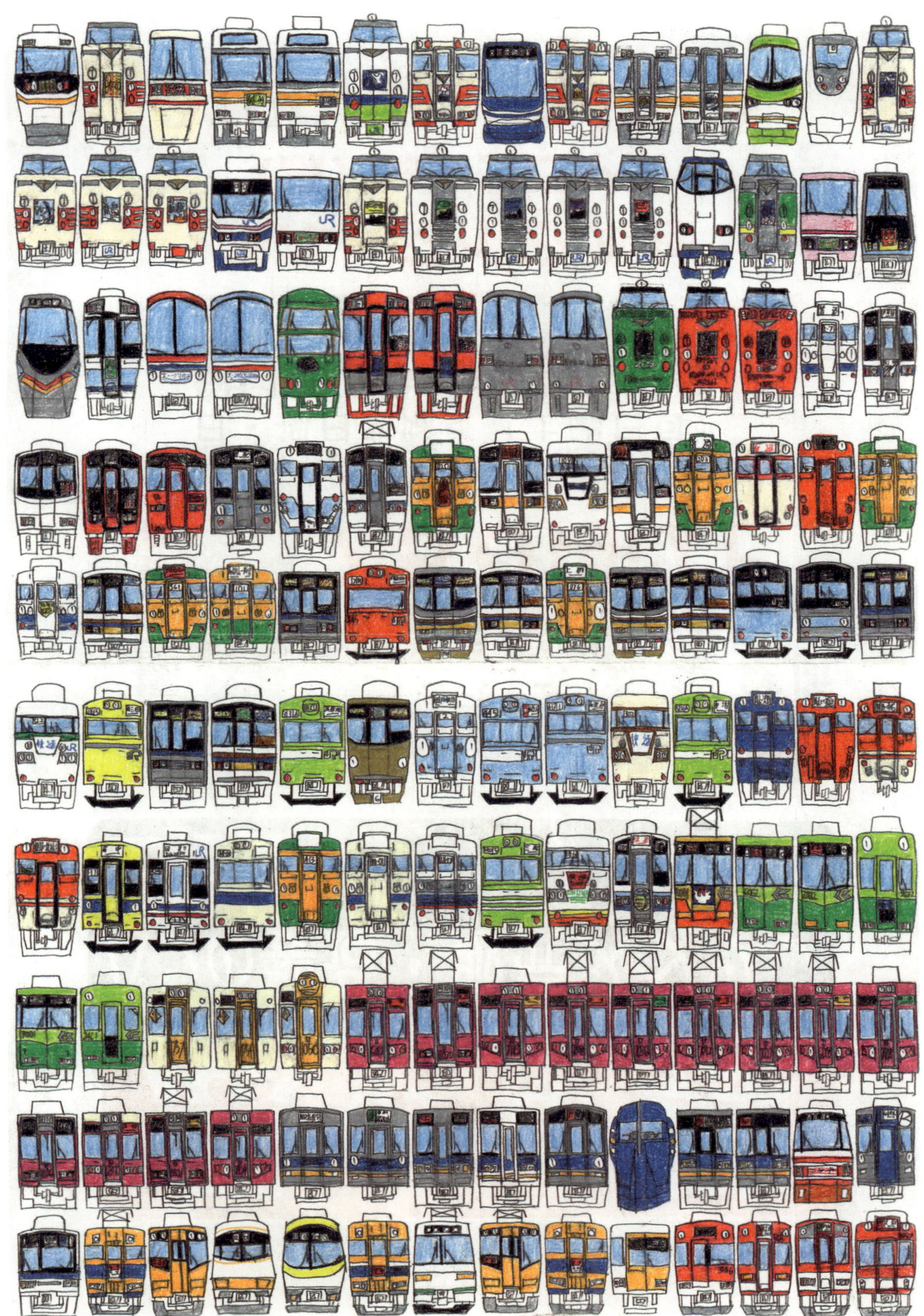

Motooka Hidenori
Trains, 1995
mine de plomb et crayon de couleur sur papier lead pencil and coloured pencil on paper
36,5 x 28 cm

Motooka Hidenori
Trains, 1995
mine de plomb et crayon de couleur sur papier lead pencil and coloured pencil on paper
36,5 x 26 cm

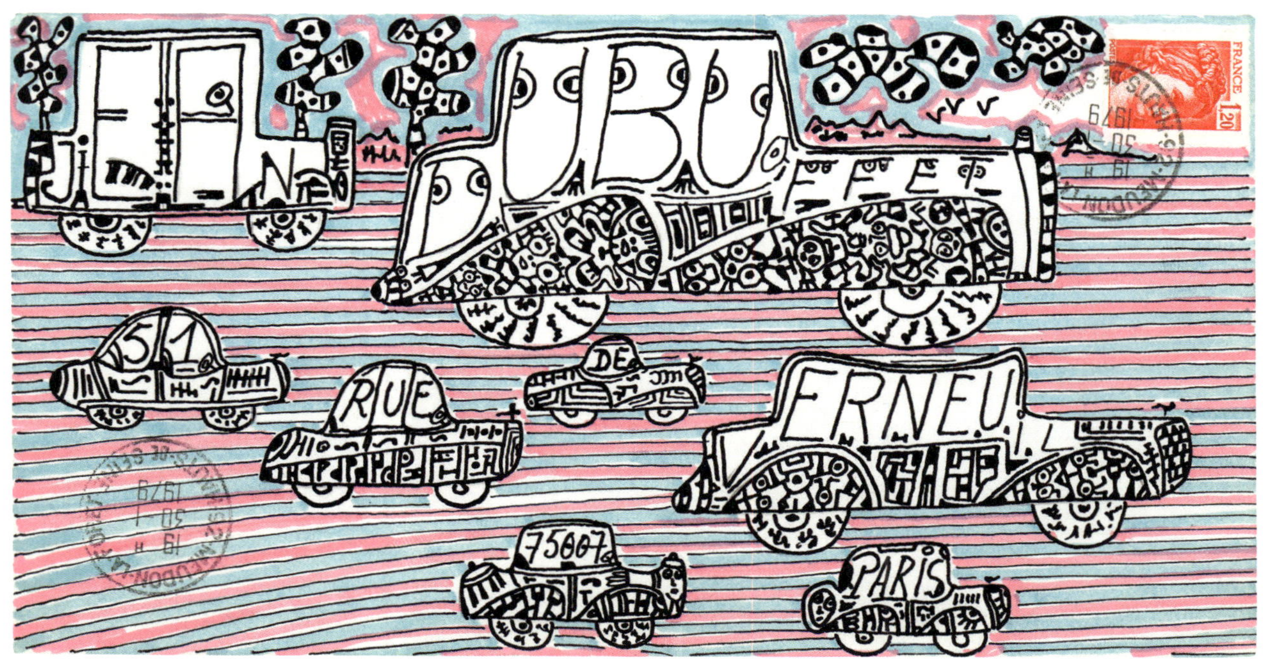

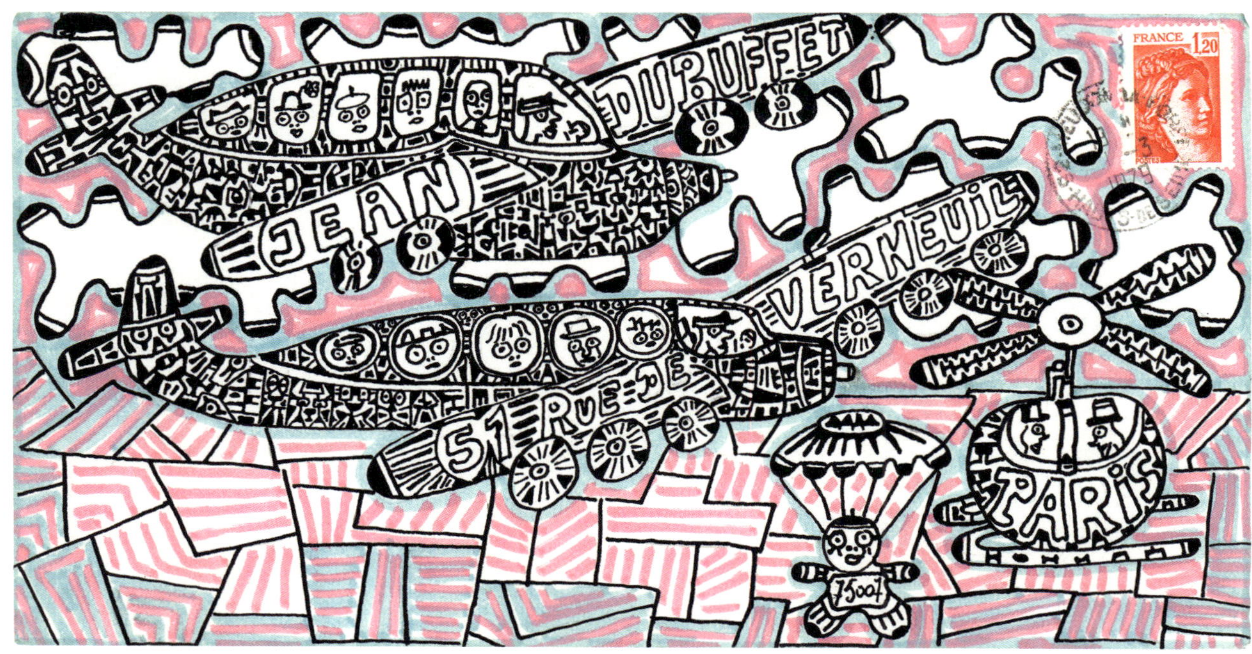

Alain Pauzié
Sans titre untitled, 1979
encre et surligneur sur papier
ink and highlighter on paper
11,3 x 22 cm

Alain Pauzié
Sans titre untitled, 1979
encre et surligneur sur papier
ink and highlighter on paper
11,2 x 22 cm

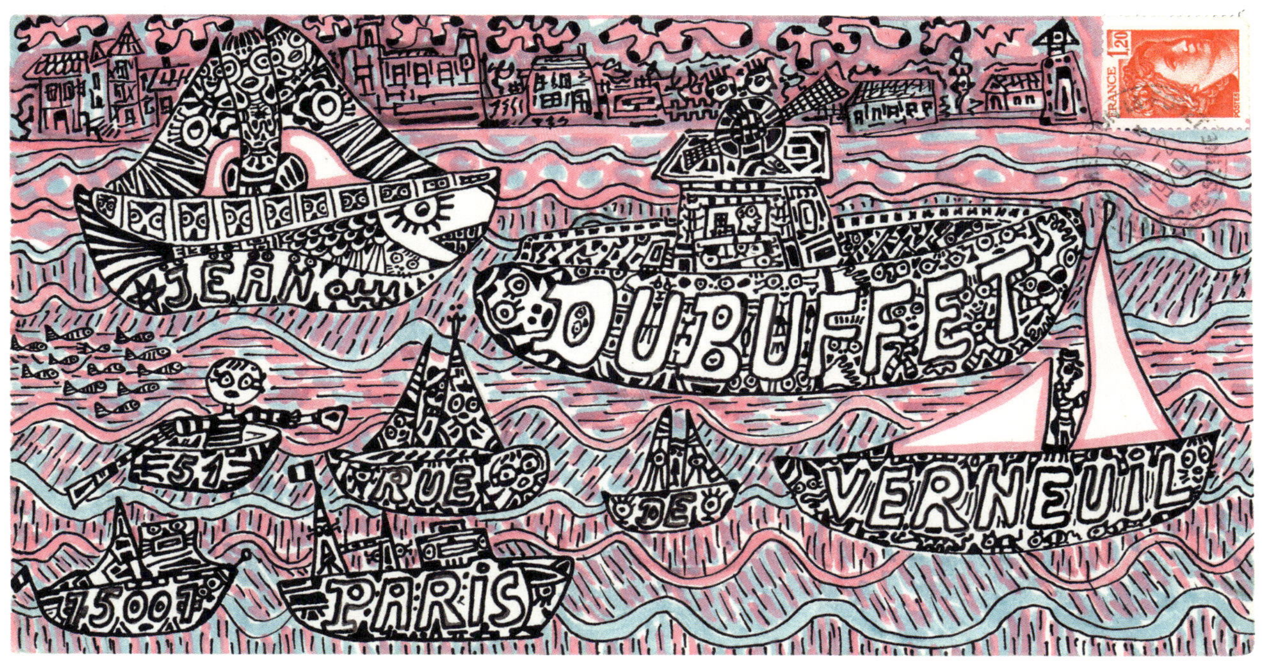

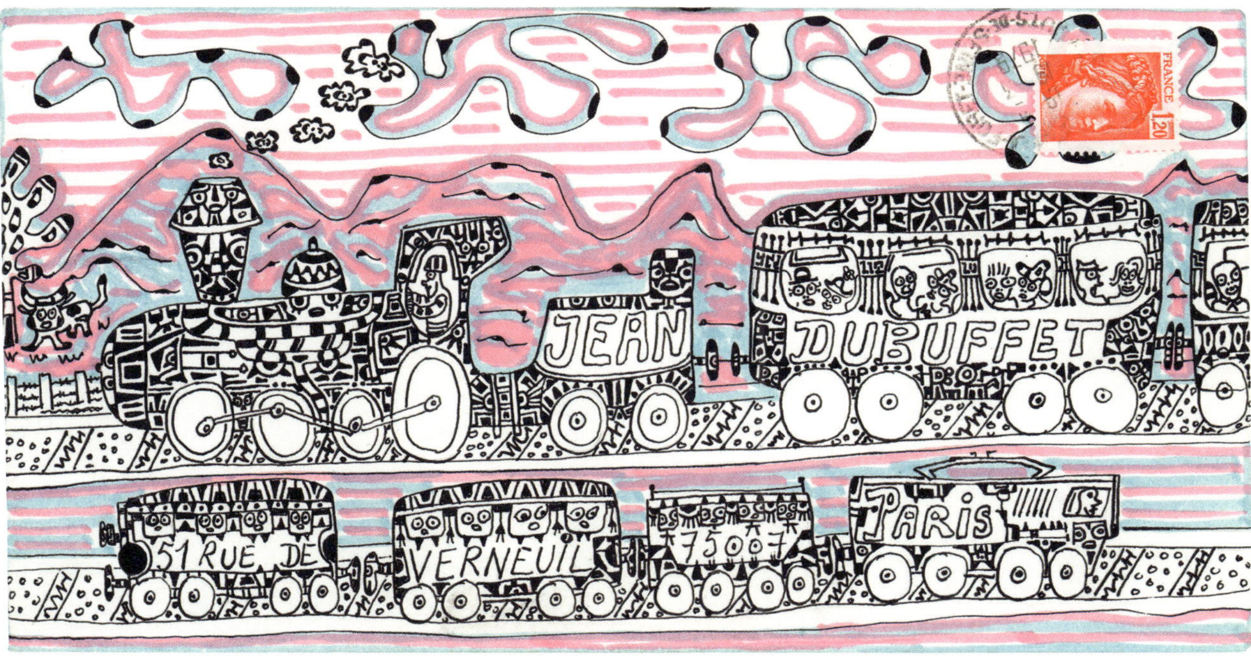

Alain Pauzié
Sans titre untitled, 1979
encre et surligneur sur papier
ink and highlighter on paper
11,2 x 22 cm

Alain Pauzié
Sans titre untitled, 1979
encre et surligneur sur papier
ink and highlighter on paper
11,2 x 22 cm

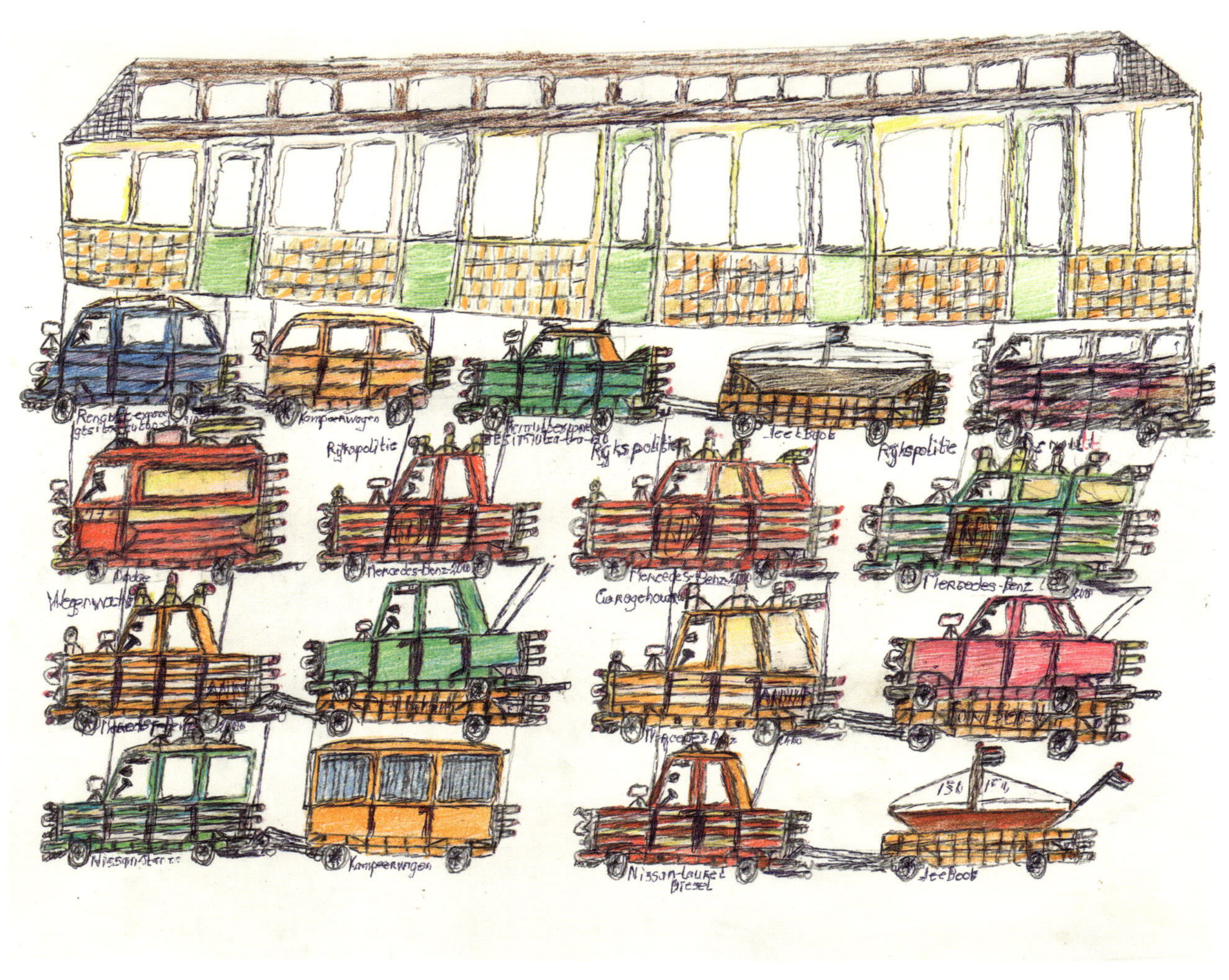

Han Ploos Van Amstel
Sans titre untitled, 2003
crayon de couleur, mine de plomb, stylo-bille sur papier coloured pencil, lead pencil, ballpoint pen on paper
50 x 65 cm

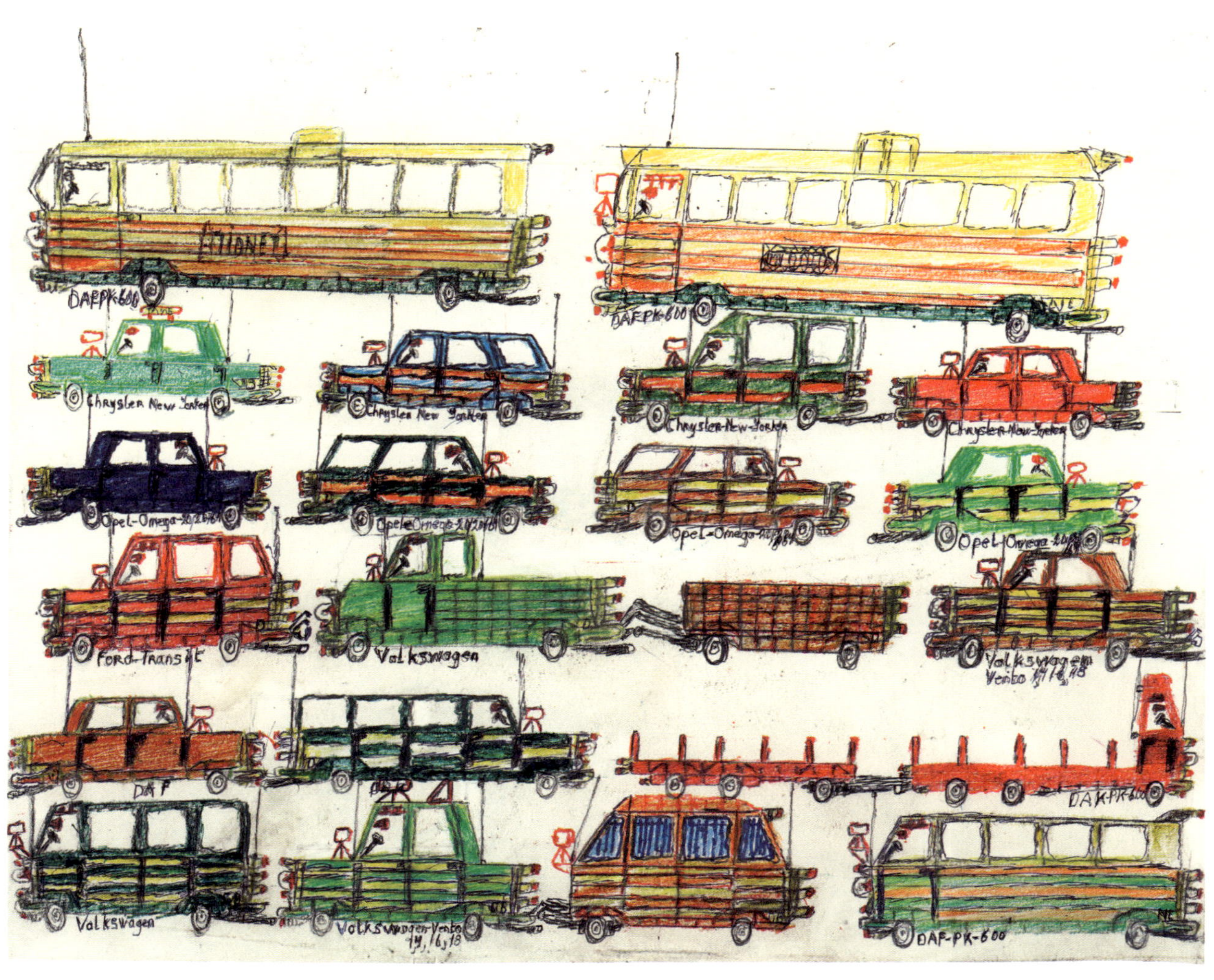

Han Ploos Van Amstel
DAF PK 600, ca. 1999
stylo-bille, feutre, craie grasse et mine de plomb sur papier ballpoint pen, felt pen, crayon and lead pencil on paper
50 x 65 cm

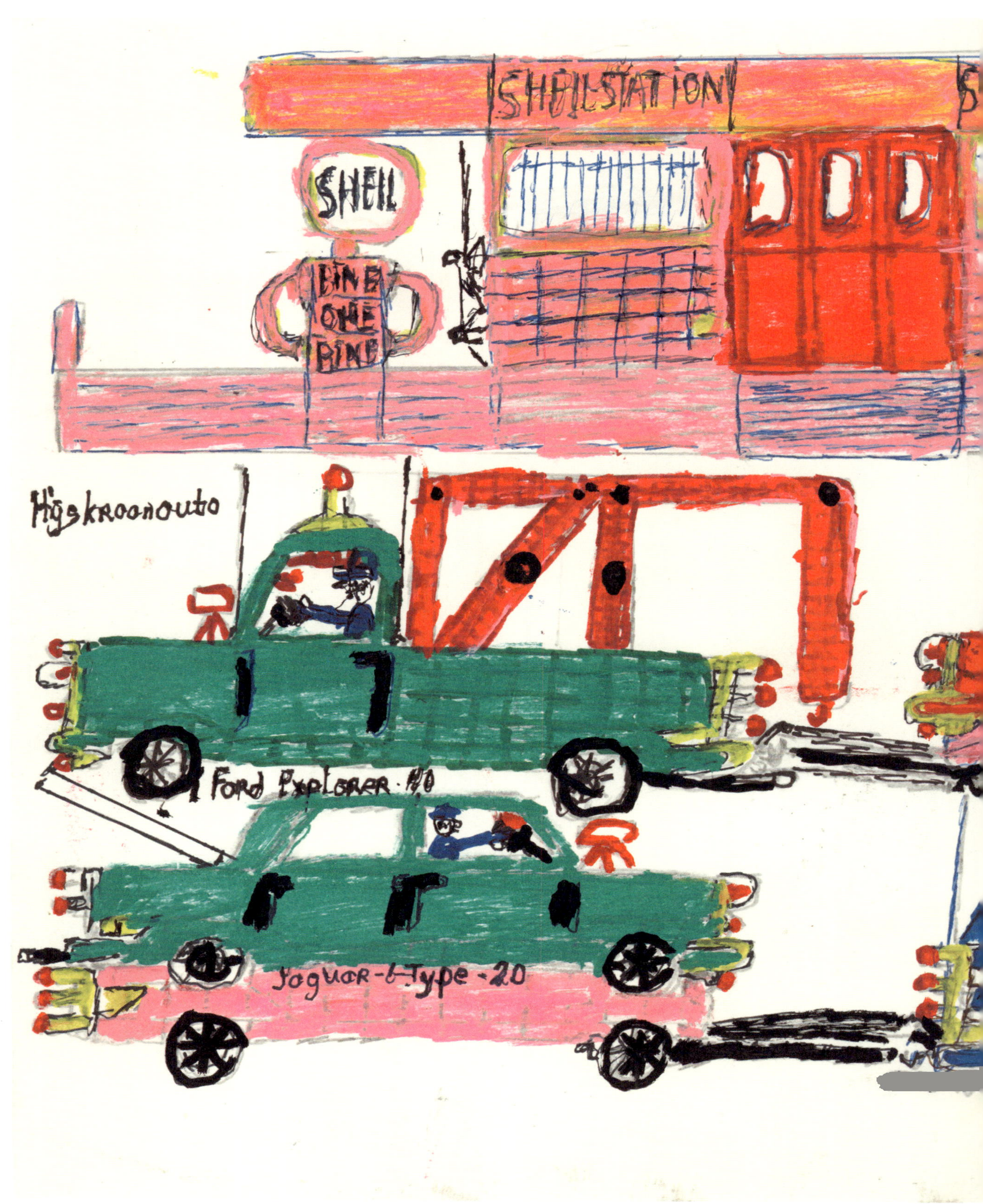
SHEILSTATION
SHEIL
Ford Explorer

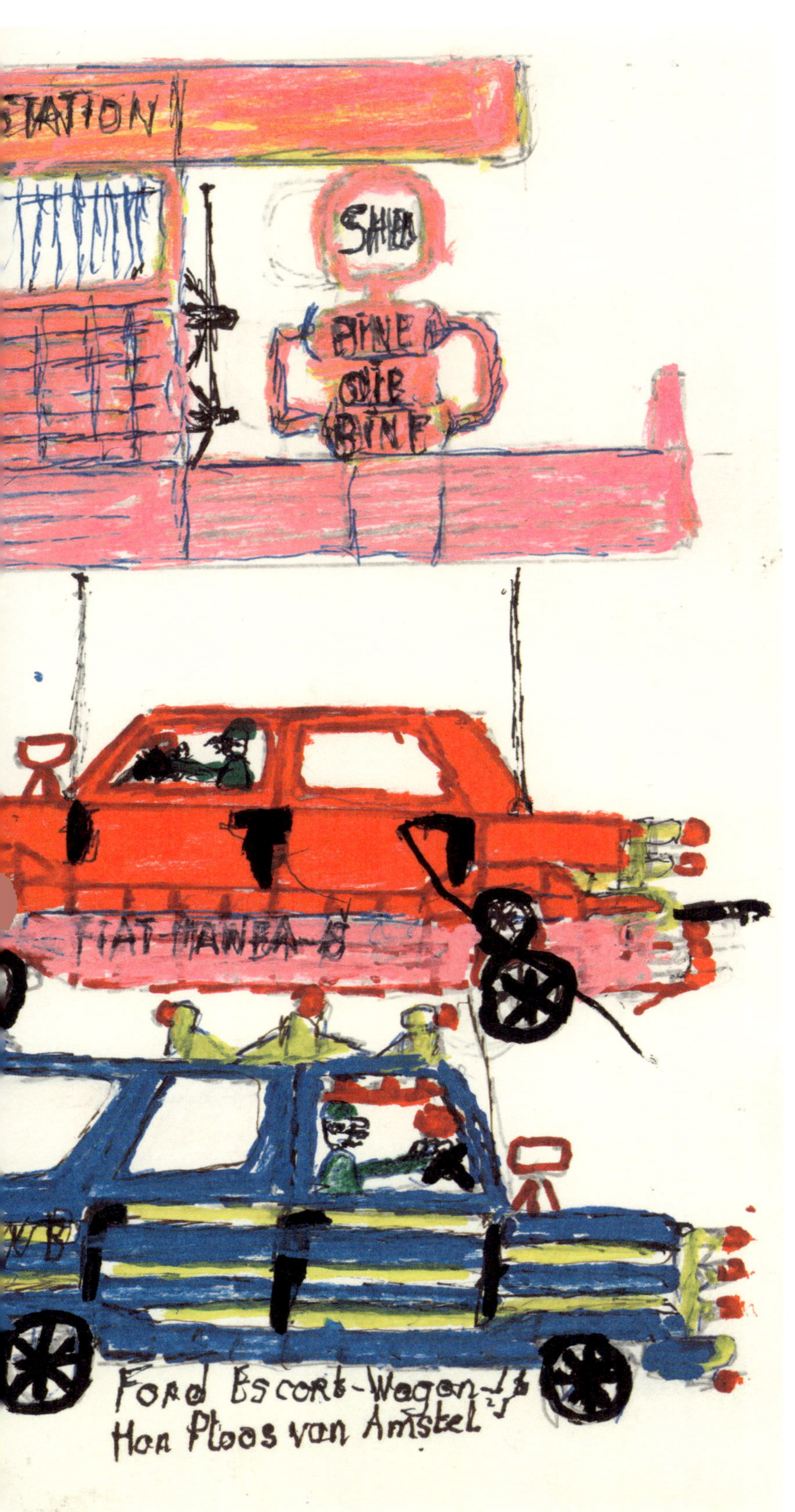

Han Ploos Van Amstel
Shellstation, 2000
gouache, stylo-bille, feutre et mine de plomb sur papier gouache, ballpoint pen, felt pen and lead pencil on paper
29,7 x 42 cm

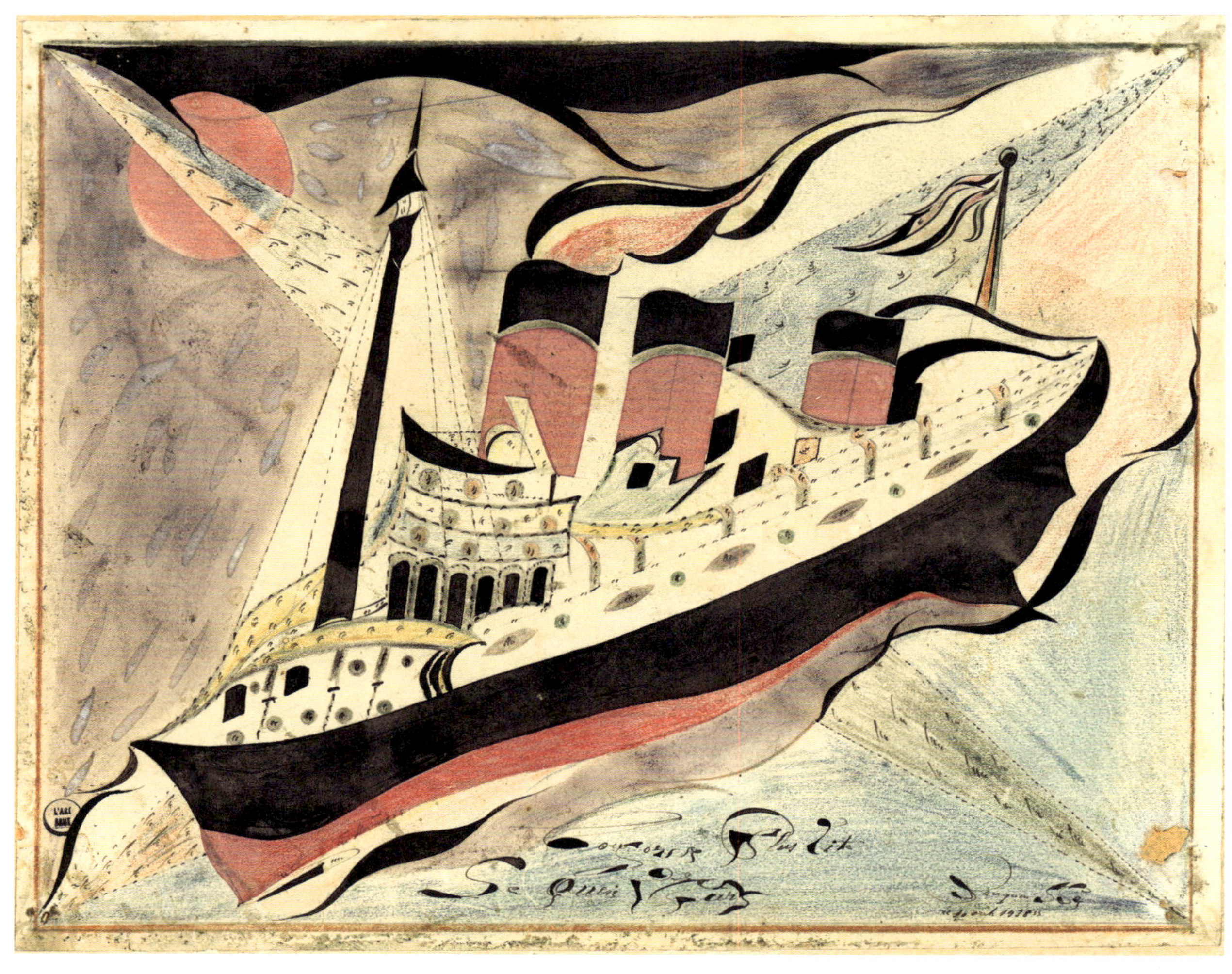

Guillaume Pujolle
Toujours plus vite, 1938
aquarelle, produits de laboratoire, encre
et crayon de couleur sur papier
watercolour, pharmaceuticals, ink
and coloured pencil on paper
24 x 31,5 cm

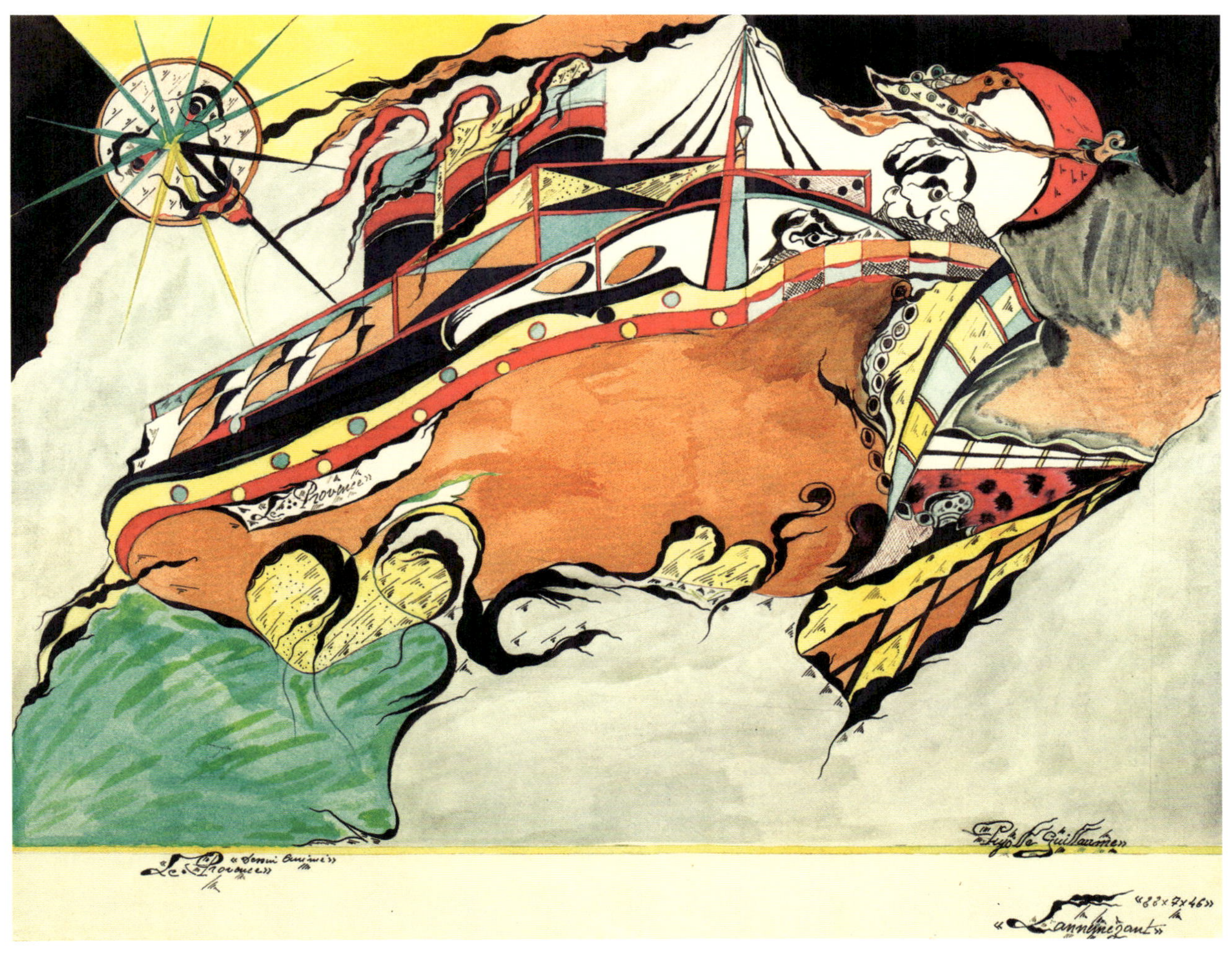

Guillaume Pujolle
Le Provence, dessin animé, 1946
aquarelle, encre et produits de laboratoire sur papier watercolour, ink and pharmaceuticals on paper
48 x 63 cm

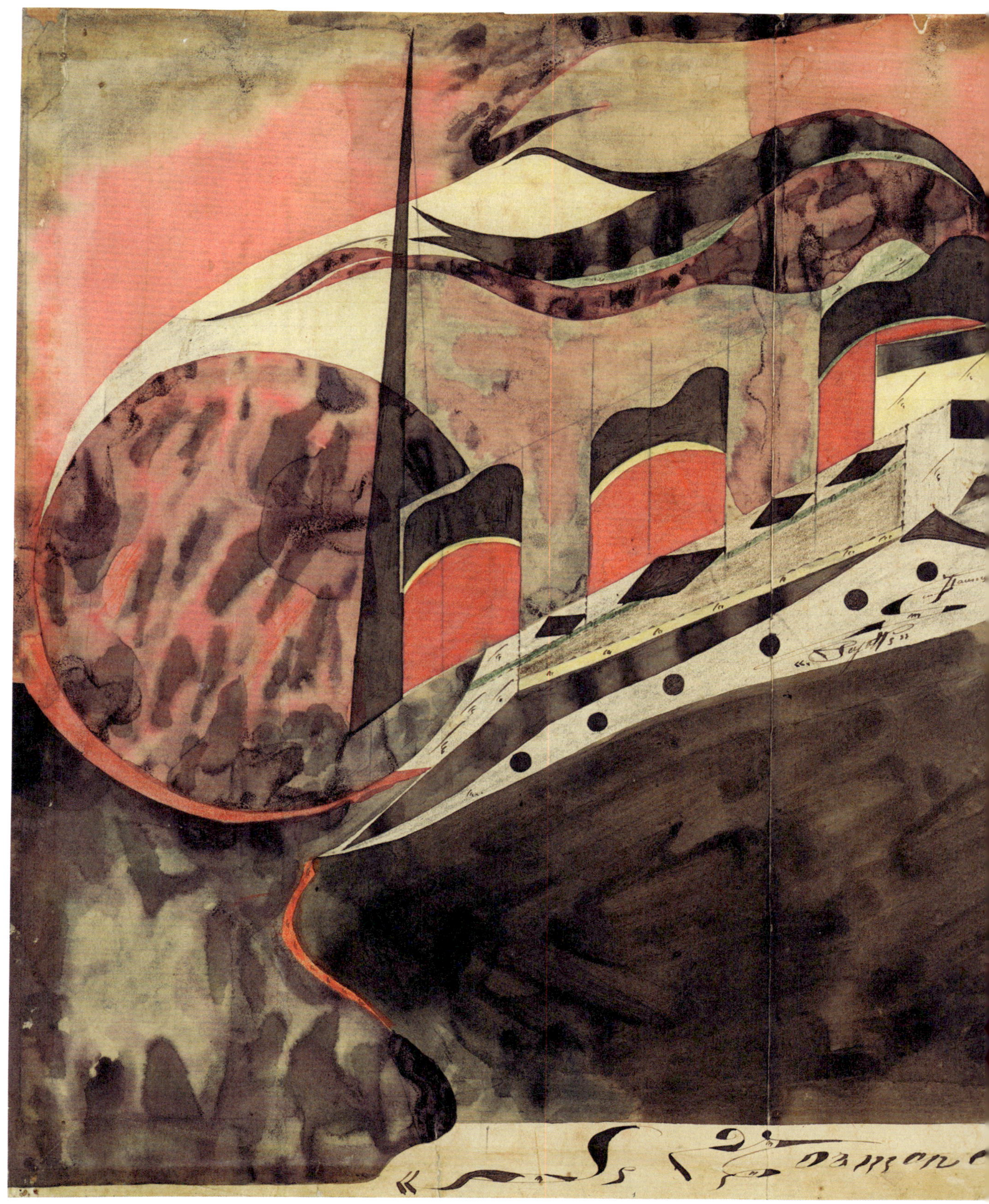

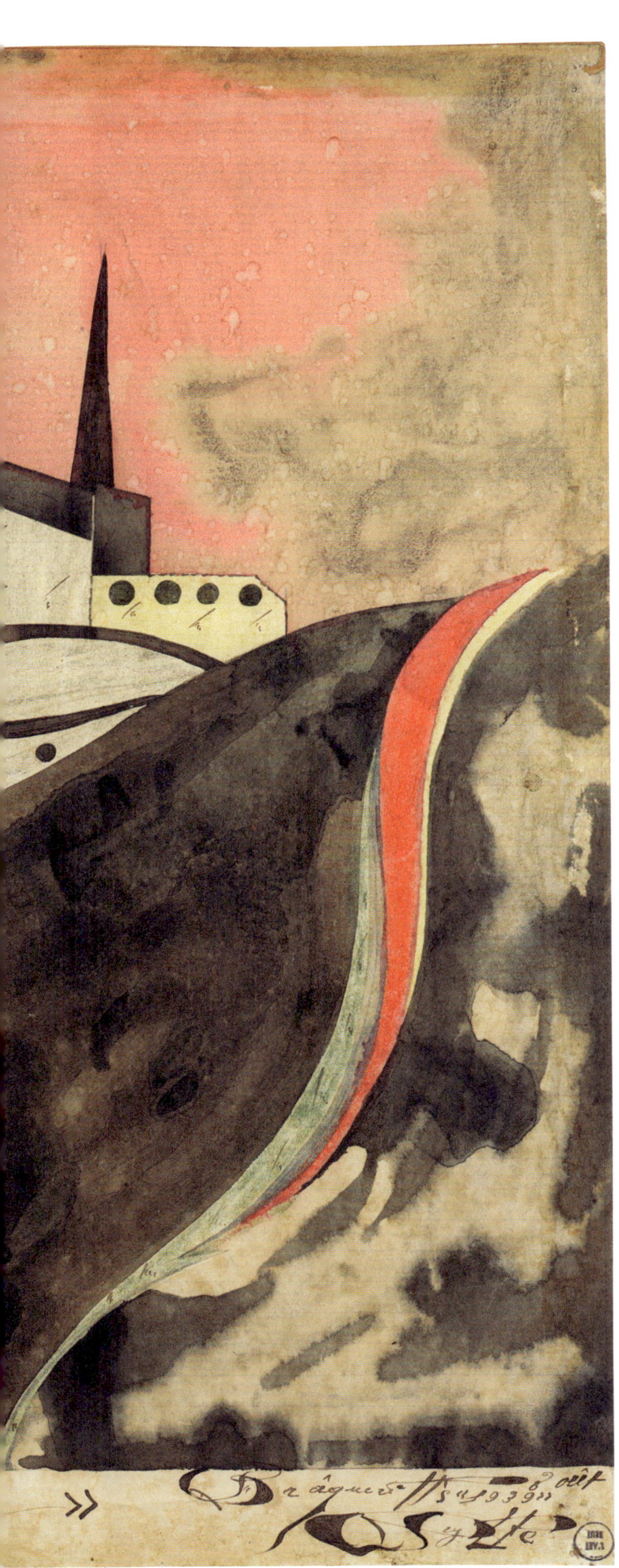

Guillaume Pujolle
La Normandie, 1939
aquarelle, encre et produits de laboratoire sur papier watercolour, ink and pharmaceuticals on paper
39 x 50,5 cm

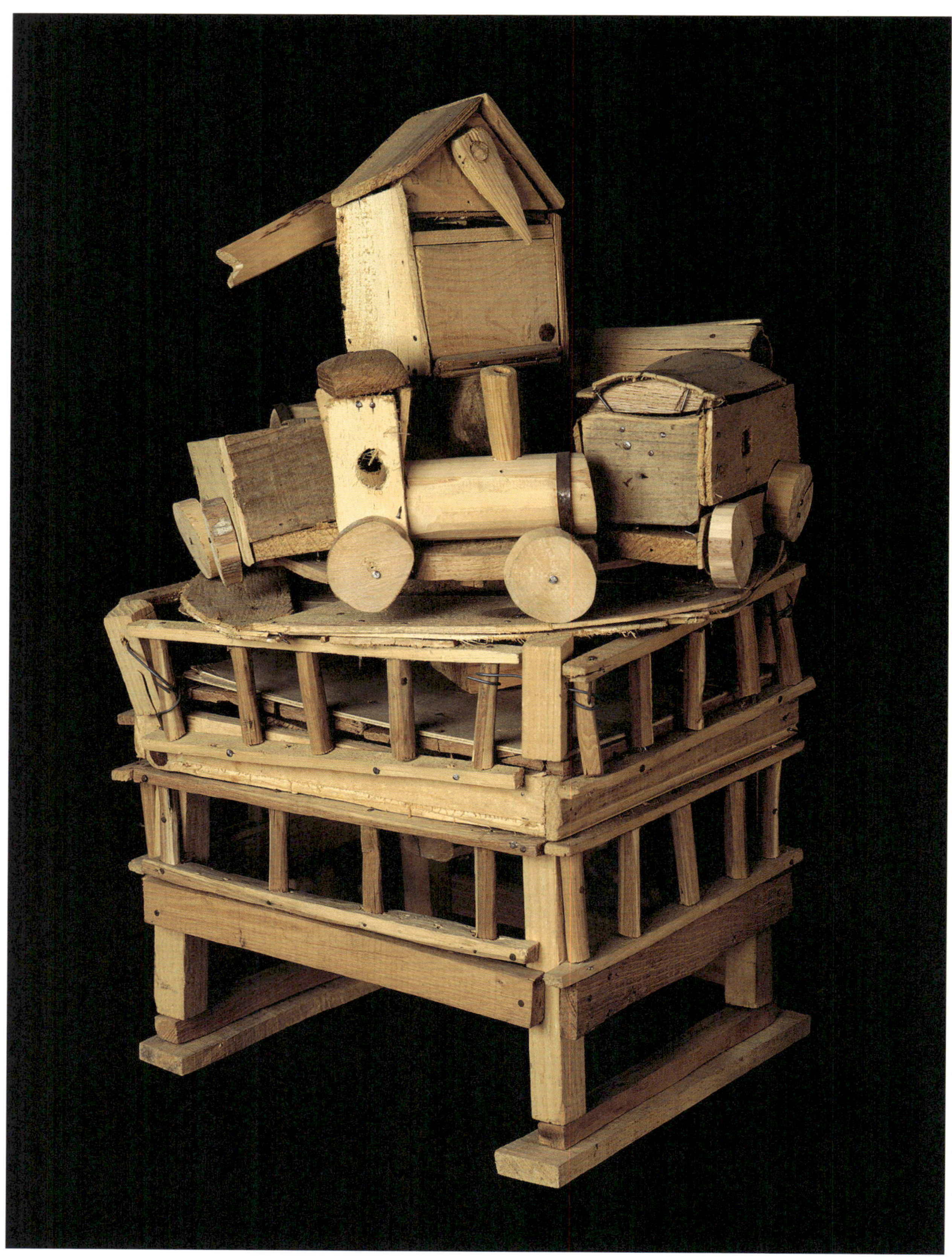

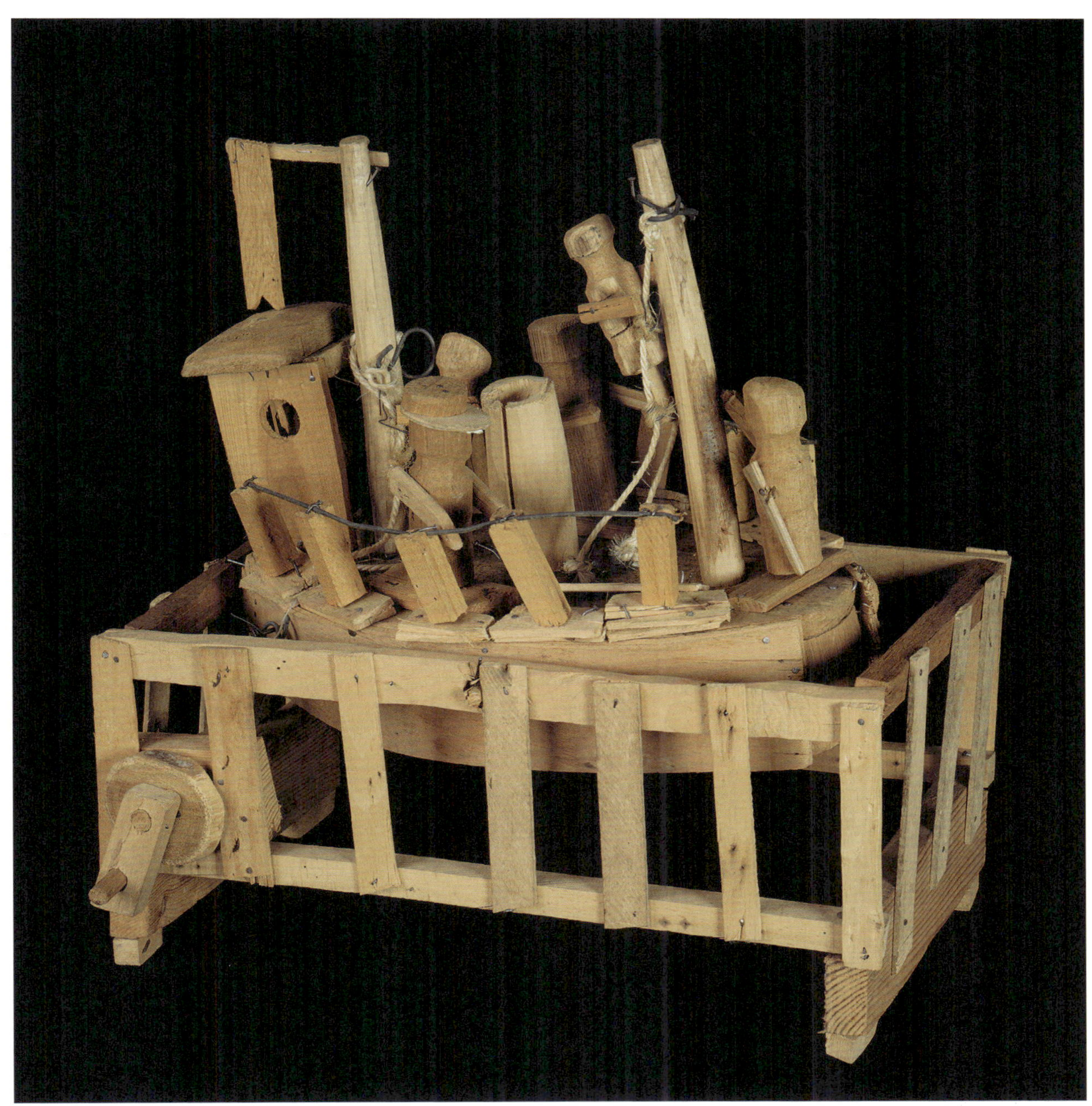

Émile Ratier
Gare et chemin de fer, ca. 1960-1984
bois et matériaux divers
wood and miscellaneous materials
64 x 38 x 42 cm

Émile Ratier
Paquebot, ca. 1960-1984
bois et matériaux divers
wood and miscellaneous materials
48 x 35 x 50 cm

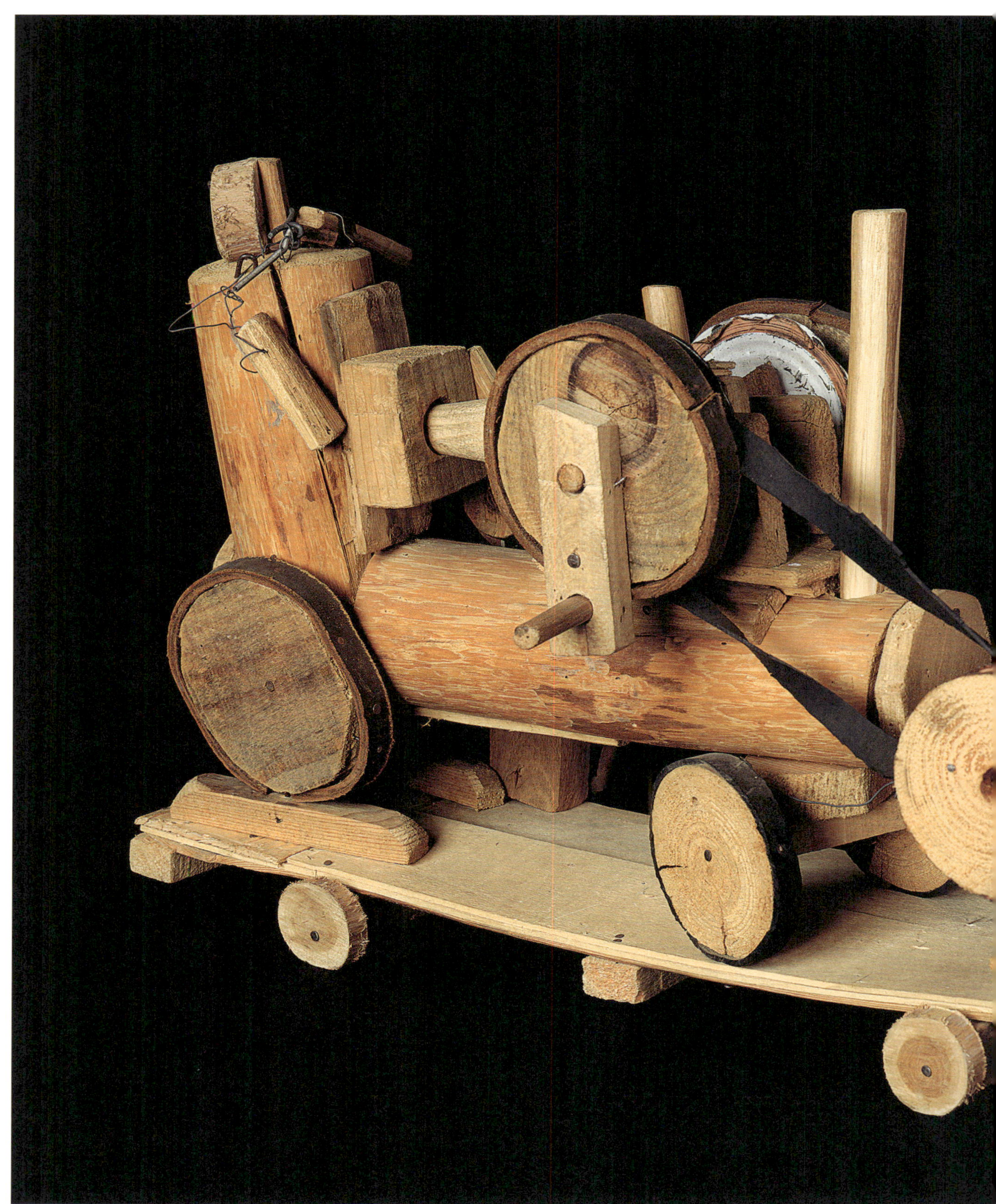

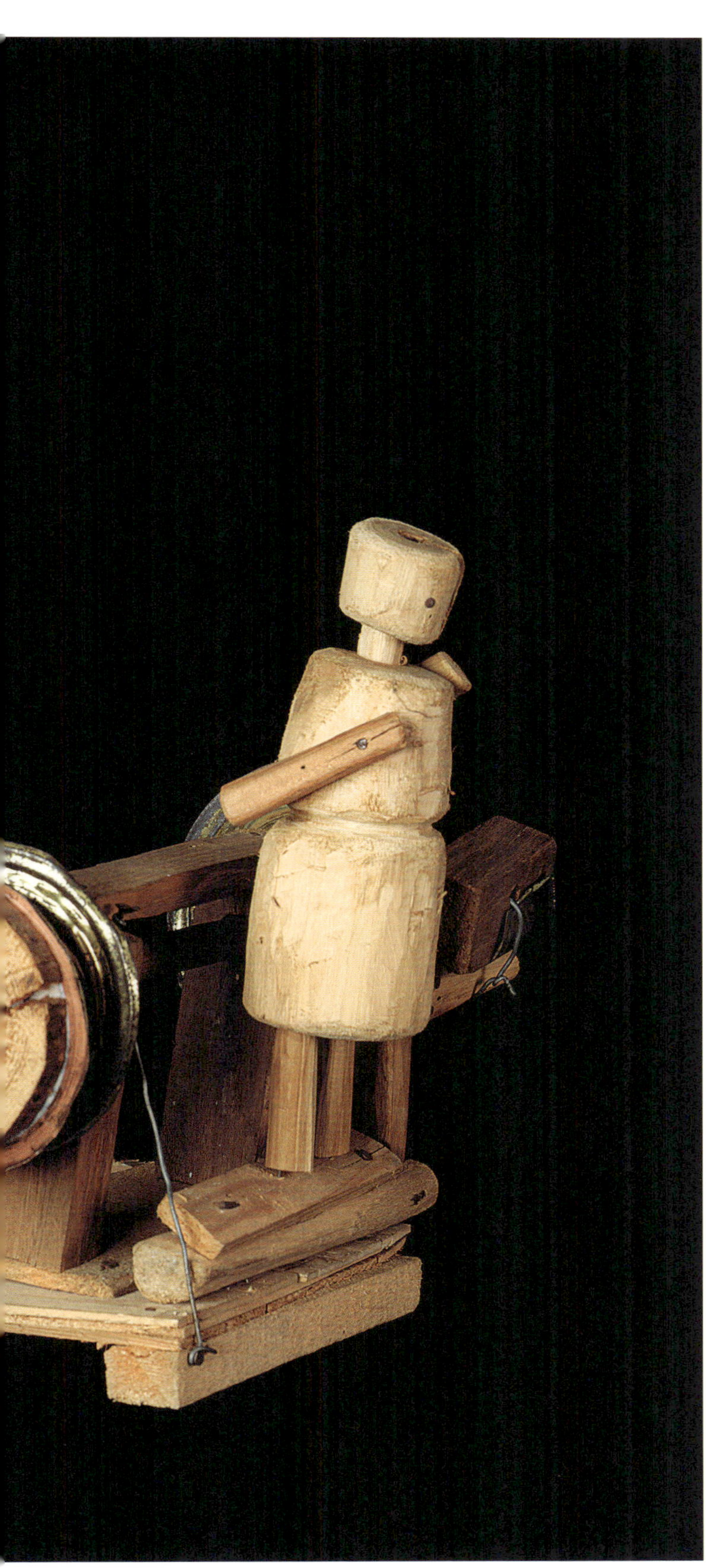

Émile Ratier
Locomotive, ca. 1960-1984
bois et matériaux divers
wood and miscellaneous materials
60 x 29 x 38 cm

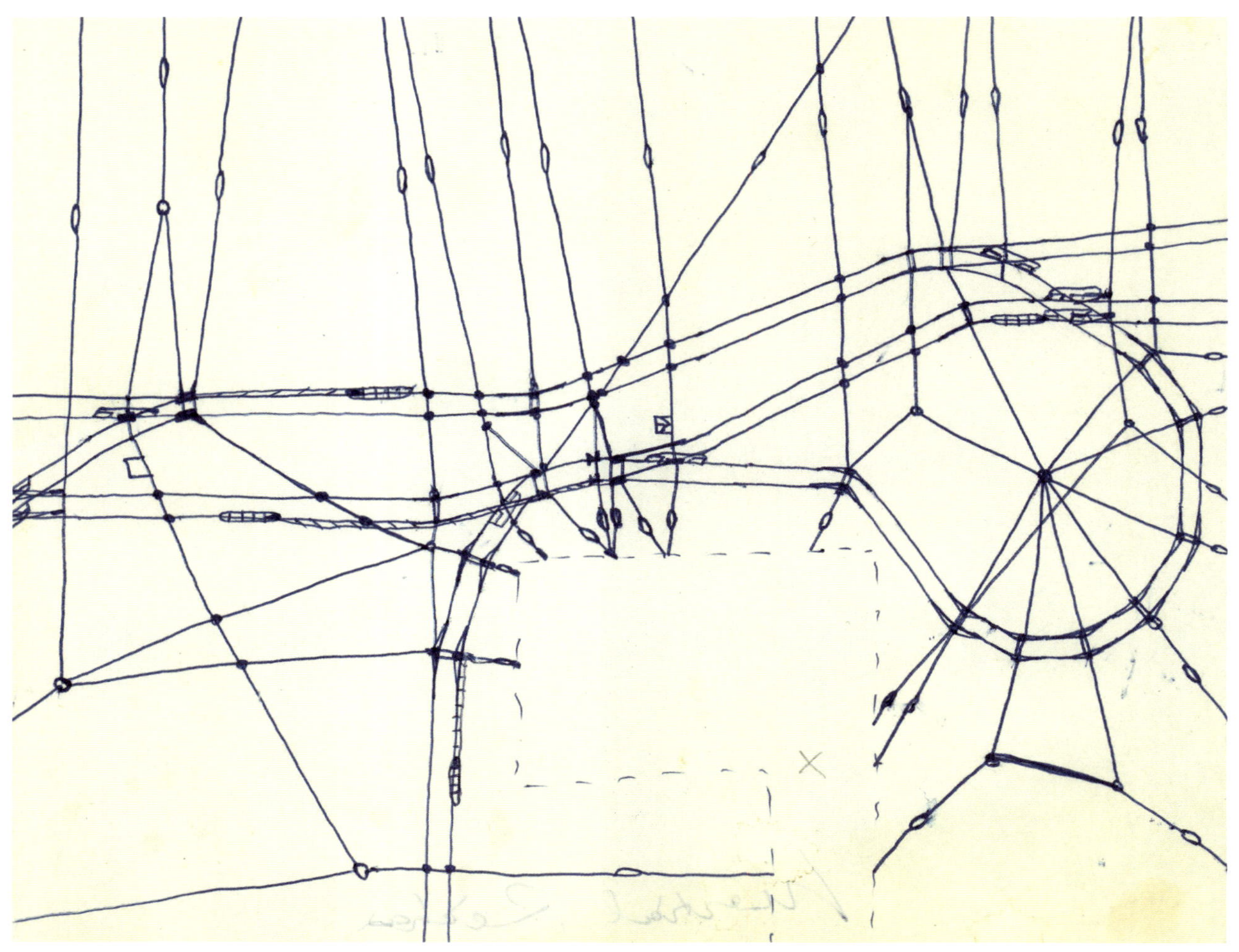

Martial Richoz
Sans titre *untitled*, ca. 1980-1986
stylo-bille sur papier
ballpoint pen on paper
22,9 x 17,4 cm

Martial Richoz
Sans titre *untitled*, ca. 1980-1986
stylo-bille sur papier
ballpoint pen on paper
22,4 x 15,7 cm

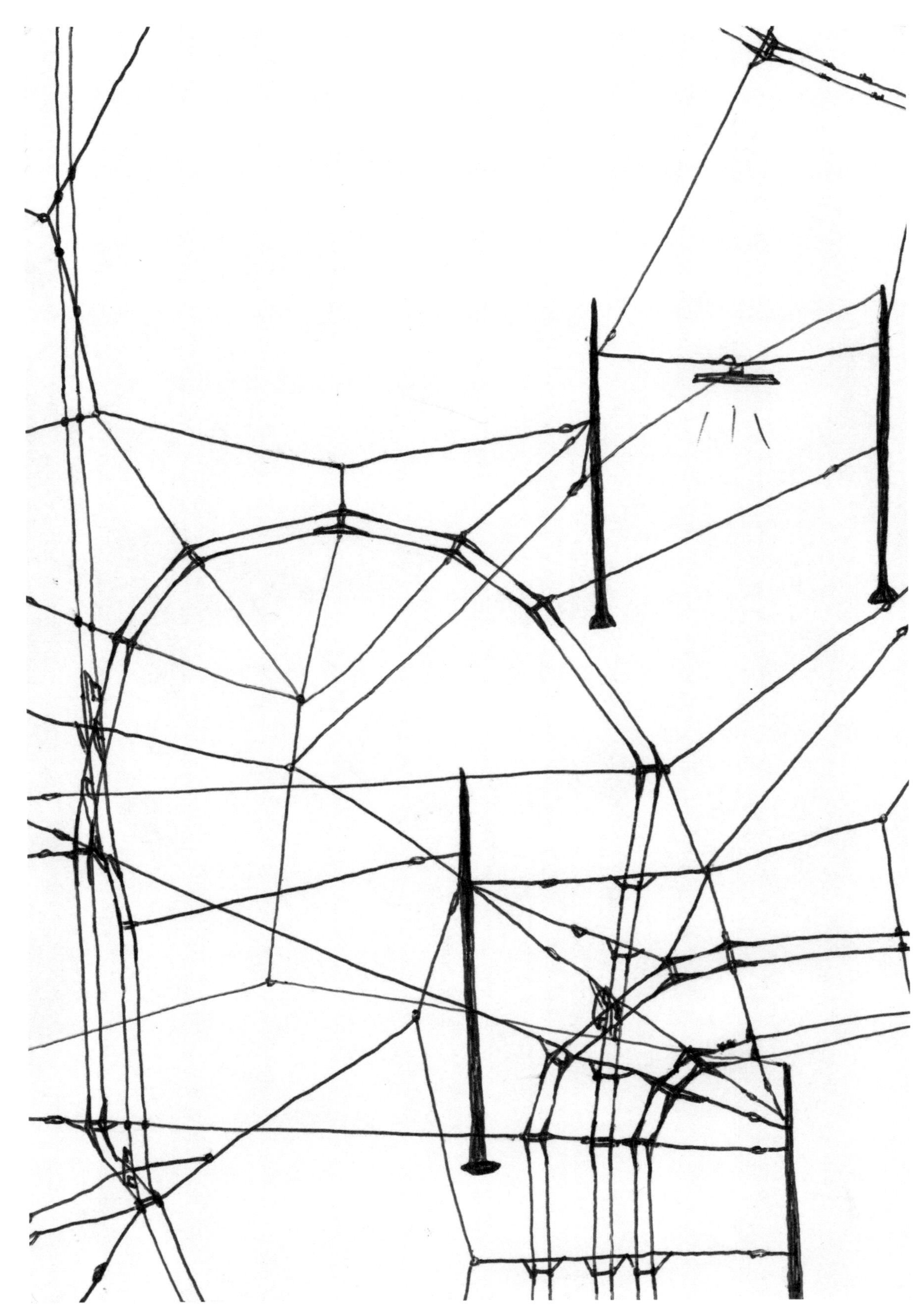

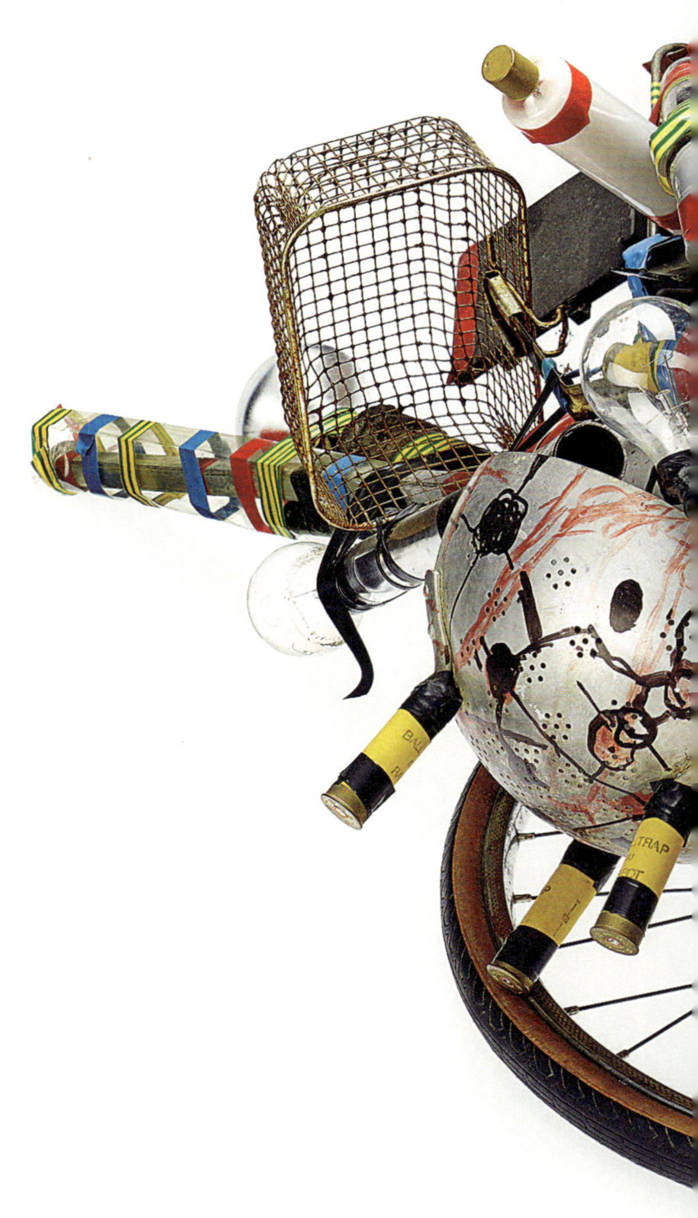

André Robillard
Spoutnik, 1994-1995
matériaux divers
miscellaneous materials
50 x 110 cm

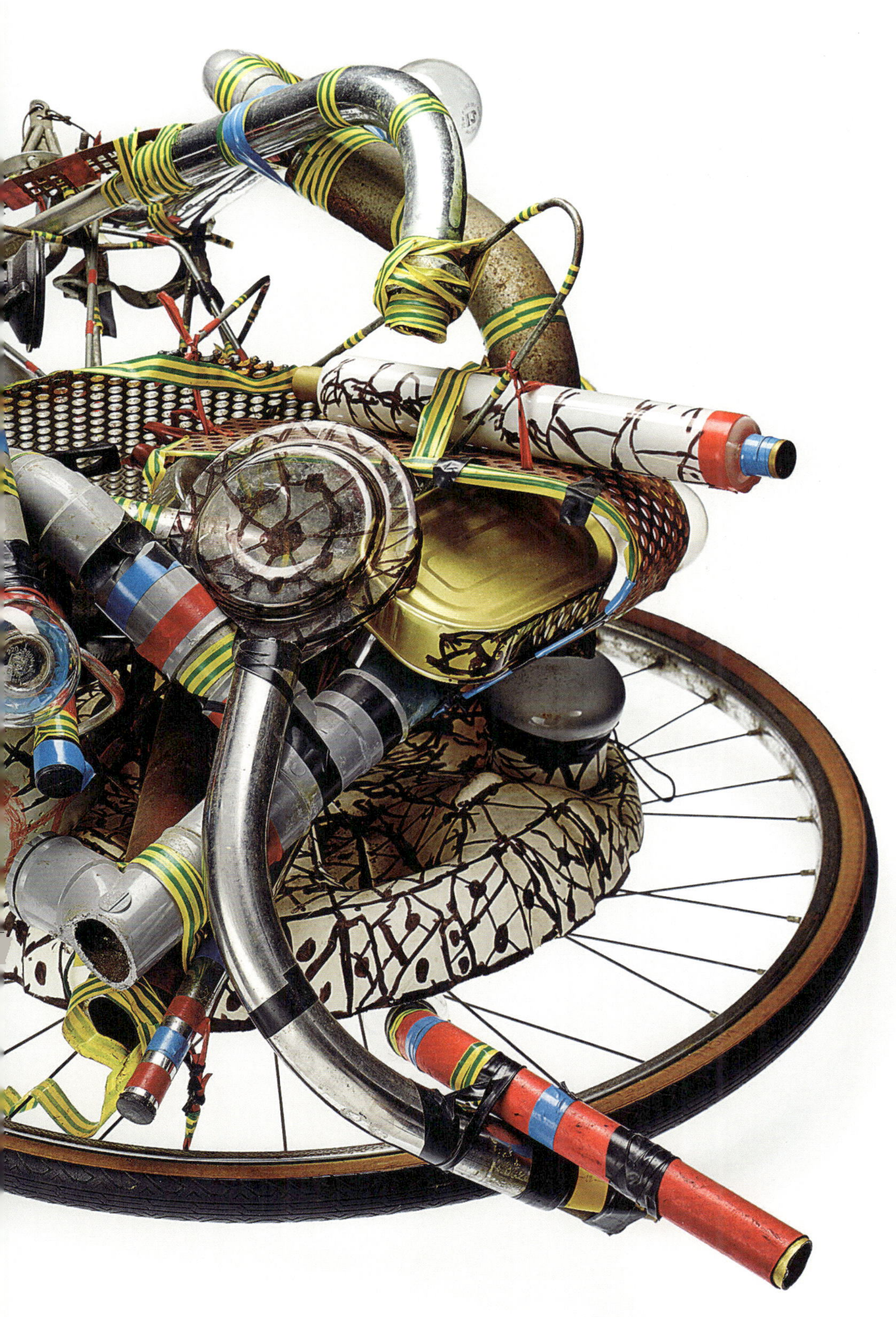

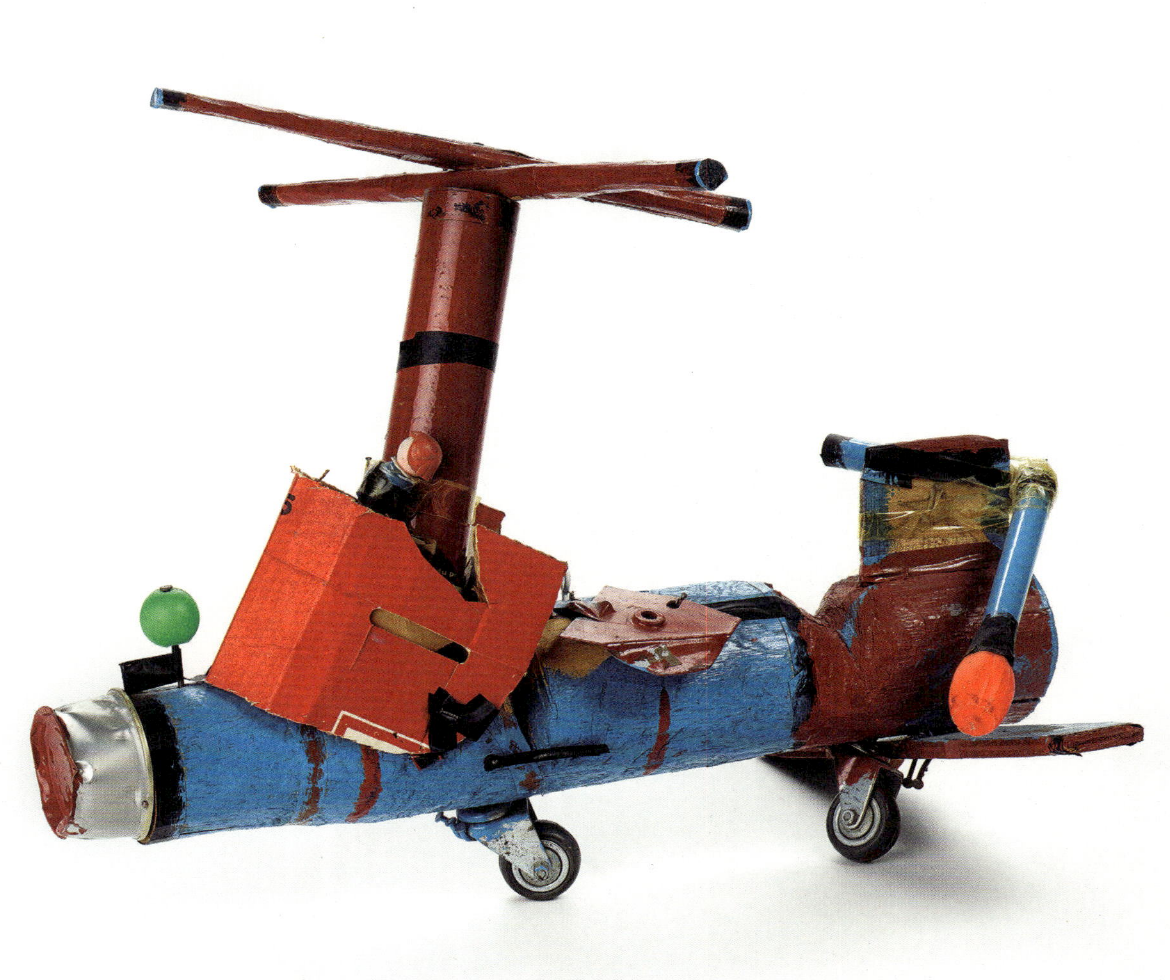

André Robillard
Sans titre untitled, 1980
matériaux divers
miscellaneous materials
55 x 40 cm

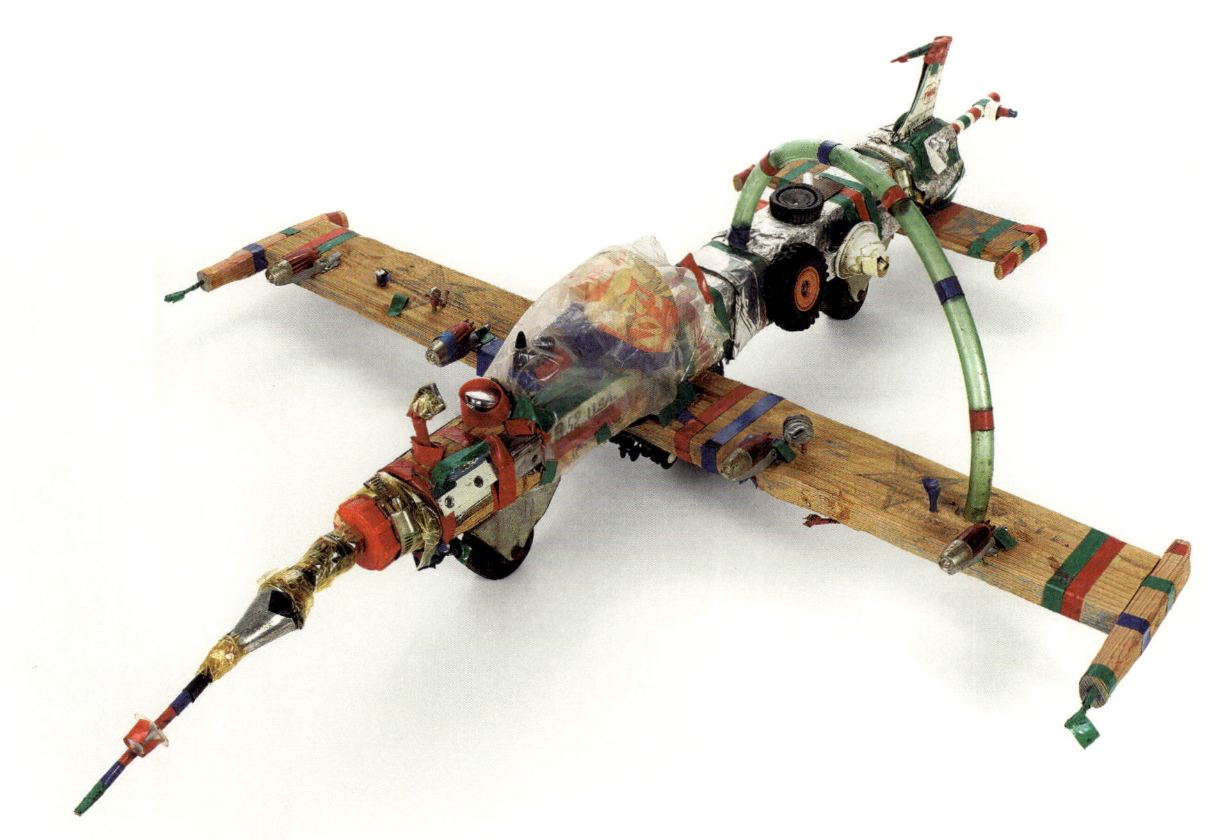

André Robillard
B52 USA, 1980
matériaux divers
miscellaneous materials
127 x 96 cm

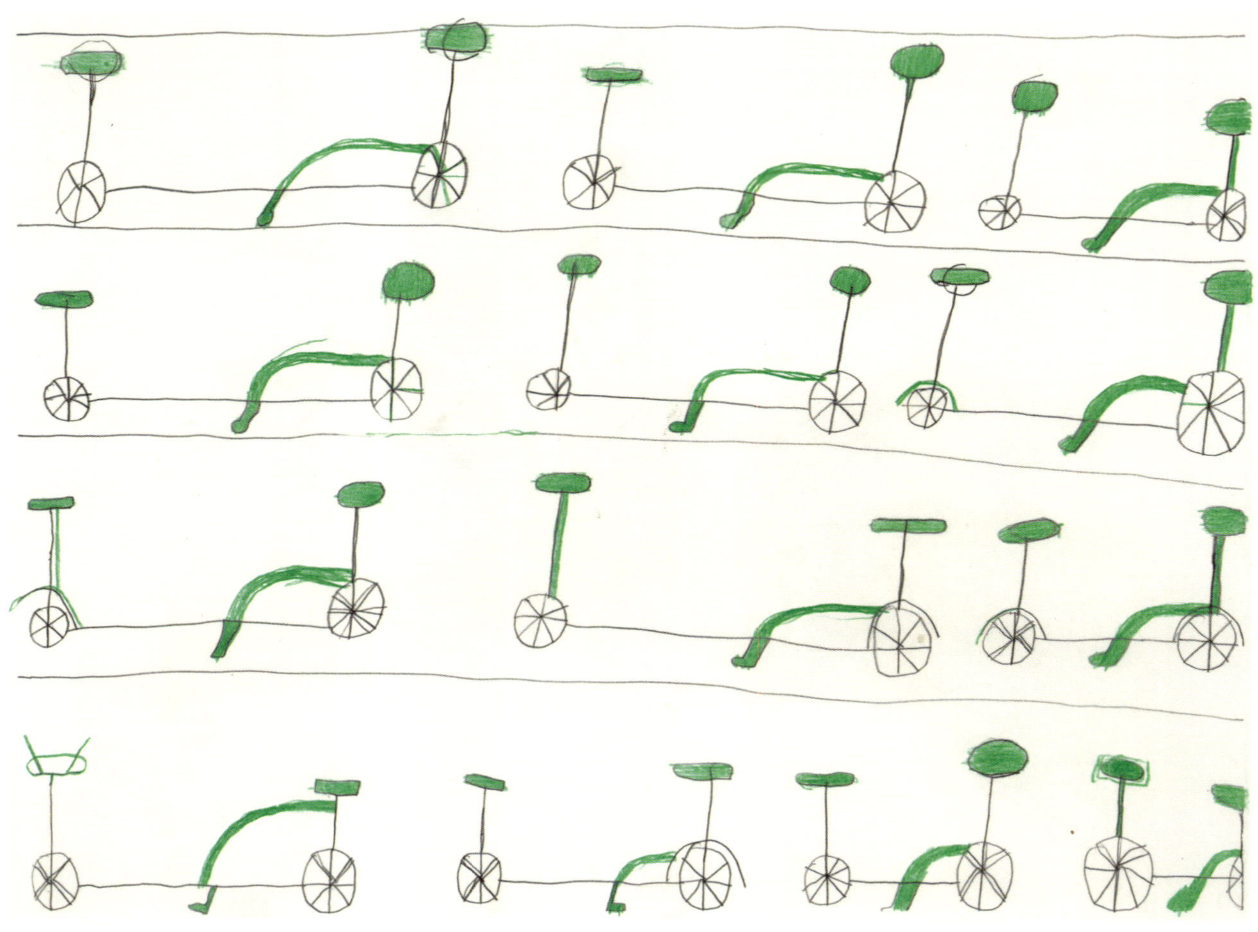

Hans Saletmeier
Sans titre untitled, 2005
mine de plomb et crayon de couleur sur papier lead pencil and coloured pencil on paper
44 x 60 cm

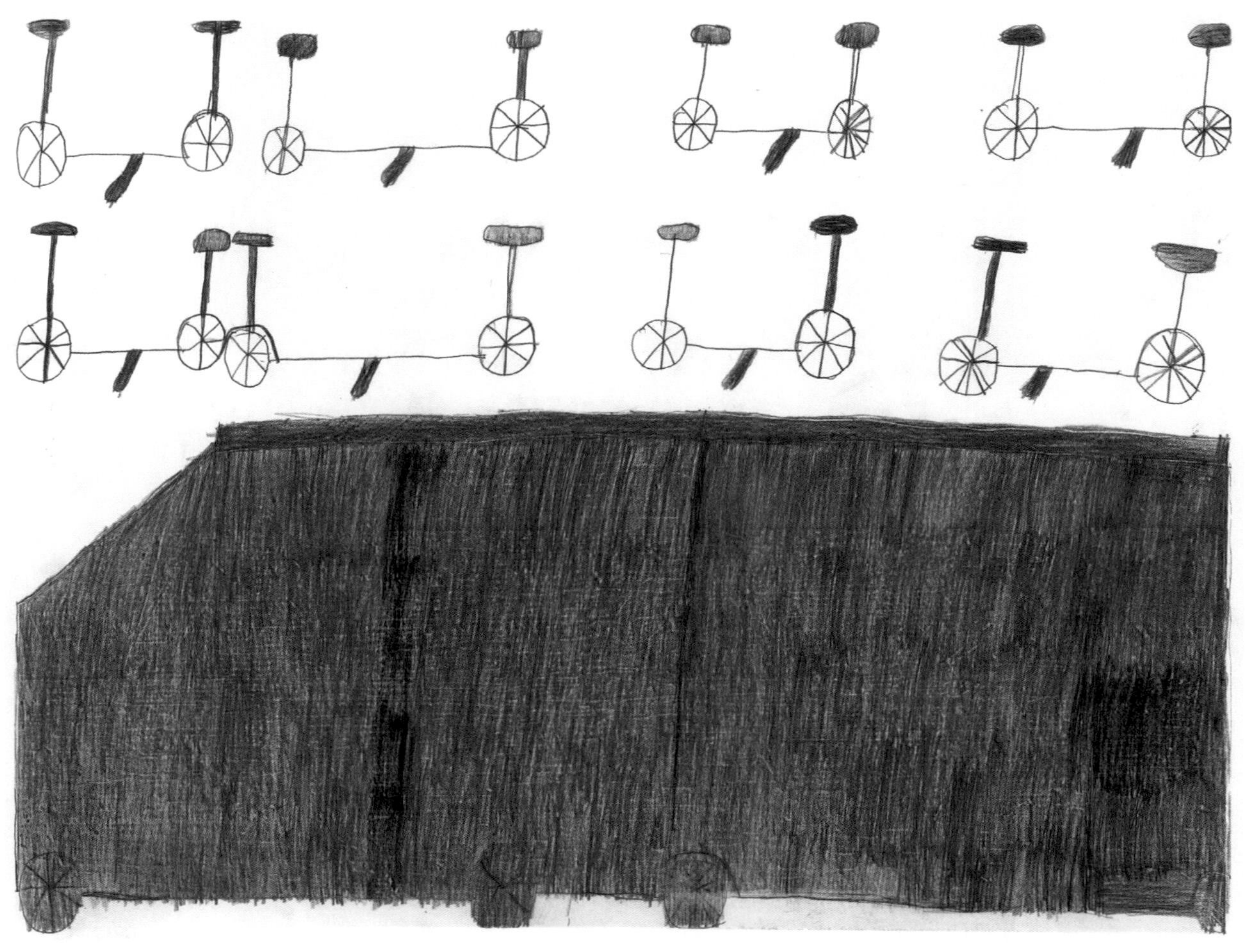

Hans Saletmeier
Sans titre untitled, 2005
mine de plomb et crayon de couleur sur papier lead pencil and coloured pencil on paper
44 x 60 cm

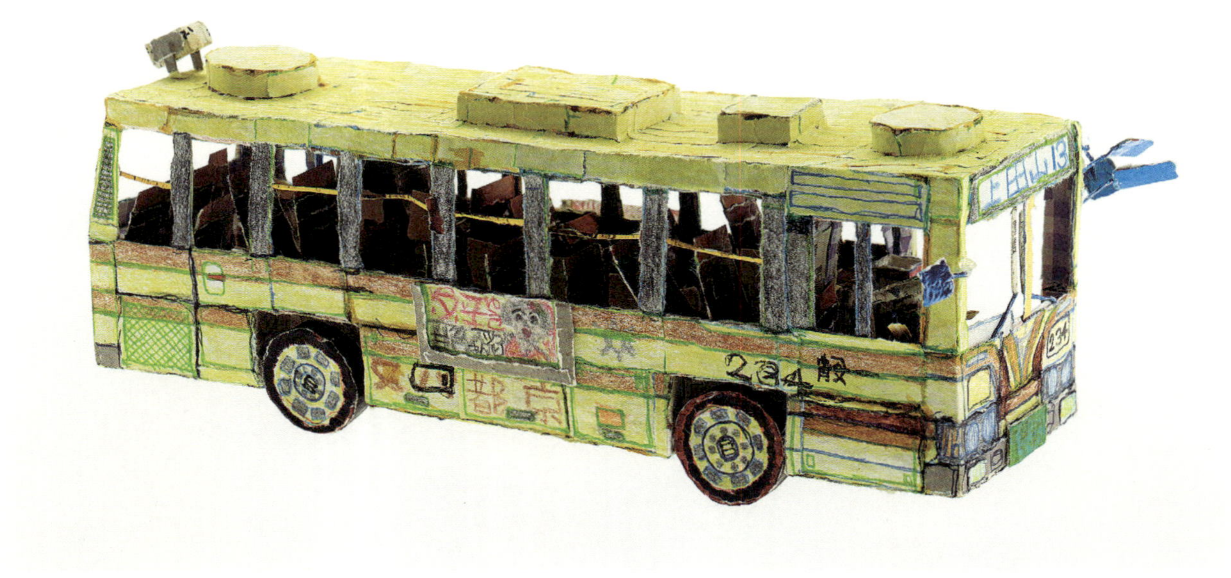

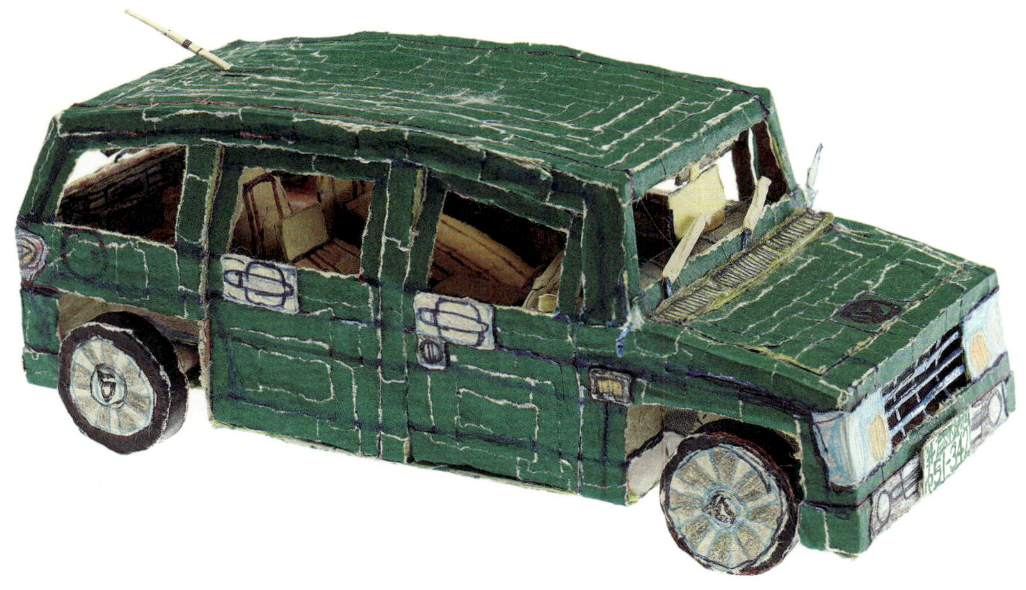

Sawada Shinichi
Sans titre untitled, ca. 1999-2000
technique mixte
mixed media
7 x 7 x 18 cm

Sawada Shinichi
Sans titre untitled, ca. 1999-2000
technique mixte
mixed media
5,3 x 7 x 12,8 cm

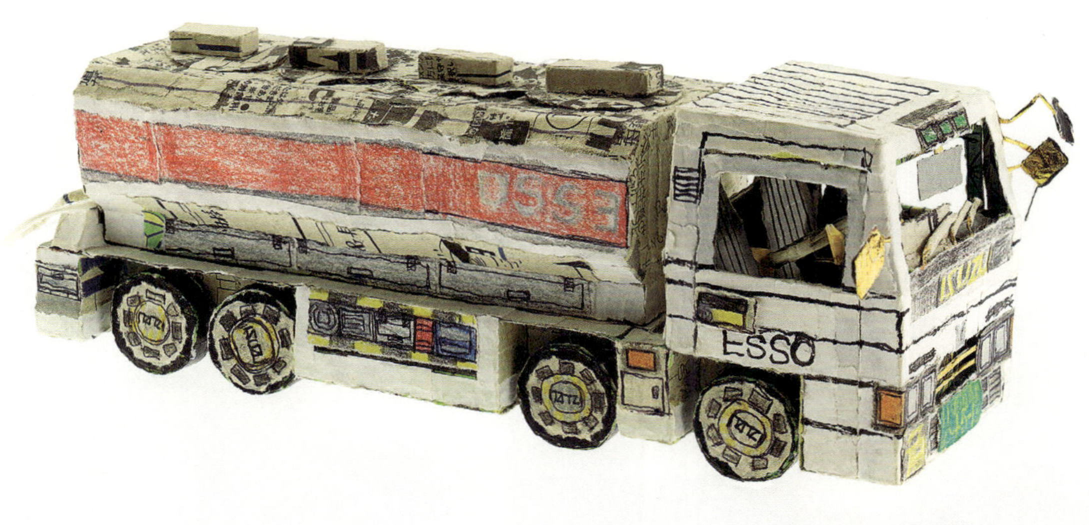

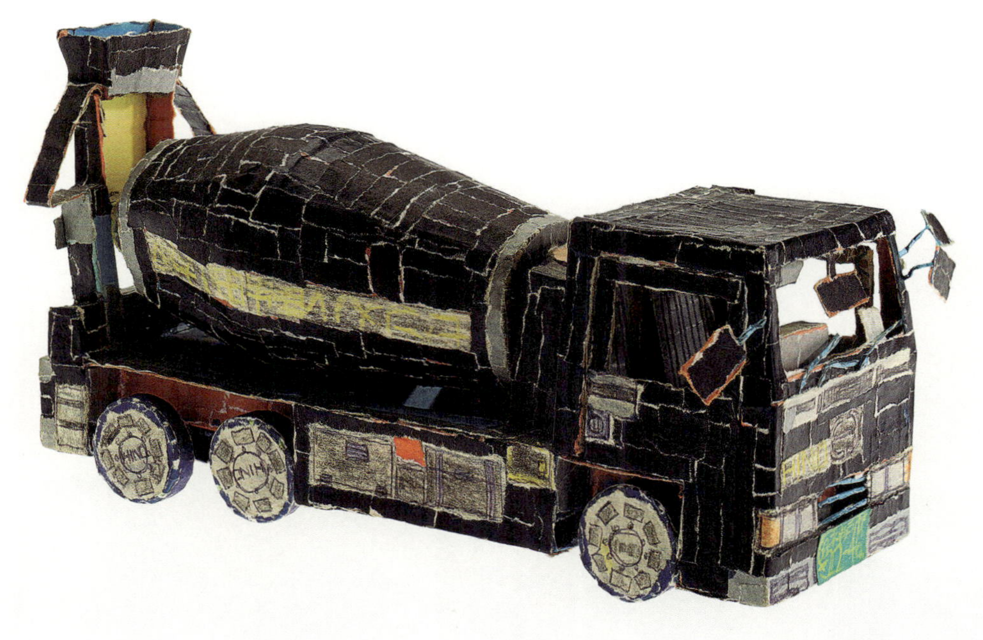

Sawada Shinichi
Sans titre untitled, ca. 1999-2000
technique mixte
mixed media
6,5 x 6,5 x 19 cm

Sawada Shinichi
Sans titre untitled, ca. 1999-2000
technique mixte
mixed media
8,2 x 6,5 x 16,5 cm

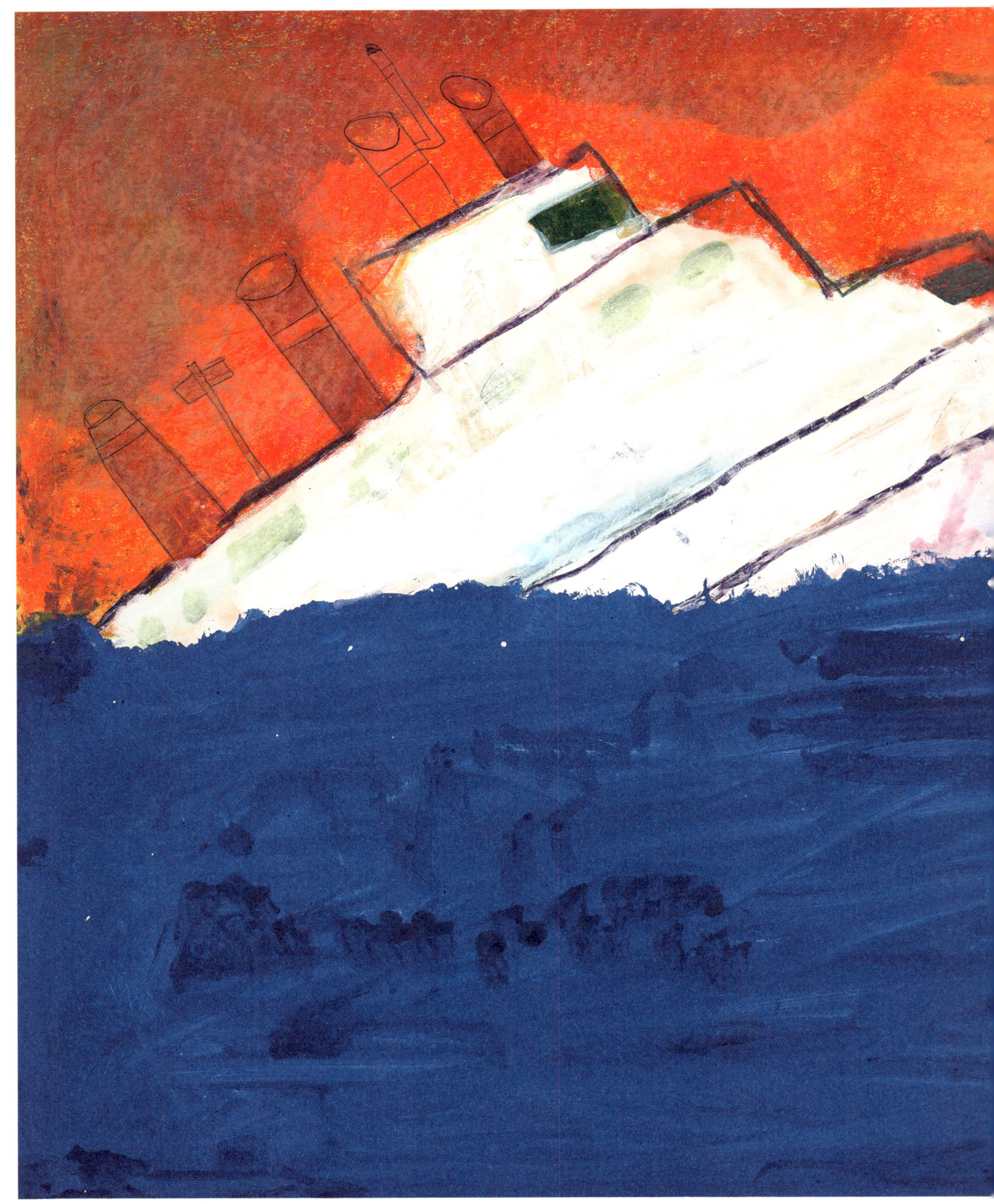

André Stanton
Sans titre *untitled*, ca. 1986-1991
pastel et gouache sur papier
pastel and gouache on paper
50 x 70 cm

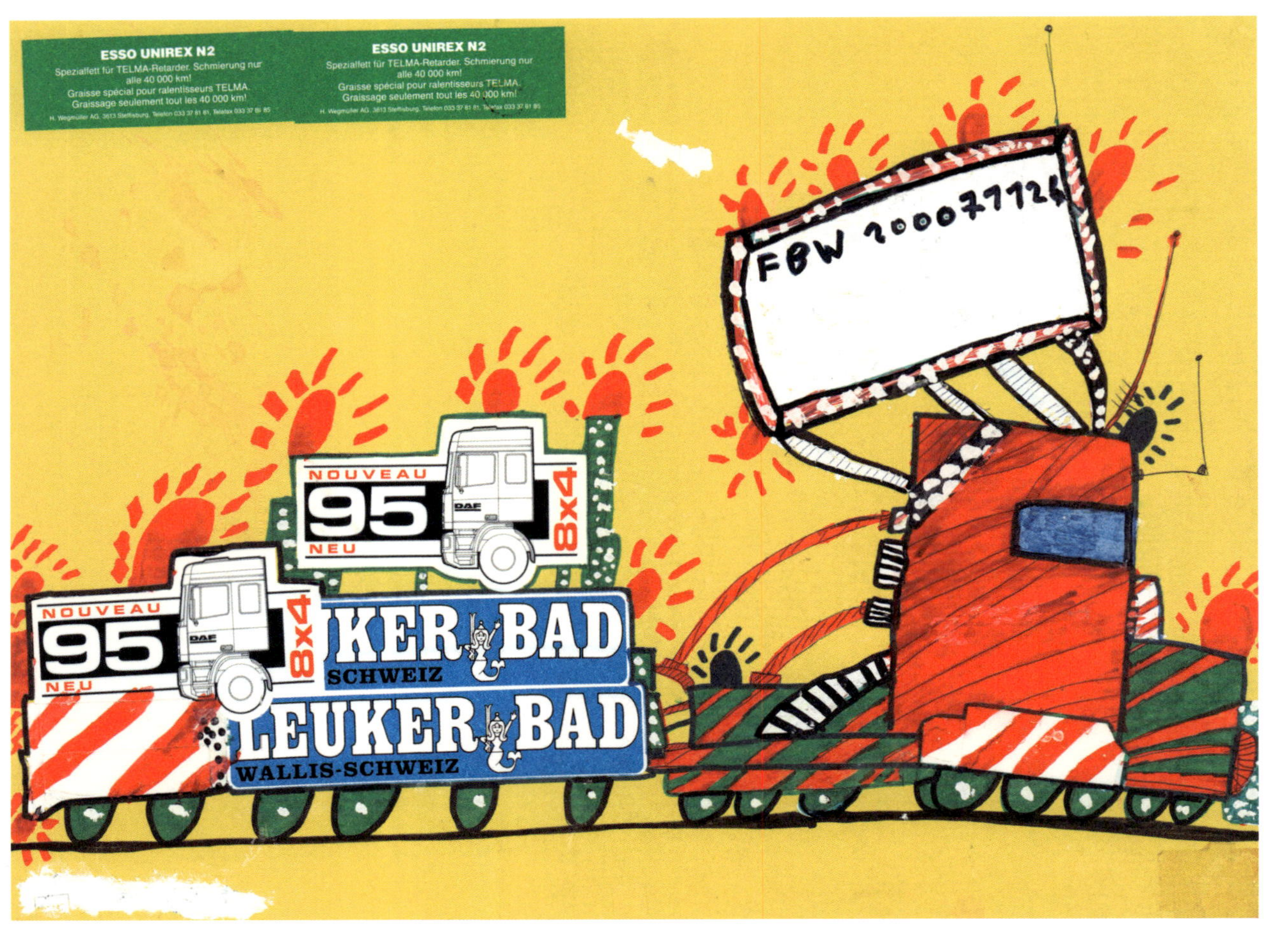

André Stanton
Leukerbad, ca. 1986-1991
stylo-bille, feutre, peinture et collage sur papier ballpoint pen, felt pen, paint and collage on paper
50 x 70 cm

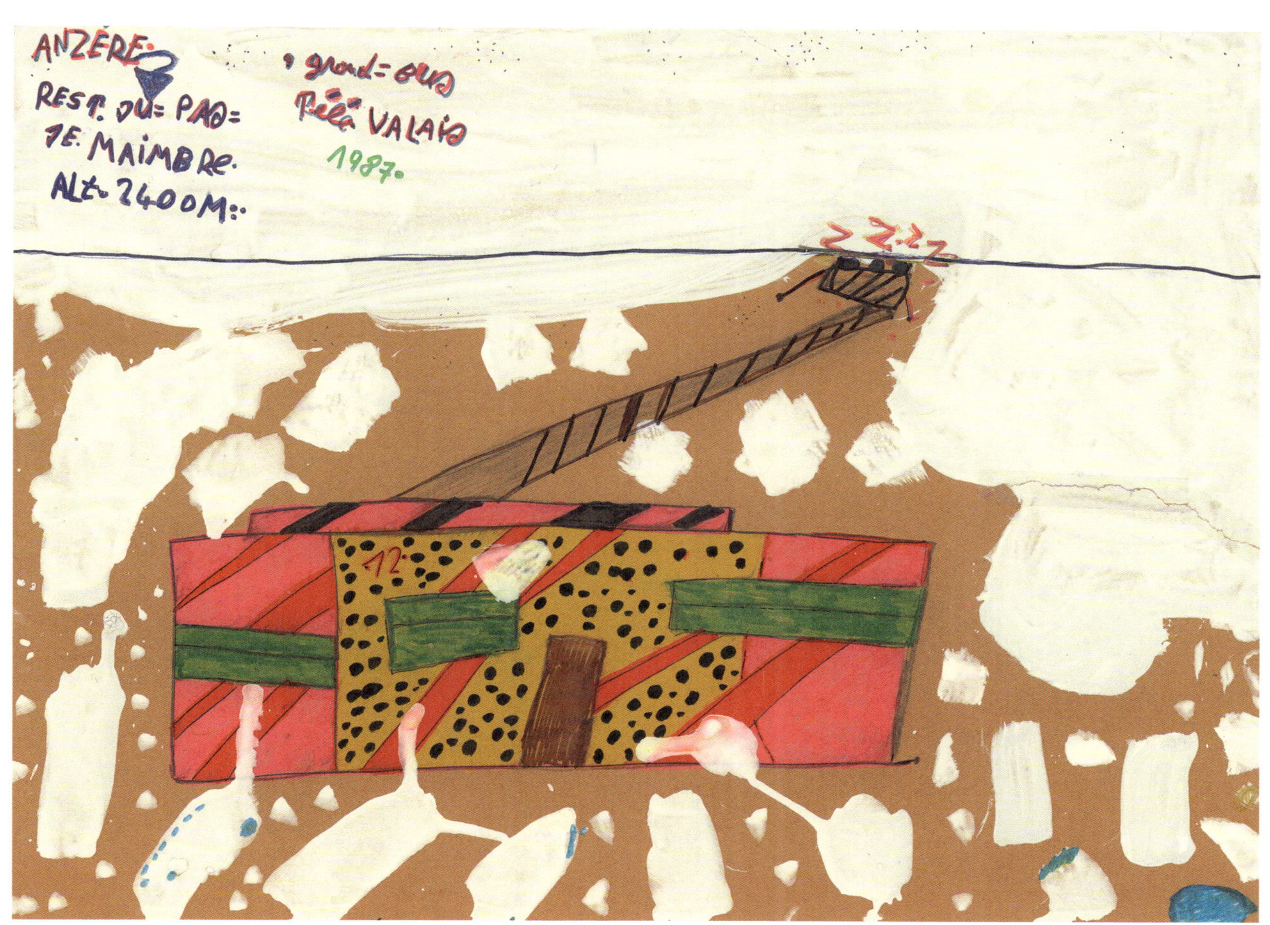

André Stanton
Anzere.rest. Du pas=de.maimbre.
Alt. 2400 m, 1987
feutre et peinture sur papier
felt pen and paint on paper
50 x 70 cm

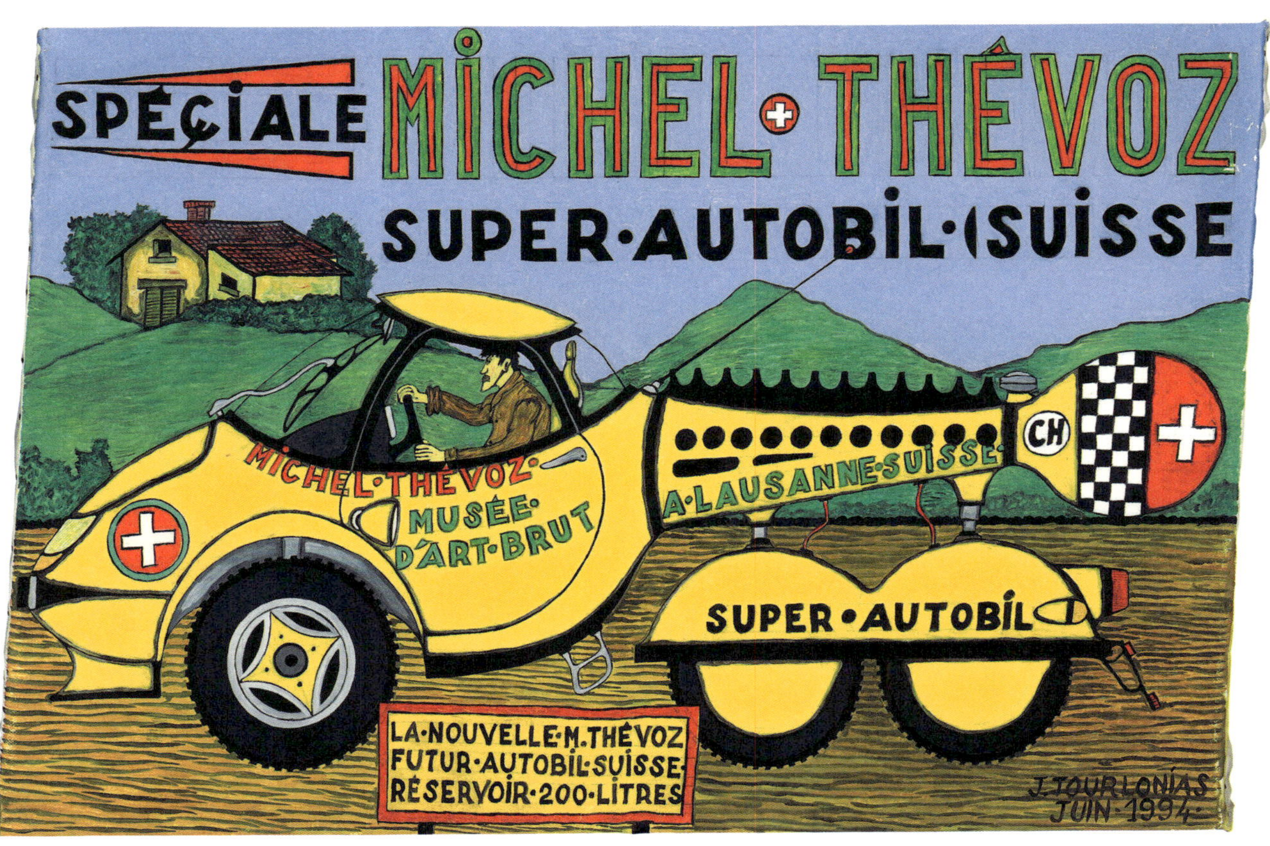

Jean Tourlonias
Spéciale Michel Thévoz super autobil suisse, 1994
acrylique sur toile cirée
acrylic on oilcloth
65 x 100 cm

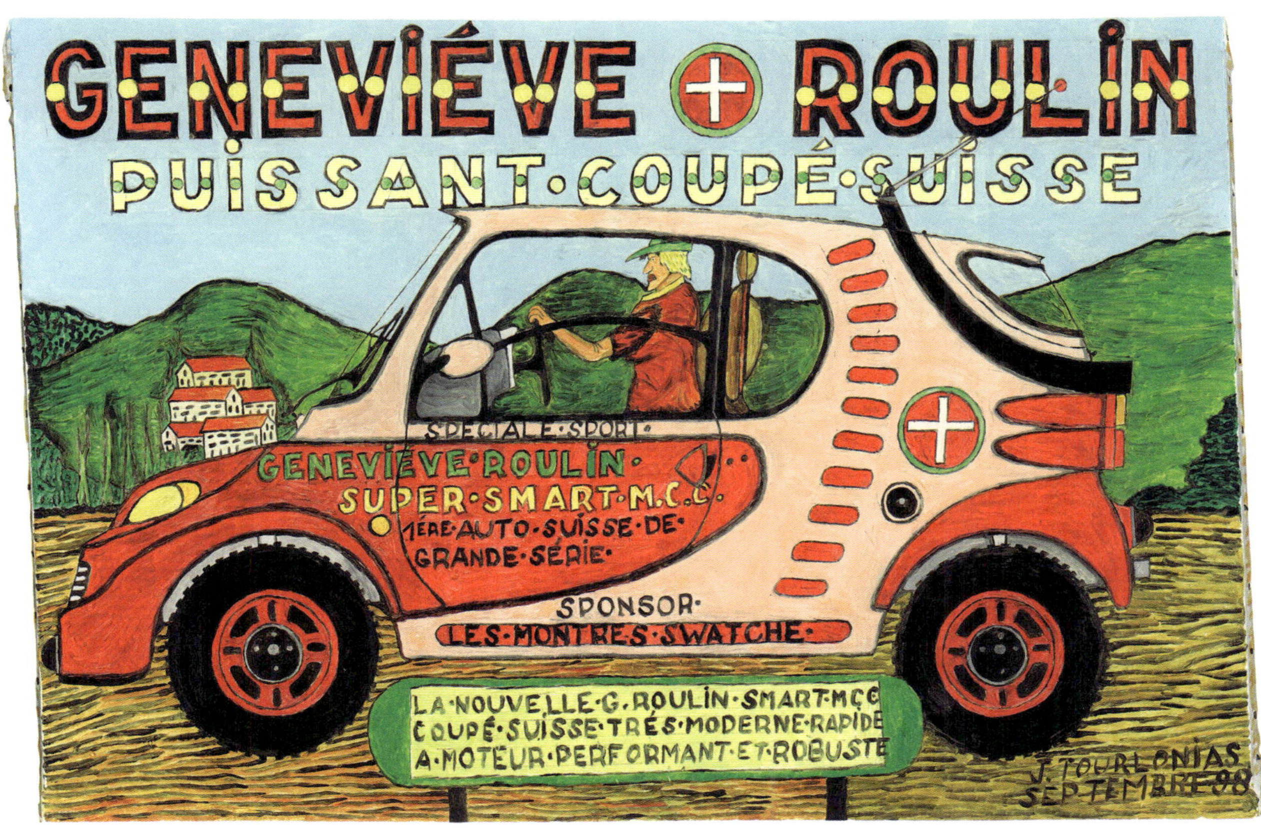

Jean Tourlonias
Geneviève Roulin puissant coupé, 1998
huile sur toile cirée
oil on oilcloth
66 x 100 cm

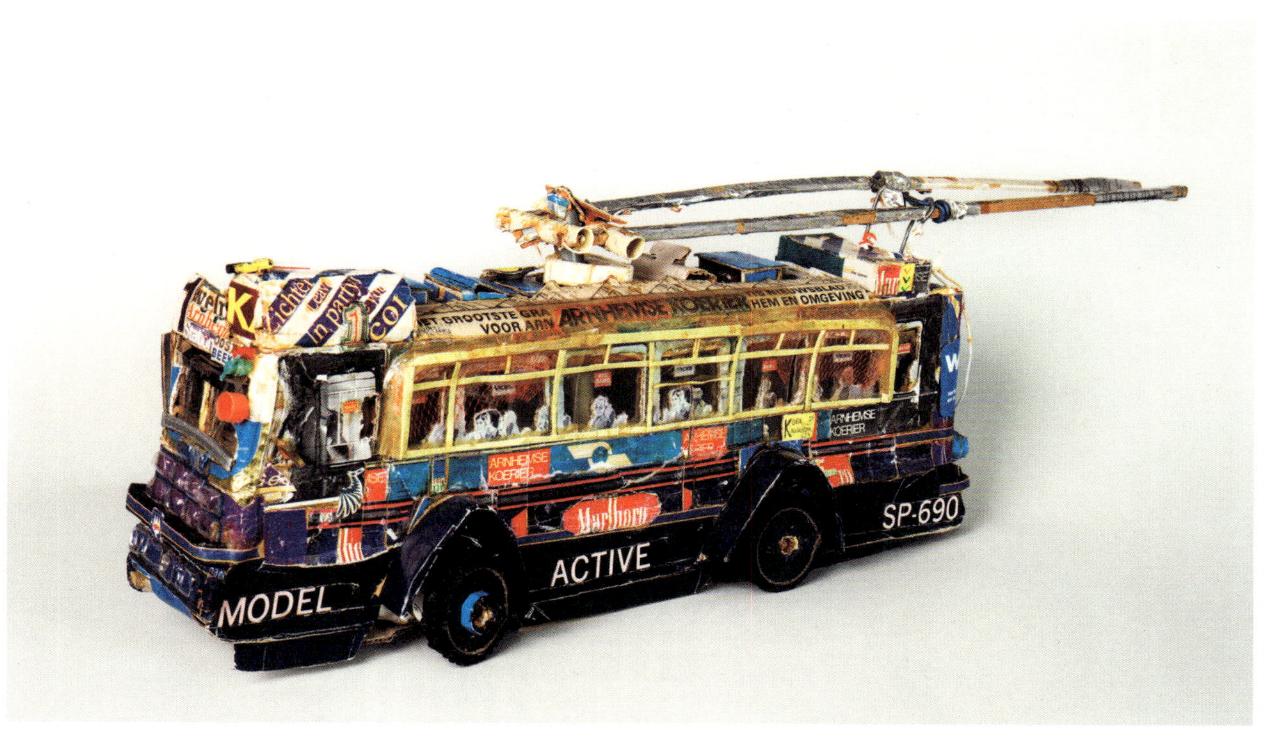

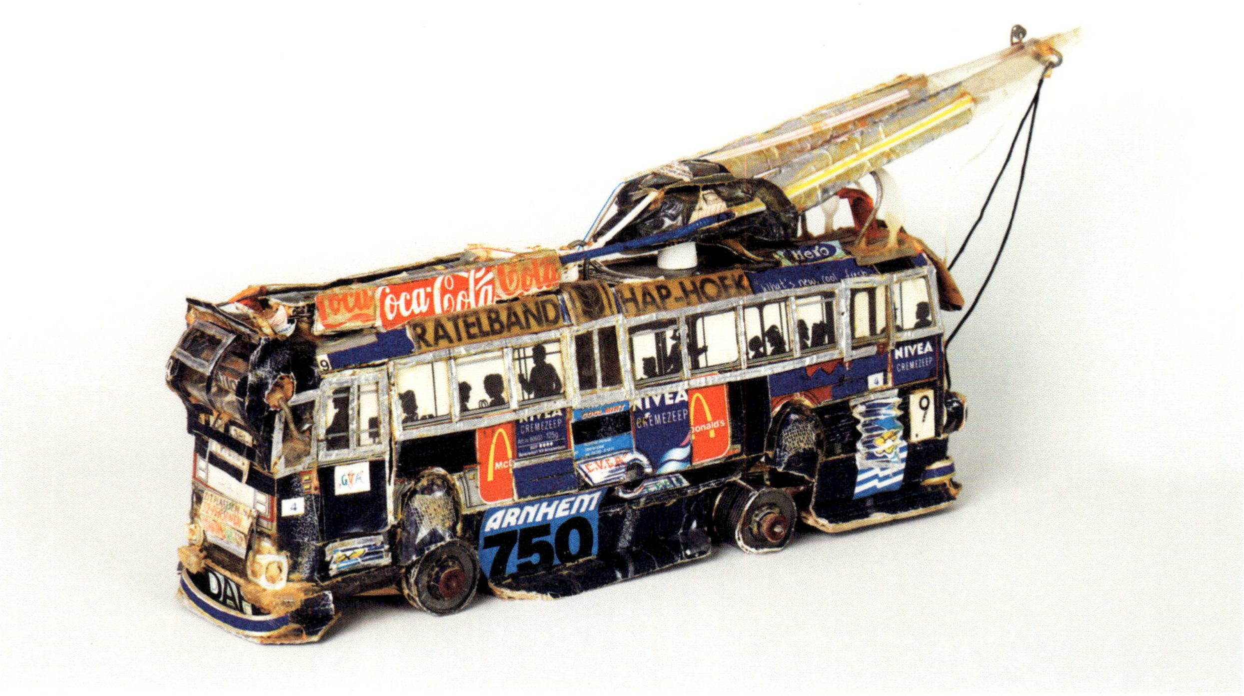

Willem Van Genk
Sans titre untitled, ca. 1988-2005
matériaux divers
miscellaneous materials
28,5 x 89 x 17,5 cm

Willem Van Genk
Sans titre untitled, ca. 1988-2005
matériaux divers
miscellaneous materials
61 x 14 x 25 cm

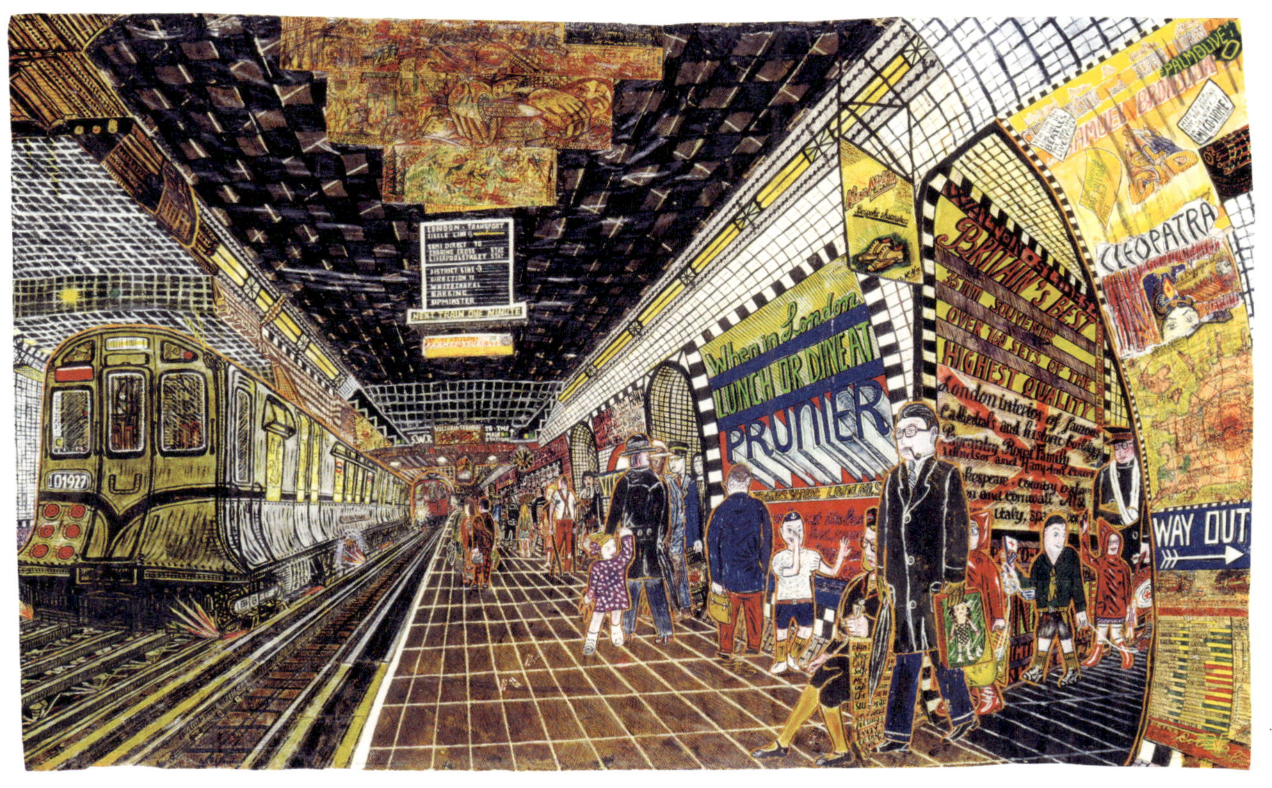

Willem Van Genk
Tube station, 1970
collage et peinture sur bois
collage and paint on wood
75 x 124 cm

Willem Van Genk >
50 jaar soviet-unie, 1967
encre et gouache sur papier kraft
ink and gouach on kraft paper
96 x 174 cm

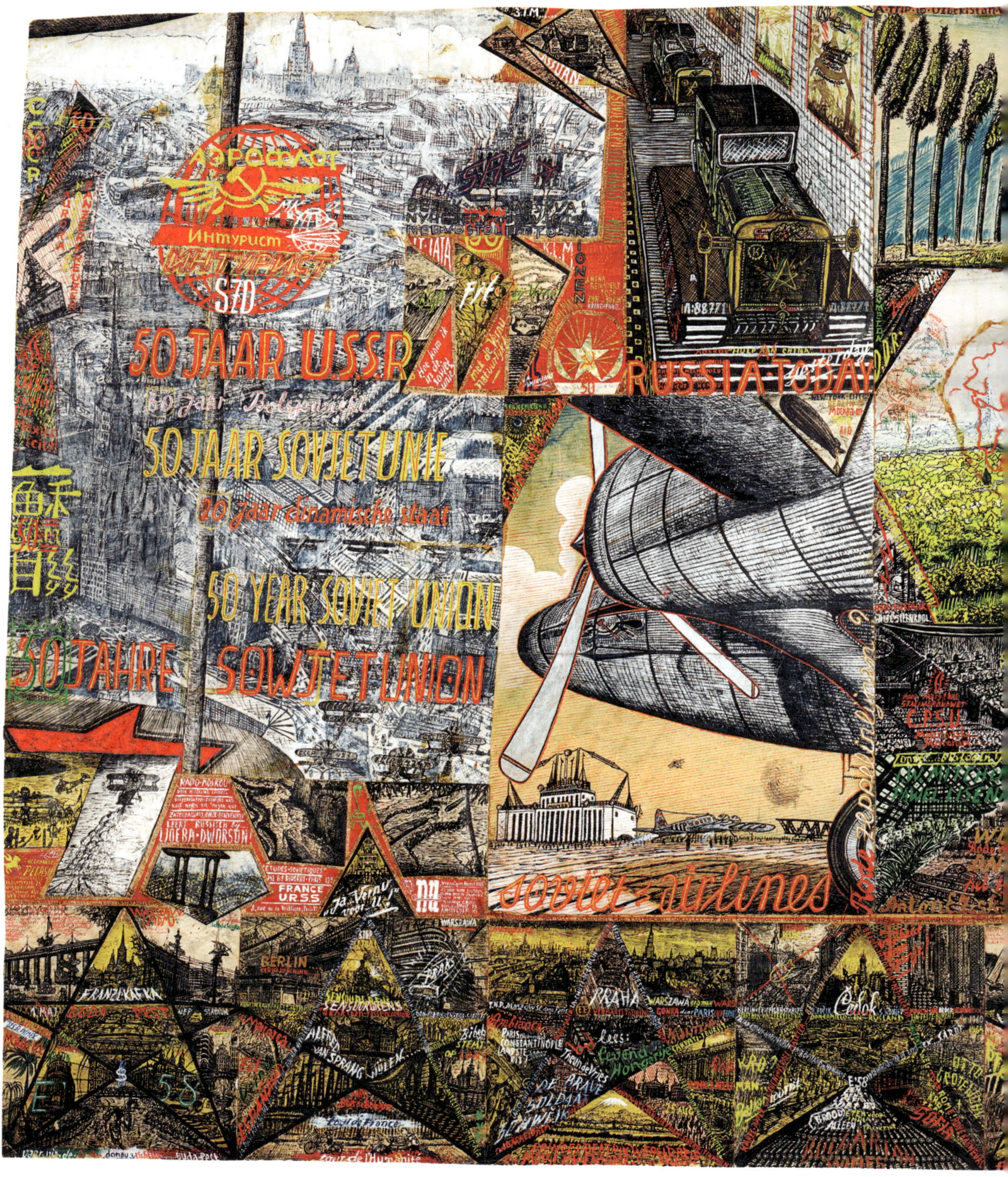
Интурист
SZD
50 JAAR U.S.S.R
50 JAAR SOVJETUNIE
20 jaar dinamische staat
50 YEAR SOVIET UNION
50 JAHRE SOWJETUNION
RUSSIA TODAY
soviet airlines
FRANCE U.R.S.S
BERLIN
FRANZ KAFKA
PRAHA
WARSZAWA

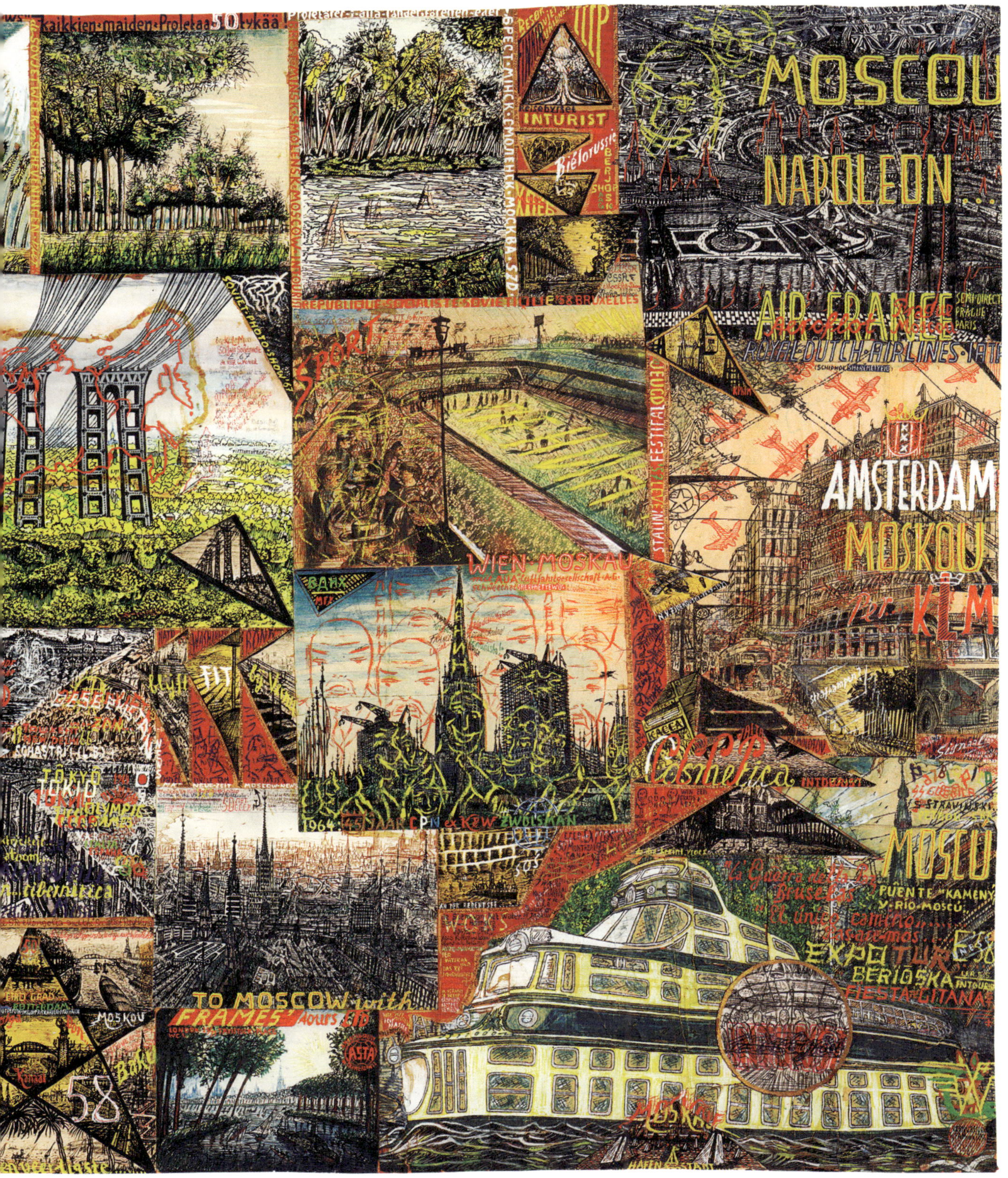
kaikkien maiden Proletaa 50 tykää
INTURIST
MOSCOU
NAPOLEON...
AIR FRANCE
ROYAL DUTCH AIRLINES
SPORT
AMSTERDAM
MOSKOU
per KLM
WIEN-MOSKAU
TOKYO
TO MOSCOW with
FRAMES
MOSCU
PUENTE KAMENY
Y RIO MOSCÚ
EXPO TUR
BERIOSKA
FIESTA GITANA
MOSKOU
58

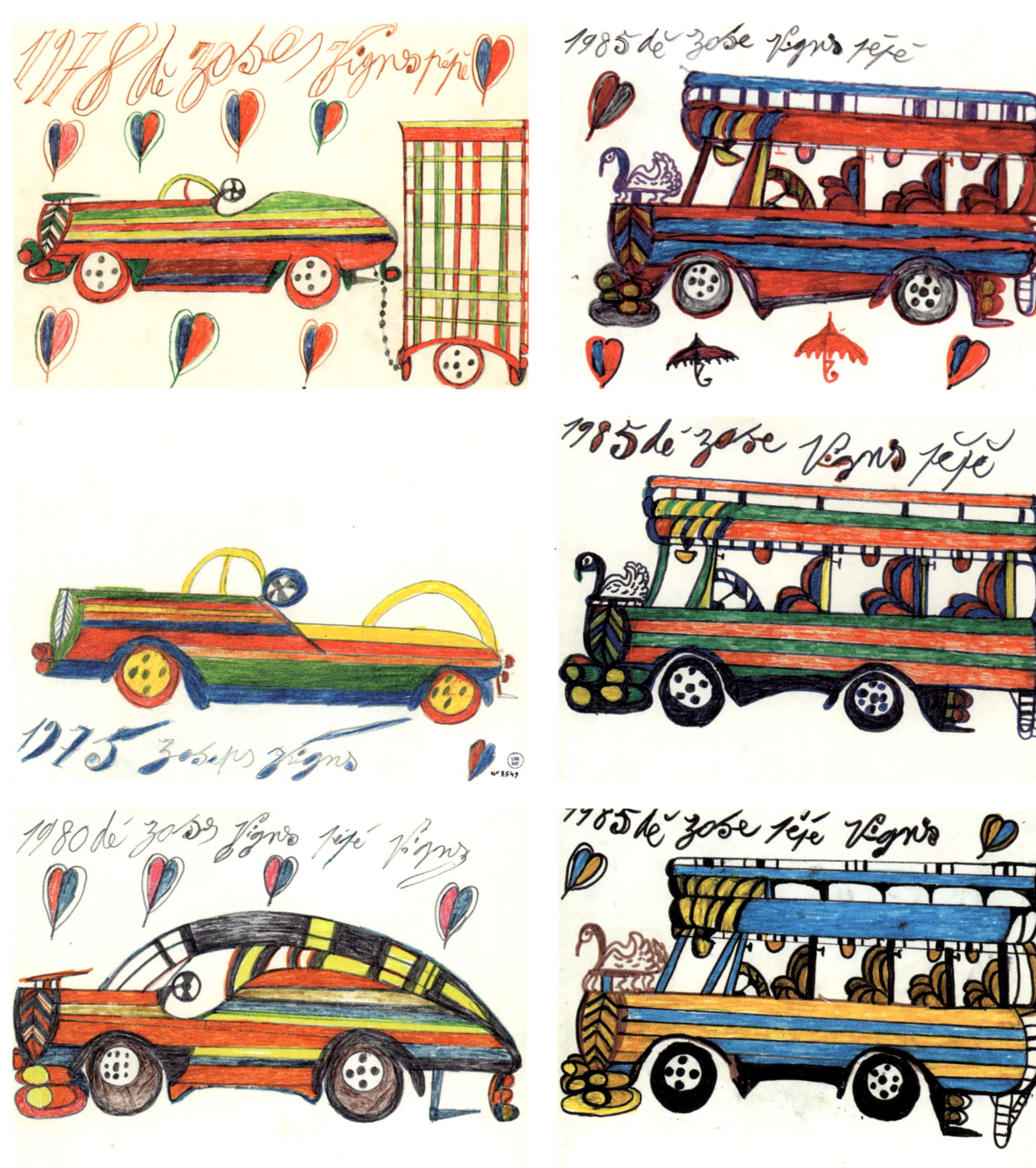

Pépé Vignes
Sans titre untitled, 1975-1985
mine de plomb, crayon de couleur, feutre sur papier lead pencil, coloured pencil and felt pen on paper
30 x 42 cm, 24 x 32 cm

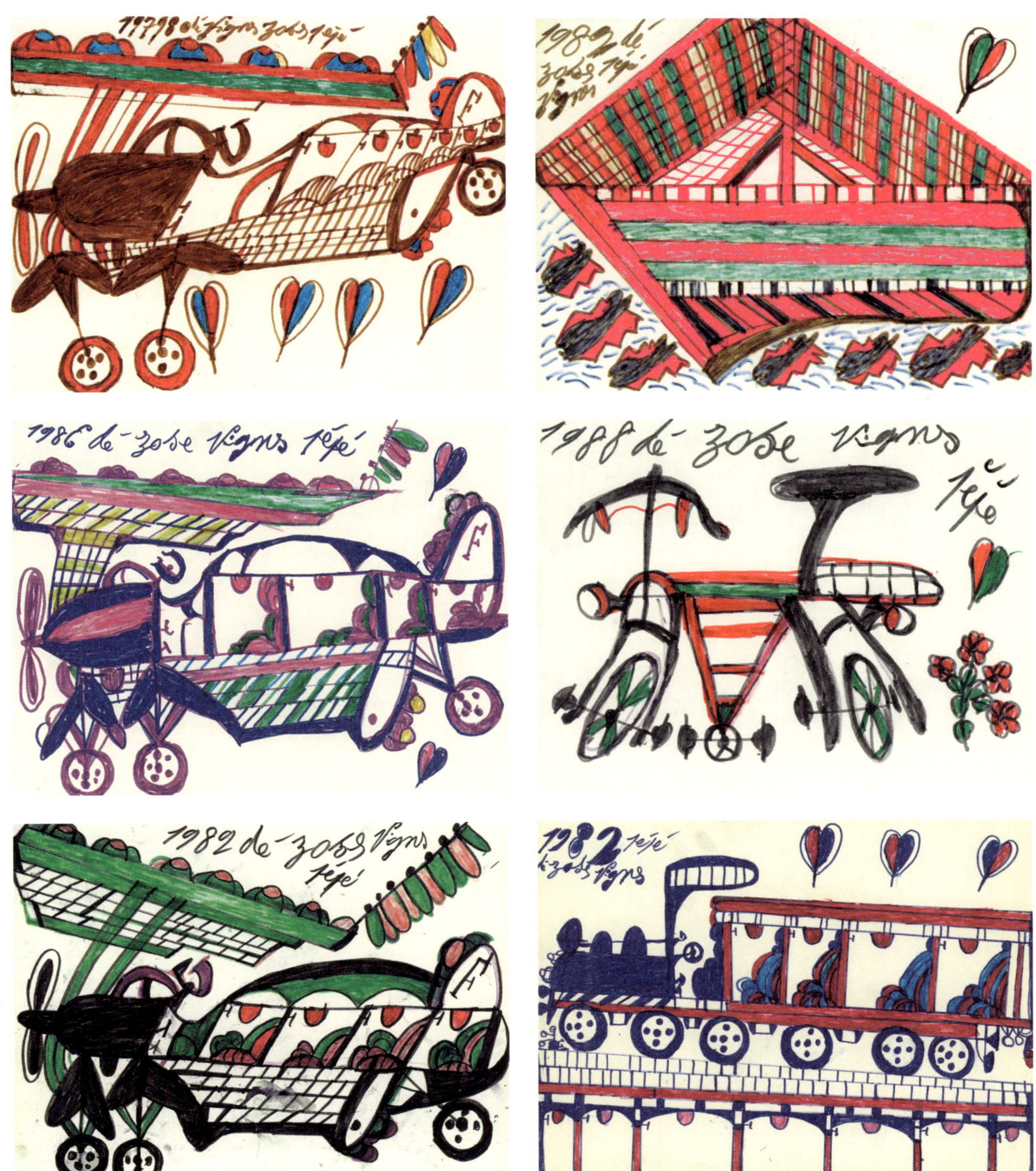

Pépé Vignes
Sans titre untitled, 1979-1988
feutre sur papier
felt pen on paper
24 x 32 cm, 21 x 30 cm, 30 x 42 cm

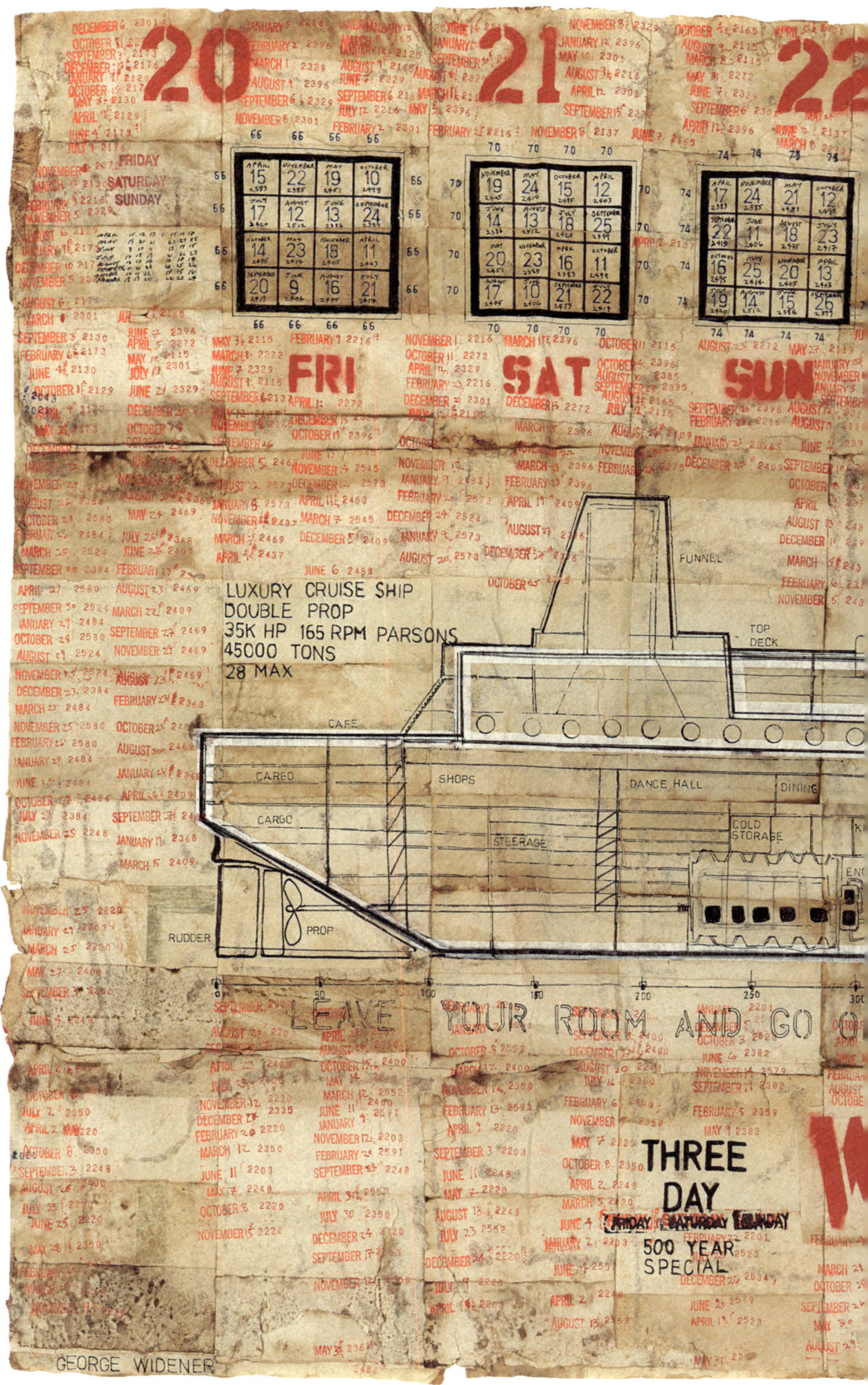

George Widener
Weekend Cruiser, 2005
encre sur papier
ink on paper
97 x 144 cm

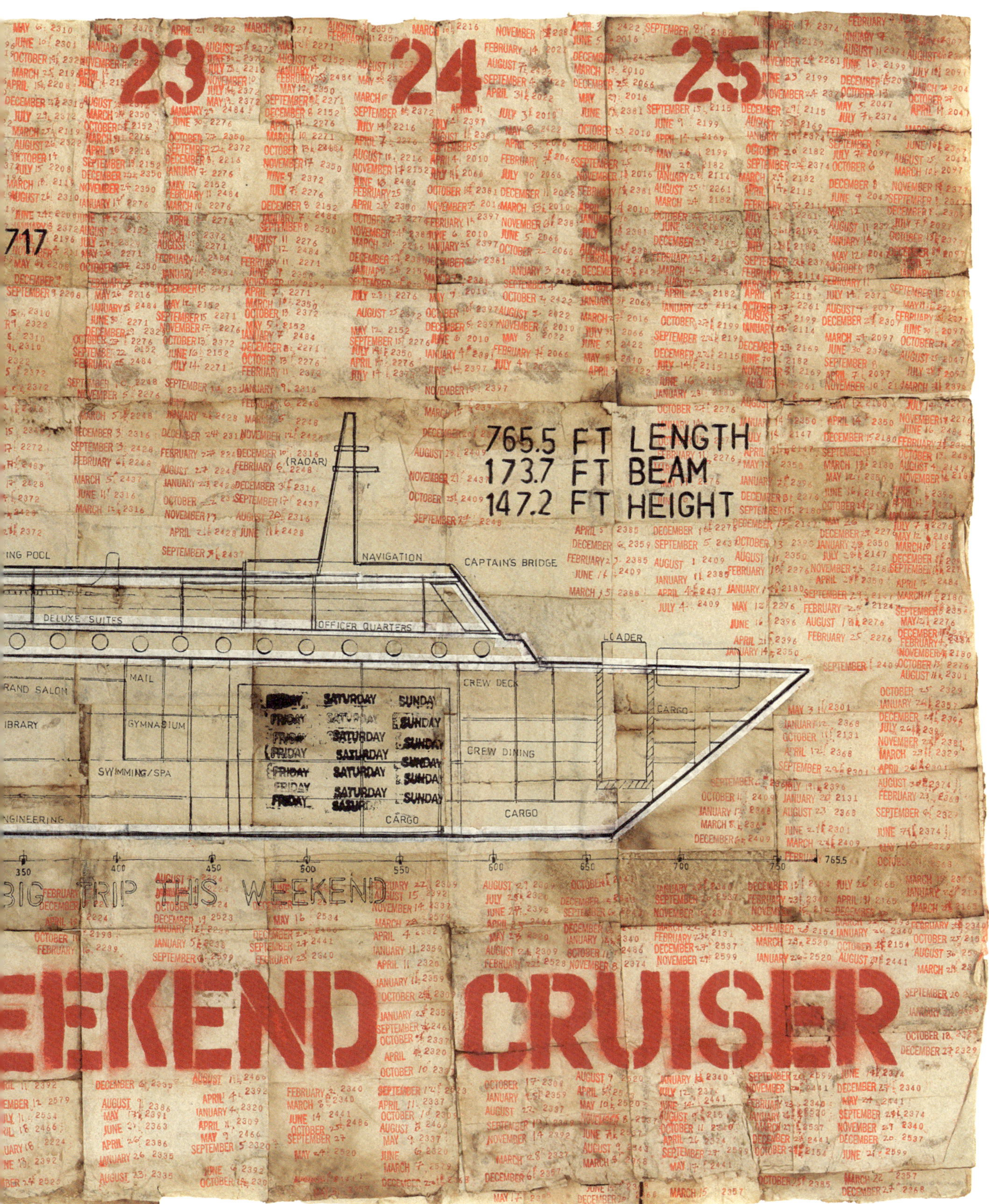
23
24
25
717
765.5 FT LENGTH
173.7 FT BEAM
147.2 FT HEIGHT
(RADAR)
NAVIGATION
CAPTAIN'S BRIDGE
ING POOL
DELUXE SUITES
OFFICER QUARTERS
LOADER
MAIL
RAND SALON
CREW DECK
LIBRARY
GYMNASIUM
CARGO
CREW DINING
SWIMMING/SPA
NGINEERING
CARGO
CARGO
FRIDAY SATURDAY SUNDAY
350
400
450
500
550
600
650
700
750
765.5
BIG TRIP THIS WEEKEND
EEKEND CRUISER

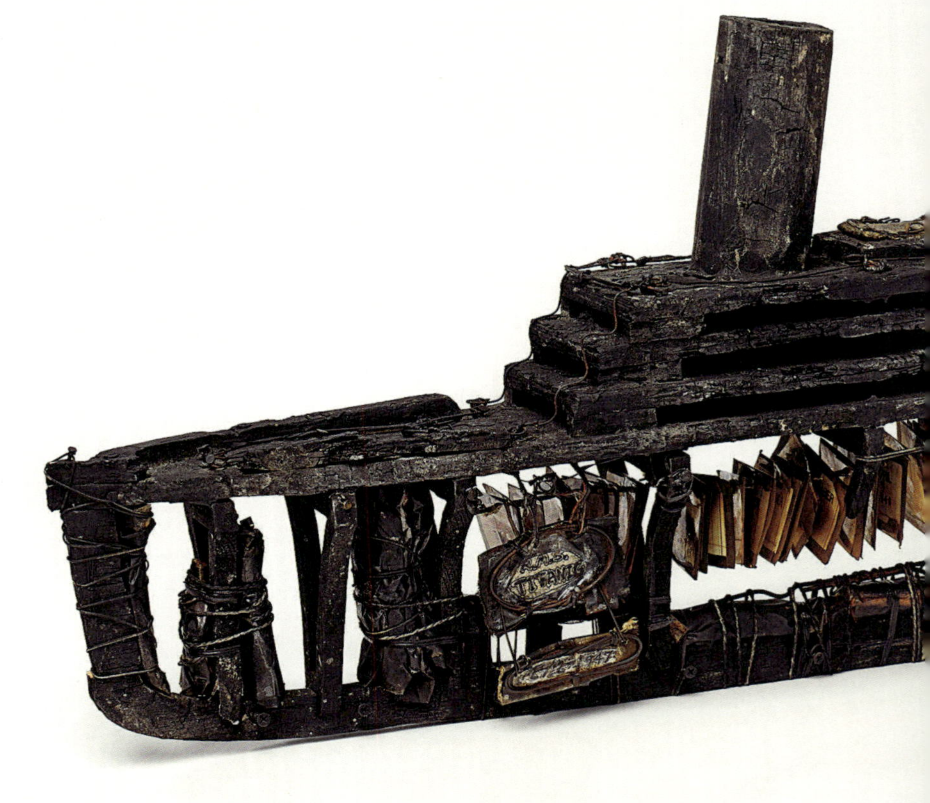

George Widener
Titanic, 2012
bois brûlé et matériaux divers
charred wood and miscellaneous materials
33 x 152 x 25 cm

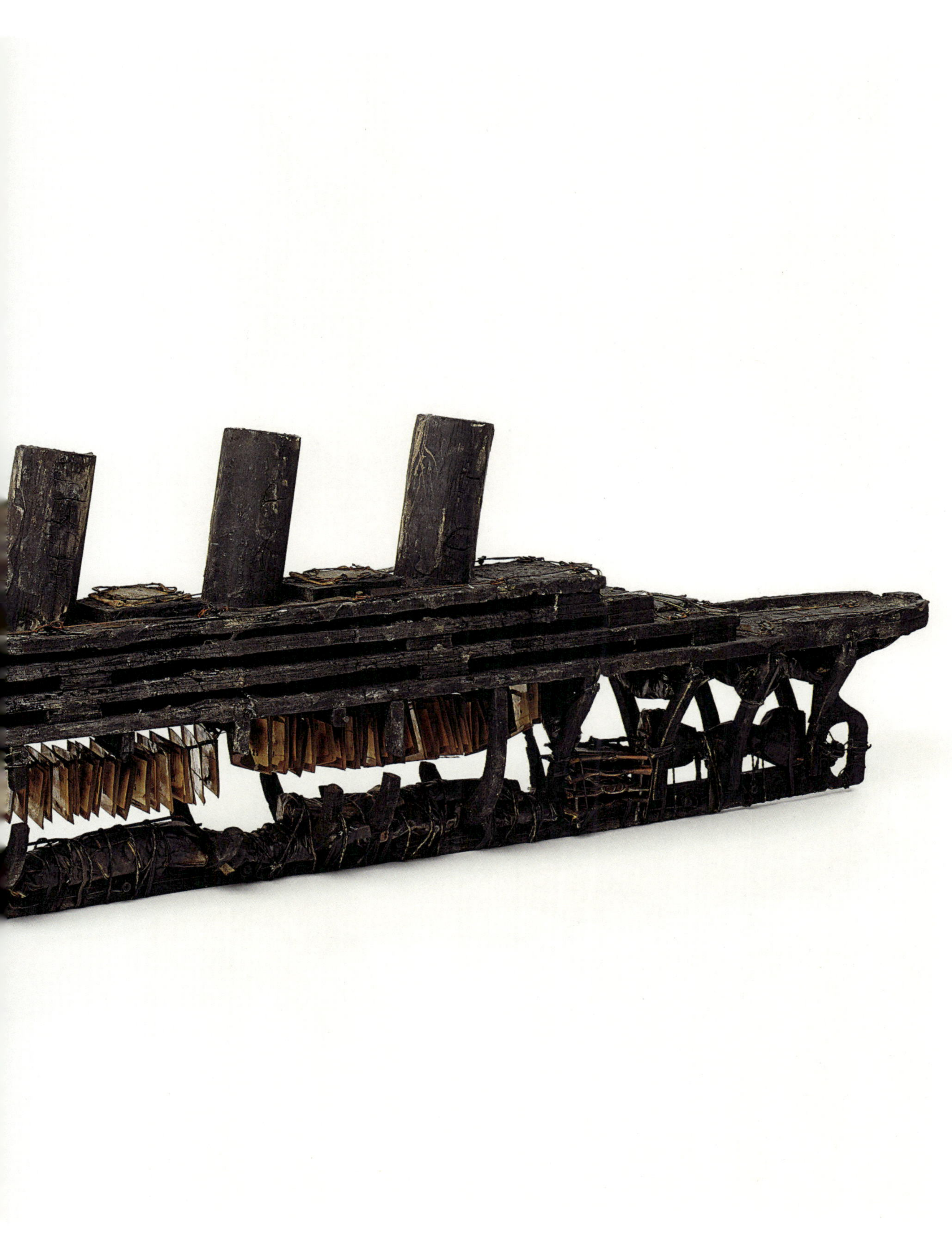

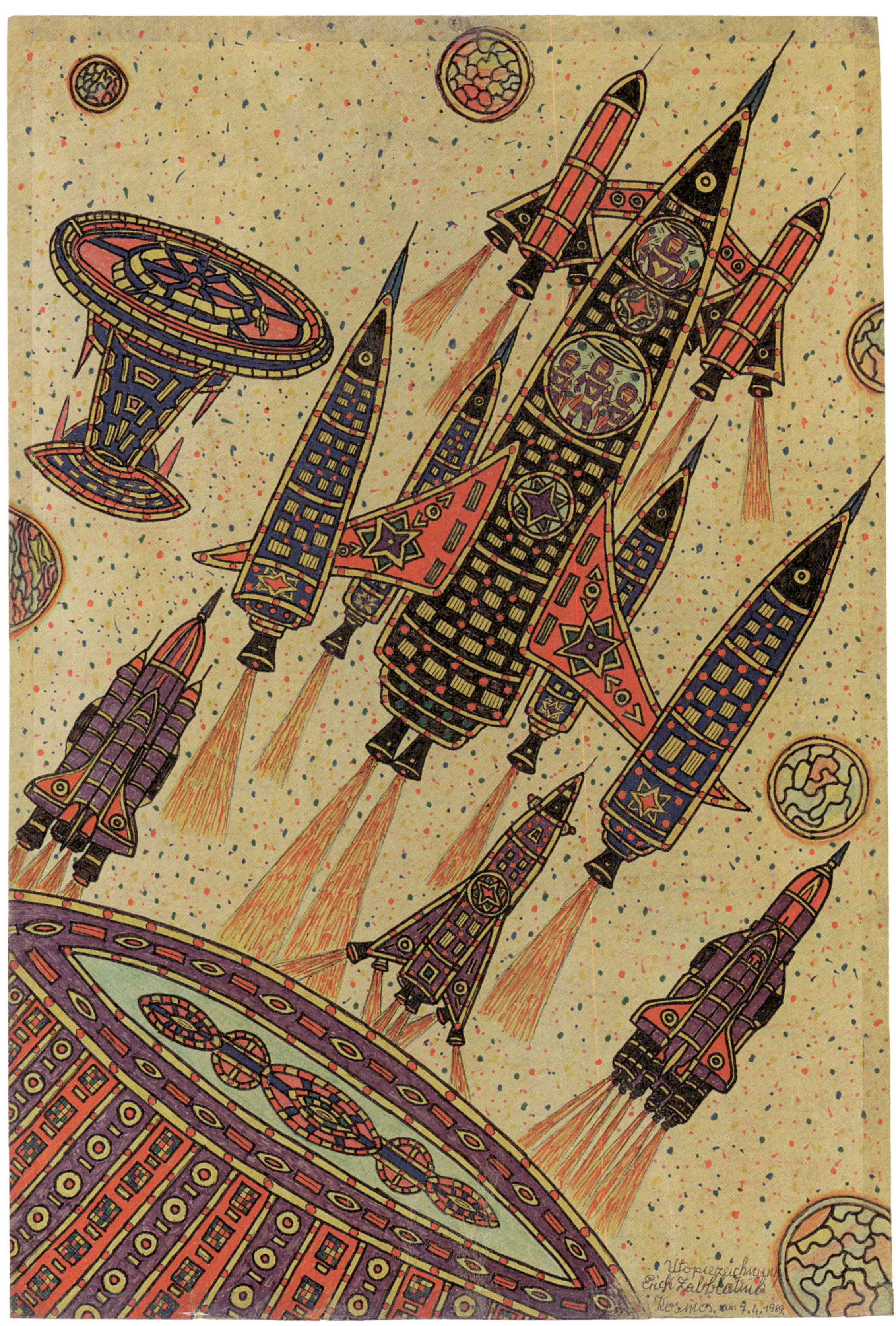
Utopiezeichnung
Erich Zablatnik
Kosmos. am 7.4.1989

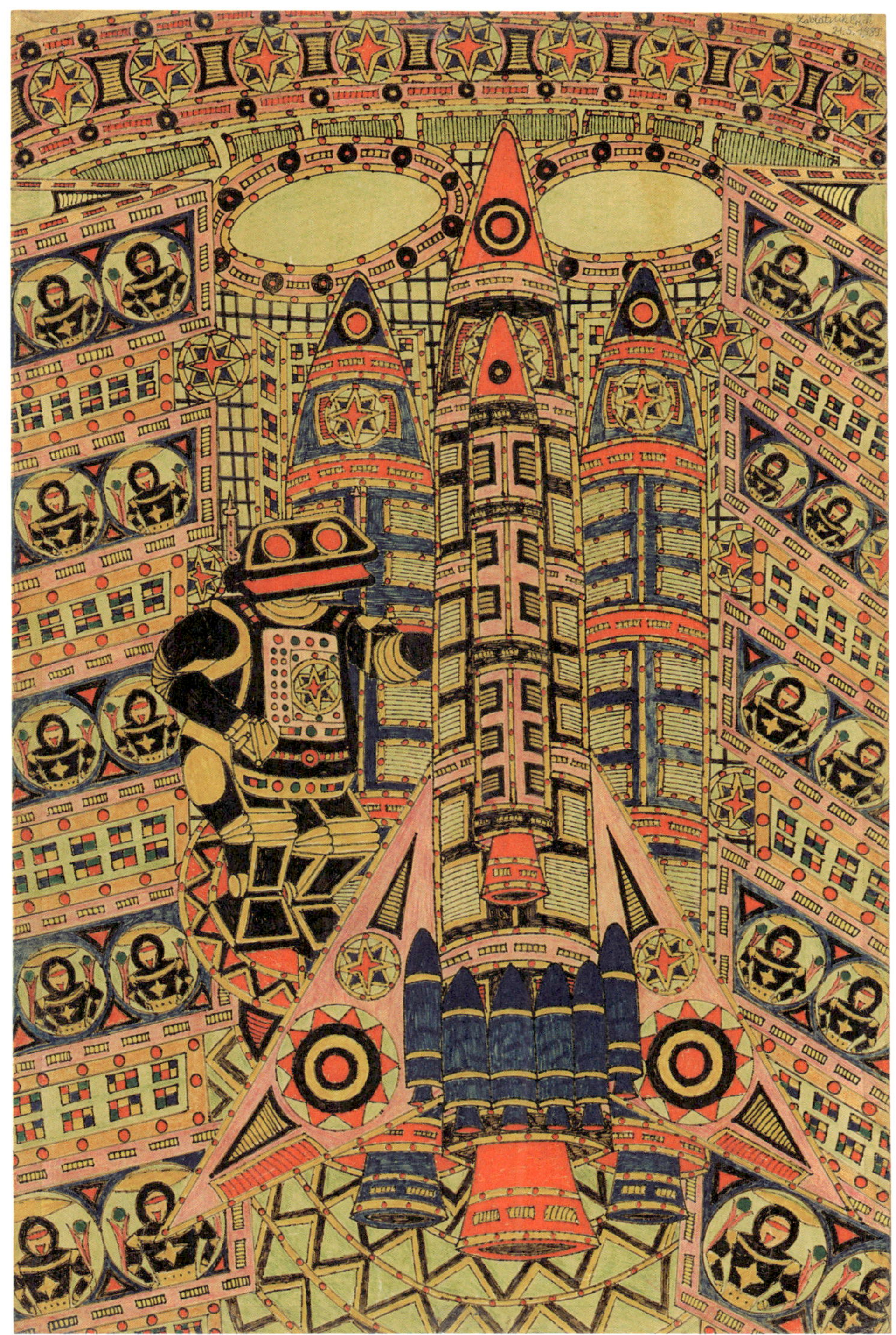

Erich Zablatnik
Utopiezeichnung, 1989
feutre, stylo-bille, vernis et crayon de couleur sur carton felt pen, ballpoint pen, varnish and coloured pencil on cardboard
60,3 x 41 cm

Erich Zablatnik
Sans titre untitled, 1989
feutre, crayon de couleur et vernis sur carton felt pen, coloured pencil and varnish on cardboard
59,8 x 40 cm

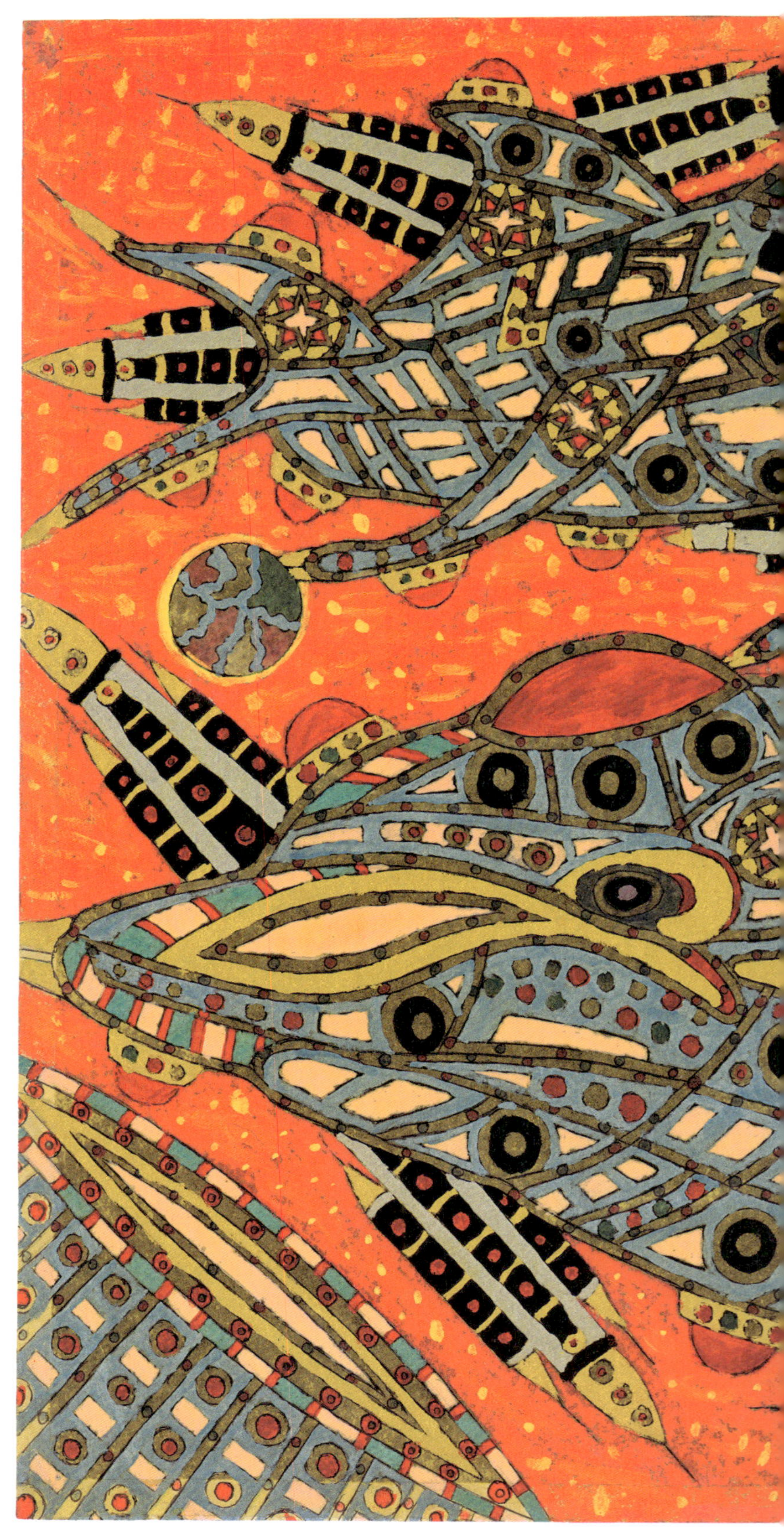

Erich Zablatnik
Sans titre untitled, ca. 1990
laque, gouache et vernis sur papier
lacquer, gouache and varnish on paper
50,1 x 70,2 cm

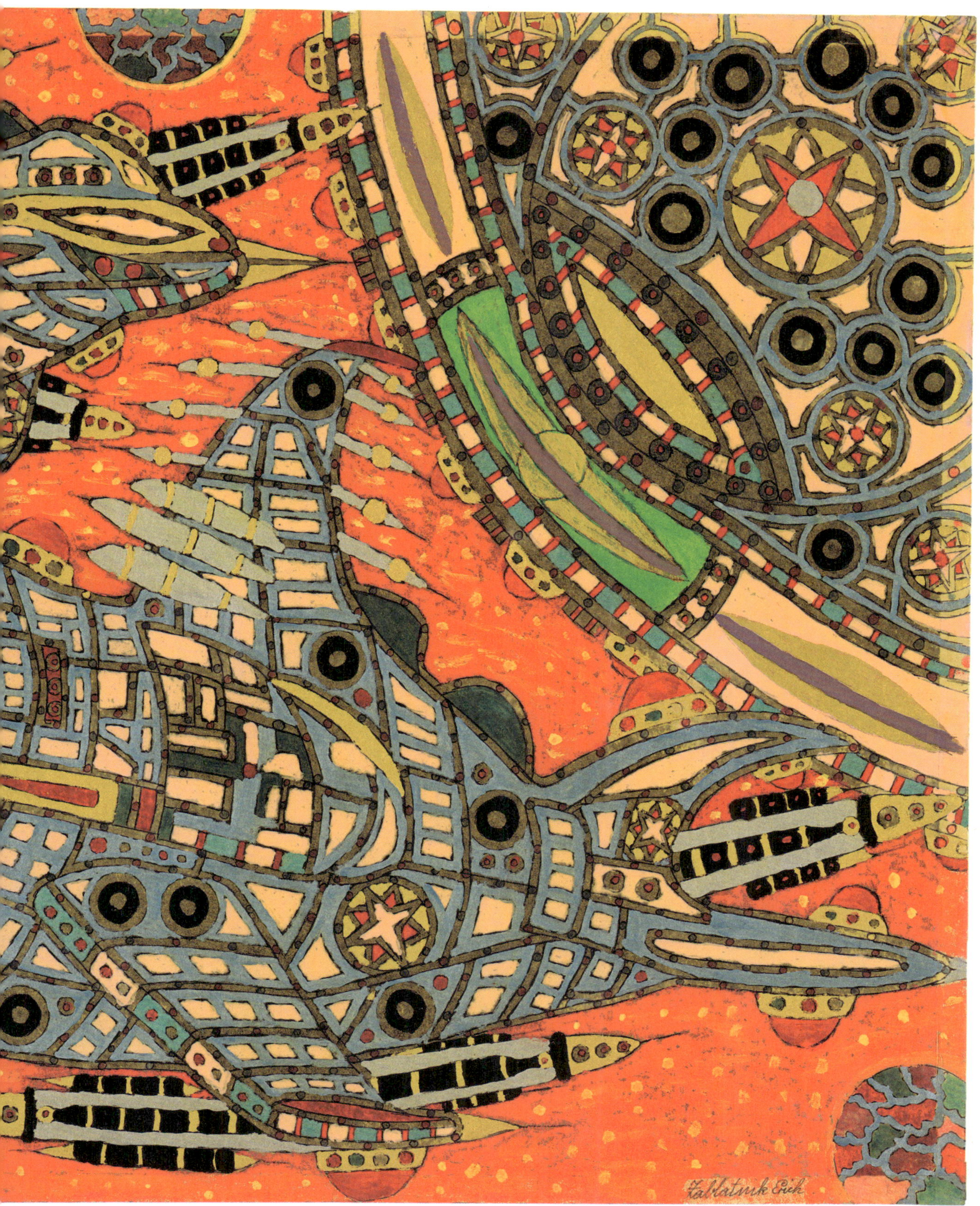
Zablatnik Erich

Annexes

Biographies

Giovanni Abrignani (1899–1977) was born in Marsala, Sicily. He worked as a mason in many Mediterranean countries. After a respiratory disease, he was taken back to Italy and put in an old people's home. In 1967, suffering from delusions, he was confined in the Trapani psychiatric hospital, where he stayed for the rest of his life. When he wanted to smoke or eat more than was allowed, he would swap a drawing for a cigarette or sweets.

His works were discovered by the Swiss sculptor Robert Müller, who spent a short spell in Trapani in 1975, after a psychotic episode. Müller was fascinated by the expressive directness and spatial control of Abrignani's compositions and decided to buy all his work. In 1982 Müller donated about twenty pieces to the Art Brut Collection.

Abrignani composed his orderly drawings with a ballpoint pen, ruler and compass, and then filled them in with coloured pencil. Transport is a recurrent theme: train, car or carriage journeys, gondola rides, cyclists in the Giro d'Italia, or a bride's car arriving at the church.

Aloïse (Aloïse Corbaz, 1886–1964) as she was known – was born in Lausanne (Switzerland). She lost her mother when she was eleven, at which time her authoritarian older sister took over running the family. After high school, Aloïse attended sewing school, although she dreamt of becoming an opera singer. She fell in love with a theology student, but her sister brutally broke the couple up and sent her off to Germany in 1911, where she found work as a teacher. Later, she became governess to Emperor William II's chaplain, promptly falling madly if impossibly in love with the sovereign—a passion she held on to all her life. Returning to Lausanne in 1913, she was confined to the Cery psychiatric hospital from 1918 to 1920, and then to the La Rosière asylum in Gimel, where she would remain until her death.

Aloïse began her creative activity in 1919 through her writings, before taking up drawing, mostly done in colored pencil. She also availed herself of flower petal juice and toothpaste, applied to the pages of school notebooks or sheets of salvaged wrapping paper that she smoothed out and patched together. She invented a highly distinctive world akin to the 'Grand Théâtre', with the feminine figure in the leading role. She tended to identify with the figures she created, be it a princess, a legendary heroine or a saint. Love was another major theme for her creativity: the fact that she placed lovers in gondolas and other means of transportation is believed to represent a metaphor for the sex act.

Benjamin Arneval (1907) was the youngest child in a farming family in Lozère, France. After his parents' death, he continued to work on the family farm which was then managed by his brother. He was mobilised in 1939, at the start of World War II, but he suffered from visions and was haunted by the feeling that the world and people were changing shape. Back on the farm, in August 1942 he mistook his brother for 'a sort of ghost', and shot him.

Arneval was then committed to the Saint Alban hospital, which he considered unjustified, but settled in quietly. In 1948 he was seized by a violent anxiety fit, feeling assailed by cows, horses, and other beasts, and was convinced the end of the world was nigh. After this attack he spent two months drawing feverishly, but this sudden burst of creativity petered out.

Arneval's drawings are minutely detailed, and sometimes show the interior of his subjects: a cow with its skeleton showing, or the inside of an aeroplane. His childhood on the farm inspired him to draw tools, vehicles, agricultural machinery, farm animals, and household furniture. Imaginary snakes and monsters haunt some compositions.

Josef Bachler (1914–79) was born in Vienna, Austria. He was orphaned and taken in by an adoptive mother, then placed in various foster homes. He trained as a roofing contractor and worked in his trade until 1938, when he was sent to the Dachau concentration camp. After the war he lived and worked in the area around Vienna, where he met the woman he eventually married. He suffered from alcoholism and was committed to the Maria Gugging hospital in 1970, and spent the last nine years of his life there.

Bachler drew working from memory or from models he chose. He preferred drawing with lead pencil, using coloured pencil only for the outlines. He used small regular strokes in a very precise, controlled manner to render variations in surfaces and textures.

According to his doctor Leo Navratil, this attention to minute detail was a way of steadying his emotional reactions and violent outbursts. Bachler had an authoritarian temperament, and his attempts to order other people about triggered numerous quarrels.

Fausto Badari (b. 1962) was born in Roverbella, Italy. His parents suffered from psychic disorders and lived in great poverty. His father was a street sweeper and his mother worked as a seasonal agricultural labourer. Badari went to school until the age of eleven, and then worked briefly in the fields. Fragile since childhood, his condition deteriorated through lack of support, and worsened when his father died in 1992. He was in and out of a home until 2004. But his mental health continued to deteriorate, and he was hospitalised in psychiatric clinics on several occasions, in particular in the Sospiro Onlus foundation, where he now lives.
In 2010 Badari began to work in the foundation's art studio. He always draws in the same manner: he sits down, studies the sheet, then gets up and draws the shapes with black pastel, which he covers entirely with white or yellow crayon. He then goes over the outlines in black and finally works on the details. Vehicles are central to Badari's work, and his only theme. He focuses on the interior and the salient parts of the vehicle: motor, radiator grill, wheels, and headlamps.

Dominique Bertoliatti (1953–2007) was born in Paris, France, the eldest of three children. He had Down's syndrome and was sent to a special school when he was ten. From 1973 he went to the vocational rehabilitation centre of the Fine Arts school in Paris, where he began to paint, with the help of an artist at the institution. Loved and supported by his family, who described him as a cheerful, sociable, affectionate boy, he learned to read and write and manage on his own.
Devastated by his father's death in 1991, Bertoliatti was put into foster care in 1993 (EDPA, an independent public institution) in Le Glandier, in the Corrèze department. His keen interest in drawing was quickly spotted.
Bertoliatti worked with felt pen, gouache, or crayon, using bright or dark colours depending on his mood. He drew black lines dividing his pages into sections, which made his pictures look like stained-glass windows. Vehicles, animals, people, and landscapes were some of his favourite themes.

Gregory L. Blackstock (b. 1946) lives in Seattle, in the United States. He was a turbulent child, later diagnosed as autistic, and spent part of his teenage years in a borstal. As an adult, he did odd jobs, before working for twenty-five years as a dishwasher in the bar of a sports club. He published his first drawing in the club magazine in 1966, and has been drawing ever since. Now, since his retirement in 2001, he spends all his time drawing feverishly.
Blackstock draws up an inventory of the world. He classes all sorts of objects, animals and plants in an order known to him alone. He systematically adds a caption in neat capital letters. The repetition and stylisation of the figures gives them great graphic power, not unlike plates in an encyclopaedia, which he freely interprets. His prodigious memory is an inexhaustible source of inspiration. Despite their orderly, methodical appearance, Blackstock's drawings surreptitiously waive the laws of science and go their own nonchalant, poetic way.

David Braillon (b. 1970) was born in Dreux, France, and grew up in a railway family. His father and brother were killed in motor accidents when he was a teenager. David Braillon's fascination for trains goes back to his childhood and he would have liked to work in the railways, but failed to find a job with the French railway company. As a young man he hung around freight stations and collected railway magazines. In 1995 he found himself in the lock-up, and spent all day and sometimes his sleepless nights drawing. He uses pieces of graph paper, which he puts together as a frieze representing army helicopters, fighter jets, and people, but his favourite subject is trains. He stacks his trains in horizontal registers in the manner of a catalogue or inventory.

François Burland (b. 1958) was born in Lausanne, Switzerland. He taught himself to draw in his late teens. In 1978 he made his first trip to the Middle East, visiting the Sinai desert, and he has been fascinated by the desert ever since. He was particularly impressed by the Tuaregs in the Sahara, and spent time among them every year until 2011. Burland has been painting for over thirty years producing a rich, protean oeuvre, mingling nomadic traditions, Swiss folklore, and Soviet imagery. His timeless compositions conjure up an imaginary past that is both mythical and magical, and studded with retro-futuristic elements.
He uses many different techniques depending on the series, working with crayon, white chalk and coloured pencil on large pieces of wrapping paper. He also uses waste materials to make vehicles which look like toys.
His works are in the collection Neuve Invention.

John Byam (b. 1929) was born in Oneonta in New York State, USA. As a boy he helped his parents, who owned a camping ground. In the 1940s he worked for a railway company. He then served the American army in Japan during the Korean War. In 1952 he went back to live with his parents and worked as a gravedigger at the local cemetery.
Byam works from memory, taking inspiration from family photographs, television, books, and magazines. He draws with a sure hand, using lead or coloured pencil. He also makes three-dimensional works in the long tradition of wooden sculpture in rural America. He assembles small, rough-hewn pieces of wood, using a mixture of sawdust and glue. The locomotives, airplanes and other craft designed by Byam suggest a powerful desire for movement. They are fragile and ephemeral-looking, and seem to have symbolic meaning.

Carlo (Carlo Zinelli, 1916–74), was born near Verona, Italy. His mother died

when he was two. Seven years later his father sent him to work on a farm, where he spent his teenage years. Later, Carlo became a butcher's apprentice at the Verona municipal abattoir. During World War II he joined the Alpini (Mountain Troops), and began to show signs of psychic disorder. Suffering from persecution delusions and hallucinations, he was committed to San Giacomo hospital in Verona when he was thirty-one.
Ten years later Carlo began to scratch graffiti on the hospital walls with a sharp stone. To accommodate this driving need for self-expression, the hospital arranged for him to work in the painting and sculpture studio it opened in 1957. He produced some three thousand drawings in fourteen years. Using gouache and holding his brush like a pencil, he covered both sides of the paper with an assortment of motifs—people, animals, and vehicles. He sometimes added collage and inscriptions. When the hospital was closed down in 1971, Carlo was transferred to another institution and then taken in by a foster family, where he died not long afterwards.

Serge Delaunay (b. 1956) was born in Charleroi, Belgium. His mother left when he was small, and his father returned to his native France in 1968, abandoning his seven children, who were put in the care of their mother's sister. Delaunay suffered deeply from this abandonment. At twenty-two he entered the Centre Reine Fabiola in Neufville and worked in the occupational workshops. But manual work bored him, and he did not do the tasks he was given, even resorting to sabotage. Redirected to the Campagn'Art studio, he began to draw and now draws passionately every day.
Delaunay uses black felt pen on large sheets of paper. Colour is rare. Cars and spaceships are his favourite subjects. He is fascinated by science, especially astronomy and mechanics, and buys science magazines every week. He adds texts and captions to his drawings. The initials GTX, often under his signature, refer to the automotive industry too.

Curzio Di Giovanni (b. 1957) comes from Lodi, Italy. He suffers from an organic disorder which retarded his development and caused an autistic withdrawal. When he was about twelve his condition worsened and he became aggressive and antisocial. In 1979, after several periods of hospitalisation, he was admitted to a psychiatric rehabilitation unit near Pavia, where he now lives. Although he had already produced some drawings, his artistic talent was fully revealed in 2001 when he joined the Adriano e Michele art studio attached to the unit.
Di Giovanni takes his inspiration mainly from photographs of animals, people, objects, or vehicles provided by the staff of the centre. He decomposes the model, marking the parts he thinks are essential with a lead pencil, then colours them with coloured pencil. The original image is then distorted and looks like a deformed stained-glass window. His compositions seem to leap off the blank white paper.

Anton Dobay (1906–86) was born in Frankenberg, Germany. His biography is vague and full of gaps. He is variously said to have been born in Germany, or Austria. He lived alone and from 1960 worked as a gardener at Paasdorf castle in Austria. He was admitted to Maria Gugging hospital near Vienna after an attack of apoplexy, when he was sixty-five.
Dobay suffered from sensorial aphasia, a major consequence of his attack, and had lost the power of speech. He was persuaded to draw as a form of therapy by Dr Leo Navratil. Drawing therefore became a new means of expression. Over time, his work attracted attention for its artistic quality.
From 1971 to 1981 Anton Dobay drew steadily and fervently, with the encouragement of his doctor, who sometimes provided him with models. He worked in grey or coloured pencil, and crayon. Having lost his ability to draw figuratively, Dobay developed a characteristically strong sense of perception of space, form, and unity.

Feng Shi Yi (1975–2008) was born in Xi'an, China. His parents were retired workers. Often feverish as a child, Feng Shi Yi suffered from an intellectual handicap which forced him to leave school and attend a special institution for two years. In 2006 he entered the Xi'an Huilin centre for the handicapped. Introverted and shy because of his lisp, he gradually opened up to other people and took part in group activities.
His favourite activity was drawing, which he did alone in peace and quiet. He drew stacks of cars, buses, aeroplanes, and helicopters, using coloured ballpoint pen on small pieces of paper or card. The vehicles were related to his everyday life: for example, an ambulance collecting a sick person or a friend taking public transport to come and see him. His drawings were a way of making contact with other people, because he enjoyed showing them to others and talking about what he did.

Auguste Forestier (1887–1958) was born into a farming family in Lozère, France. He was fascinated by trains and ran away from home several times by simply boarding a train. One day in 1914 he caused a derailment by piling stones on the rails. This incident landed him in a psychiatric hospital, where he stayed for the rest of his life.
Forestier did labouring work in the hospital and helped in the kitchen. In his spare time, he drew with coloured pencils, made medals, which he wore proudly, and carved objects out of bones he had scrounged in the hospital kitchen. At a later stage, Forestier set up a small workshop in a corridor in the hospital and carved figures, animals, and boats from odd pieces of wood with the aid of a

shoemaker's paring knife. He also used fabric or leather, medals, string, and objects salvaged from the rubbish bin.

Clément Fraisse (1901–80) was born in a village in Lozère, France, into a farming family with fourteen children. After elementary schooling the boy worked on the family farm, and then became a shepherd. When he was twenty-four he tried to burn down his parents' farm with a bundle of burning banknotes. Following this incident he was sent to the Saint-Alban psychiatric hospital.
Because of his violent, uncooperative attitude and attempts to escape, from 1930 to 1931 he was confined to a narrow cell measuring 2 by 3 metres, lined with wainscoting. For two years Fraisse carved the walls of his cell, using a broken spoon handle or toe plates, which he sharpened on the stone. When his makeshift tools were confiscated, he used the handles of his china chamber-pot, which he ground to an edge in the same way.
After this period of close confinement, Fraisse did odd jobs around the hospital, working especially as a bricklayer and grave-digger. In 1945 he left the hospital and took up work on a local farm.

Johann Hauser (1926–96) was born in Pressburg (now Bratislava, Slovakia). He was put into a special school and never learned to read or write. Regarded as simple-minded, he was committed to a psychiatric institution when he was seventeen. Johann Hauser is described as a dreamy, impulsive, quarrelsome person.
In 1949 he was transferred to the Maria Gugging psychiatric hospital near Vienna, where he stayed for the rest of his days. He later spent time in the artists' studio adjacent to the hospital (Das Haus der Künstler), where Dr Leo Navratil encouraged him to draw.
Hauser took inspiration from pictures of film stars, newspaper cuttings, photos of war machines and vehicles in illustrated magazines. Ignoring the principles of representation, proportion and perspective, he invented his own graphic system. His formal repertory includes elements suggesting male and female sex organs. The expressive power of his work swings between uncontrolled infantile urges and undeniable graphic skill.

Helmut (Helmut Nimczewski, 1945 or 1946) was born in Heidelberg, Germany. He was brought up by his mother and never knew his father. Retarded, probably as a result of brain damage caused by his epilepsy, he was put into various specialised institutions. After a long stay in a psychiatric hospital, he moved to a sheltered home in Hamburg. He likes going for walks and takes his camera along with him. He is very devout and never misses a service.
Helmut is a stickler for order, uniformity and exactitude. He is fascinated by crowds and draws in great detail the spectators at a football match or swimming championship sitting in tight-packed rows on the stands. The drivers and the passengers of the vehicles he draws always seem to be travelling in perfect harmony along clearly marked roads, straight rails, or over smooth seas. Helmut works directly with coloured pencil and felt pens, using bright colours, and spends about eight weeks on each drawing.

Lorna Hylton (1963–2007) was born in Castro Valley, California. She was mentally handicapped and attended a special educational programme. She spent most of her time drawing, and had done so since she was a child. Later she spent several years in an art centre in Castro Valley, then joined the Creative Growth Art Center in Oakland in 1991. Lorna Hylton's colourful compositions depict parades of vintage cars and chaotic traffic jams. She drew bird's-eye views of her objects and worked with areas of solid colour. The figurative subjects are freely outlined with a felt pen in a near-abstract manner, forming masses of colour that hum with energy. Crayon was her favourite medium. The name of the car and the year of the model are often written on the drawing.

Franz Kernbeis (b. 1935) was born in Prigglitz, Austria. He was the youngest child in a family of seven. After eight years of primary schooling he started work on his parents' farm. In 1955 he was admitted to the Maria Gugging hospital in Austria, suffering from psychic disorders. At the beginning of his stay he was withdrawn and mute, remaining perfectly still for hours on end, or walking in circles with his eyes closed. He started producing artwork when he was forty-four, at the House of the Arts (Das Haus der Künstler), where some of the patients lived and worked.
Kernbeis produces large coloured pencil drawings of people, animals, and vehicles. His condition has improved over the years. When he is not drawing, he likes going for long walks and looks after a flower bed in front of the hospital.

Sylvain Lecocq (1900–50) was born in Boulogne-sur-Mer, France. He grew up in poverty and suffered from adjustment disorders. He worked as a shop assistant, married, and fathered three children. In 1942, after an operation for an ulcer, he stopped work altogether and withdrew into an imaginary world. He was put in a psychiatric hospital in Lille in 1947, and committed suicide three years later. In hospital he went on several hunger strikes, and ran away several times, travelling hundreds of kilometres to reach his wife's or sister's place. Each time he was caught, locked up, and tied to his bed.
From 1948 to his death, Lecocq worked feverishly, producing poems, love letters, songs, and drawings. He scrounged notebooks, scraps of Kraft paper, blotting paper and cardboard, which he ruled with straight lines in lead pencil, then covered the entire surface with a regular childish handwriting that contrasts with the delirious content. In

one unusually large work, *Tour de France Bocycliste,* sixty cyclists in weird costumes are scattered over a historiated map of France.

Philippe Lemaire (b. 1954) was born in Montreal. Suffering from schizophrenia with autistic traits, he was hospitalised for the first time in 1975, then transferred five years later to the Louis-H. Lafontaine Hospital, where he has continued to live to this day. Since 1992 he has attended the hospital's art studio, called 'Les Impatients'. He has few interests, seldom communicates, and exhibits repetitive behaviour, which can be seen in his work: the only vehicle he draws is the car his father used to drive when he came to take him out for a ride. He calls it 'my father's car' (he uses the word *char*, Quebec slang for 'car').
Lemaire always begins by drawing two horizontal lines with gouache, and two wheels. After a short pause, he completes the car, outlines his father and himself, then stops again for a few minutes. He then adds the background: a garage, a tree or a fast- food store sign. Once he has finished his drawing, he leaves the studio and does not come back until closing time. 'My father's car' seems to bring back a happy memory that he enjoys reliving. Over the years he has occasionally drawn other subjects, such as a sugarhouse, a pumpkin, or a tree.

Dwight Mackintosh (1906–99) was born in Hayward, California. Until he was sixteen he lived at home, and then was sent successively to three psychiatric hospitals in the region. After fifty-six years of institutional care, Dwight Mackintosh was admitted to the Creative Growth Art Center in Oakland, California. Withdrawn and almost inarticulate, Mackintosh expressed himself solely through drawing. He drew with an incessant to-and-fro movement of the hand, and his favourite subject was a naked figure with an erect penis. He paid particular attention to the eyes, eyelashes, nose, and navel, as well as the fingers and toes. He sometimes placed his figures inside a train or a car, showing an 'x-ray' view of the interior of the vehicle.
The texts he often added to his ink drawings express more in terms of the rhythmic writing style than of the actual meaning of the words.

Francis Mayor (1904–95) was born in Lausanne, Switzerland, to a single mother. He spent his early years with her in Algeria before returning to Switzerland. She made several attempts to be rid of him, once trying to drown him in Lake Bret. He was saved by a doctor and put in a foster family, and then in an orphanage, which he ran away from. He was finally taken in by two brothers. In 1923 he left Switzerland to go to the naval school in Sables-d'Olonne. He became a helmsman and travelled back and forth between France and the Pacific islands. He returned to his homeland in the 1930s, married and worked for the Compagnie Générale de Navigation du Lac Léman. He divorced shortly afterwards, and nothing is known of his life until 1986, when he was put in an old people's home. He was a loner, spending his days drawing and hoarding meat in his room to feed various animals.
The main themes of Francis Mayor's collages are the sea, boats and religion. He collected pictures from magazines, scandal magazines, and television programmes. He sometimes added pieces of plants, sand, or everyday objects such as cotton-buds or drinking-straws. He then coloured his assemblages with gouache or pencil.

Gene Merritt (Clyde Eugene Merritt, b. 1936) was born in South Carolina, in the United States, where he now lives. A bout of high fever when he was about five left him with a mental handicap. His childhood was marked by his parents' alcoholism, regular stays in foster homes, and his mother's suicide. After this dramatic event, he went to live with his father in Fort Mill, and likewise lapsed into alcoholism.
In 1972, when he was thirty-six, Merritt found himself alone and dependent on social welfare. Later he moved into a caravan at Rock Hill. He started to draw, using a ballpoint pen, developing a highly individual graphic style: the faces of television, film or music stars are put together from thousands of fragments, like a jigsaw puzzle, each one named in a short caption placed in round or square brackets. He also draws vehicles, mainly collector's cars. His pictures are done from memory, mostly on tablemats or lined paper. In his spare time he plays both the electric guitar and the bass.

Motooka Hidenori (b. 1978) was born in Hyôgo district and now lives in Kôbe in Japan. As a small child, he was intrigued by trains. He often goes to the railway station to photograph them, always front view, and then files the photographs with great care. As soon as a new model comes into service, he rushes to photograph it. He also works as a dishwasher in a hotel kitchen, taking his job very seriously.
Motooka Hidenori began to draw shortly before 1995. He shows trains from the front, crowding them together on photocopying paper or on the back of advertising leaflets. He has drawn nearly a hundred different locomotives from the local Hankyu line. Motooka wants to put all the models he knows in the same picture. In his more recent work, he has joined several sheets of paper together and compressed the vehicles so as to fit as many as possible into the available space.

Alain Pauzié (b. 1936) was born in the Aveyron region, France. He grew up in Albi, where his family moved in 1942. He was keen on rugby, studied law and political science in Toulouse, and married in 1961. He then went to work at the Atomic Energy Commission near Paris.

He started to draw in 1967 on perforated printing paper and envelopes. Although he drew for his own satisfaction at the beginning, he soon felt the need to exhibit his work and share his ideas and difficulties with others. He had his first show in 1976. The next year he met Jean Dubuffet, with whom he had been corresponding for three years. The French artist decided to include Alain Pauzié's work in the collection Neuve Invention.
Pauzié's world swarms with symbols and figures with great graphic power, intensified by sharply contrasting colours. He draws with ballpoint, felt pen, and paint on envelopes and salvaged material such as shoe soles and plastic bottles. He also carves bone with a dental drill.

Han Ploos van Amstel (1926–2004) was born in Amsterdam, in The Netherlands. He was mentally handicapped and worked in a protected workshop making brooms and doormats, and lived with his mother. When his mother died, he moved into a semi-independent home, and then in 1992 he went to a day-care centre, where he began to draw. Although he had collected miniature cars for many years, it was when he was flicking through an automobile catalogue only two years after he joined the centre that vehicles became his favourite theme. From then on, he never stopped drawing them, and talked with pleasure about his fascination for vehicles.
Van Amstel's pictures feature cars, vans, trucks and trailers, and ambulances and buses, viewed from the side and neatly aligned in rows, with alternate rows facing in the opposite direction. He drew the outlines of the vehicles in black and coloured them in with acrylic or pencil, then added details such as rear lights, aerials and rear-view mirrors.

Guillaume Pujolle (1893–1951) comes from Saint-Gaudens, France. He first worked as a cabinetmaker, then joined the army in 1913 and set off for the front. On his return he took a job as a customs officer and married in 1924. He was hospitalised for psychic disorders, and then, at the age of thirty-three, committed to the psychiatric hospital of Toulouse, where he spent the rest of his life. Seven years after his admission he began to draw. A doctor encouraged him in this activity and began to collect his works.
Pujolle used photos or illustrations as a starting point, working with gouache when he could, as well as various pharmaceutical products such as iodine or mercurochrome. He made brushes from a lock of hair, with tightly rolled paper as a handle. He also used compasses, setsquares and rulers, which he kept with him at all times. His compositions are like inlay work, forming a pattern of lines and arabesques. From 1947 he carved astonishing sculptures from discarded materials and chunks of wood. He also used everyday objects in strange ways, giving them a different meaning. After fourteen productive years, Guillaume Pujolle ceased all artistic activity.

Emile Ratier (1894–1984) was born into a peasant family at Soturac in the west of France. He worked on the farm, leaving it only once to go to the front in 1914. After the war he returned to the family farm where he worked as a wood merchant and then a clog maker. After 1960, Emile Ratier went through a period of depression, while his sight gradually failed until he was completely blind.
When his eyesight weakened, he started to work with wood, especially young elm, from which he made mobile sculptures worked by means of cranks and other mechanisms, using the sounds they made to guide his work. Most of his pieces represent carts, merry-go-rounds, and animals, but he also made a model of the Eiffel Tower and all sorts of odd vehicles. Emile Ratier's workshop was in a barn at the back of his farm. He found his way to it by running his hand along an ingenious system of dangling wires.

Martial Richoz (b. 1963) was born in Lausanne, Switzerland, where he was brought up by his grandmother. The people of Lausanne know him well because in the 1980s he could be seen dressed in the city bus company uniform pushing a handcart transformed into a trolleybus with various mechanical parts. He took the same route at set times and mimicked the sounds of a trolleybus: the opening of the doors, the hiss of the brakes and the click of the indicators. His psychiatric disorders landed him in the Cery hospital in 1986. After that episode, on the doctors' instructions, he gave up acting as a bus driver.
Fascinated by trolleybuses since he was a child, Martial Richoz made his own vehicles by attaching salvaged material to handcarts or stepladders on wheels. Using ballpoint pen, felts and paper, he also drew diagrams of the trolleybus overhead cables and their complex criss-crossed network of wires.

André Robillard (b. 1931) grew up near Orléans, France. His father was a forest ranger, and the family lived in a council house. When he was nineteen Robillard was committed to the specialist Fleury-les-Aubrais hospital (near Orléans), where he did odd jobs and was employed part-time to manage the water-treatment plant. This job gave him a measure of independence: he lived in lodgings of 150 square metres at the edge of the hospital grounds. In 1989 he moved into a flat, and devoted his time to his art.
This is where the rifles, spaceships, and sputniks he has been making since 1964 are now kept. He rummages in the public tip for tin cans, old lightbulbs, scrap wood, plastic hose, and metal bars, which he assembles with adhesive tape and wire.

Hans Saletmeier (b. 1950) was born in Kirchdorf, Austria. He was the youngest in a family of seven children. Physically and mentally handicapped from birth, he lived at home sheltered by his mother's tender care until he was thirteen, when he was sent to a children's home. He learned the rudiments of reading, writing, and arithmetic, but he suffered from the separation from his parents and went home again three years later.
In 1992 Saletmeier went to the Lebenshilfe hostel in Ried. When an art studio was opened there in 1997, he immediately took part, having already shown an interest in drawing. He gave up drawing in 2009, but still lives in Lebenshilfe. Saletmeier draws with black and coloured pencils on sheets of paper, in a slow, careful manner. His style is clear and simple. He often portrays large figures, writing their names on the edge of the sheet. Some of his pictures show series of vehicles and include cars, ambulances, and police vans.

Sawada Shinchi (b. 1982) was born in the Shiga district and now lives in the city of Kusatsu, in Japan. He is autistic and seldom communicates with the people around him. After a few years in a special high school, he took a job in the bakery of the home for the mentally handicapped where he lives. He also assembles parts for electrical appliances. Sawada Shinichi is clever with his hands, and has always made small objects like paper cars. But his creativity was revealed in his work with clay in a pottery studio. He makes sculptures bristling with prickles, representing strange beings and animals from another world.

André Stanton (1948–91) was born in London, England. His family moved to Switzerland when he was five. As the son of the artist Hélène Stanton, he led an independent life despite his mental handicap. Sociable and agreeable by nature, he took part in local life in Coppet, in the canton of Vaud. Between 1978 and 1985 he built models out of pieces of wood, and in 1986 he began to paint, sometimes adding collages to his pictures. He often represented vehicles and construction equipment in bright colours, emphasising details such as aerials and flashing lights.

Jean Tourlonias (1937–2000) was born into a peasant family in Cébazat, a little village near Clermont-Ferrand, in France. After a brief spell at school he helped his parents on the farm. When he was twenty-three he was mobilised for nine months during the Algerian war, then returned to his parents' farm in Auvergne. He began to paint in his spare time, but nobody was interested in his paintings, and he temporarily gave up this pastime.
Tourlonias was a motor sports fan. He rode a motorcycle and regularly bought specialist magazines. Naturally he began to paint high-power machines that sprang out of his imagination. In 1986 his works were noticed by art enthusiasts who began to commission work from him. Working on the fringe of the art world, thinking of himself as a craftsman, he painted on demand at a set hourly rate. After 1986 he painted nothing but racing cars. He combined drawing and writing by dedicating his canvases to television stars or patrons, and flanking his machines with enthusiastic advertisement-like slogans.
His works are in the collection Neuve Invention.

Willem Van Genk (1927–2005) was born in Voorburg, Netherlands. He developed serious health problems and behavioural disorders at an early age. He started to draw at school and at home, as an escape from a lonely, difficult childhood.
Later he was put in an orphanage, then in a Christian technical school, where he studied commercial art. But he was a misfit and ended up in a workshop for the mentally handicapped in The Hague. Van Genk worked in his flat, painting and making complex cut-outs and collages. He drew inspiration from his many journeys to the former Soviet Union, Rome, Paris, Madrid, Copenhagen, Cologne, and Prague, and from various tourist guides or photographs he had collected.
In 1988 he stopped painting and started to make models of buses from waste materials.

Pépé Vignes (Joseph Vignes, 1920–2007) was born in Paris, France, one of five children. He played the accordion at public dances and worked as a singer, then took up his father's trade as a barrel-maker. After a strike in the factory he was working in, the young man decided to leave the city, and moved to the small village of Elne, in the eastern Pyrenees.
In 1960, when he was forty, he began drawing with ballpoint pen and coloured pencil. His favourite themes were flowers, boats, cars, aircraft, trains, churches, whales, fish, musical instruments, gas cookers, and hearts.
He was severely short-sighted and worked with his nose almost touching the paper. He also used pieces of cardboard and scraps of plywood. His house was filled with stacks of his drawings, packed in plastic bags.

George Widener (b. 1962) was born in Covington, in the United States. His father died when he was nine, and his mother was hospitalised with drinking problems. When he was twelve he was sent to live with his grandparents, and later with his aunt. He went to a special school, where he showed particular skill in arithmetic and drawing. From then on he drew in his spare time. In 1979 he joined the US Air Force as a technician, but his instability led to several stays in psychiatric institutions. It was not until 2001 that he was diagnosed as suffering from Asperger's syndrome, a form of autism characterised by very high intellectual ability, which

explains his outstanding memory and his gift for mental arithmetic. He now lives in Asheville, North Carolina, where he continues his artistic activities.
Widener draws calendars, diagrams, inventories, and tables of figures, letters and symbols which often refer to historical events, usually disasters such as the sinking of the Titanic or plane crashes. He works with pen and ink pads, and draws on paper towels, which he glues together in layers.

Adolf Wölfli (1864–1930) was born in Bowil, in the canton of Bern, Switzerland. He came from a poverty-stricken family of seven children. Orphaned at eight, he worked as a domestic, a goatherd and a farm servant on various farms. At times mistreated, he led a life of misery and had several socially ill-fated love affairs. Attending school in fits and starts, during this period he nevertheless learned to read and write. He enlisted for military duty in 1883; seven years later, he was arrested for indecent assault and condemned to two years in prison. In 1895, a second offence had him interned in Waldau, a psychiatric hospital near Bern; diagnosed with schizophrenia, he remained there for the rest of his life.
Upon entering the hospital, Adolf Wölfli set about developing his personal mythology, beginning with his literary output and, four years later, taking up his graphic production. In all, he put out over 25,000 pages as far-ranging in kind as drawing, music, philosophy, literature, mathematics and geography. He created fantasy architectural elements, city maps and geometric compositions in strictly delineated lines deriving their graphic impact from the brightly coloured pencils he used on them. Between the various elements, he was wont to slip in faces whose eyes he would outline in black, like masks.

Erich Zablatnik (1942–95) was born in Klagenfurt, Austria. He attended school to secondary level, then did odd jobs until his military service began. He then moved to Germany and worked for several years as a miner. Later he trained as a rotisserie cook and worked in a chain of grill restaurants for twenty years. Devastated by the accidental death of his wife and son, he tried to kill himself in 1989 by driving his car into a wall. He survived his grievous injuries and returned to Klagenfurt, where, no longer able to work, he lived in a Caritas hostel.
That was where Zablatnik started to produce paintings of his utopian, futuristic dreams. He drew on cardboard with ballpoint, felt pen, gouache, or acrylic paint. He sometimes added cardboard or aluminium foil shapes, and finished his pictures with a layer of glossy varnish.

Selected Bibliography

General Catalogues of the Art Brut Collection

Peiry, Lucienne, and Sarah Lombardi. *Collection de l'Art Brut*. Paris: Skira / Flammarion; Lausanne: Collection de l'Art Brut, 2012.

Thévoz, Michel. *La Collection de l'Art Brut, Lausanne*. Postface by Lucienne Peiry. Geneva: BNP Paribas (Suisse) SA; Zurich: Institut suisse pour l'étude de l'art, 2001.

Thévoz, Michel, Geneviève Roulin, Lucienne Peiry, et al. *Neuve Invention*. Lausanne: Collection de l'Art Brut, 1988.

Thévoz, Michel, *Collection de l'Art Brut*. Preface by Jean Dubuffet. Lausanne: Collection de l'Art Brut, 1976.

L'Art Brut series collection

L'Art Brut series was created in 1964 by Jean Dubuffet. These reference books are monographs on the artists whose works are comprised in the Collection. The detailed index with the entry for each work is available on the Collection's website: http://www.artbrut.ch

L'Art Brut, nos. 1–9. Paris: Compagnie de l'Art Brut, 1964–73. Rev. eds. *L'Art Brut*, no. 1, Lausanne: Collection de l'Art Brut, 1975 and *L'Art Brut*, no. 7. Lausanne: Collection de l'Art Brut, 1989.

L'Art Brut, nos. 10–22. Lausanne: Collection de l'Art Brut, 1977–2007.

L'Art Brut, nos. 23–24. Lausanne: Collection de l'Art Brut; Gollion: Infolio, 2011–13.

Exhibition Catalogues of the Art Brut Collection

Aloïse. Lausanne: Collection de l'Art Brut, 2012.

Aloïse. Le ricochet solaire. Milan: 5 Continents Editions; Lausanne: Collection de l'Art Brut, Musée cantonal des Beaux-Arts, 2012.

Guo Fengyi. Lausanne: Collection de l'Art Brut, 2012.

Nannetti 'colonel astral'. Lausanne: Collection de l'Art Brut; Gollion: Infolio, 2011.

Nannetti. Lausanne: Collection de l'Art Brut; Gollion: Infolio, 2011.

Ataa Oko. Lausanne: Collection de l'Art Brut; Gollion: Infolio, 2009.

Art Brut fribourgeois. Fribourg: La Sarine; Lausanne: Collection de l'Art Brut, 2008.

Art Brut du Japon. Lausanne: Collection de l'Art Brut; Gollion: Infolio, 2008.

L'Art spirite. Lausanne: Collection de l'Art Brut, 2005.

Dubuffet & l'Art Brut. Milan: 5 Continents Editions; Lausanne: Collection de l'Art Brut, 2005.

Le Royaume de Nek Chand. Lausanne: Collection de l'Art Brut; Paris: Flammarion, 2005.

Écriture en délire. Milan: 5 Continents Editions; Lausanne: Collection de l'Art Brut, 2004.

Josef Hofer. Lausanne: Collection de l'Art Brut, 2003.

Louis Soutter (1871–1942). Ostfilern: Hatje Cantz, 2002.

Podestà. Lausanne: Collection de l'Art Brut, 2003.

La Foule. Lausanne: Collection de l'Art Brut, 2002.

Le Nouveau Monde. Lausanne: Collection de l'Art Brut, 2002.

Joaquim Vicens Gironella. Lausanne: Collection de l'Art Brut, 1998.

Art incognito. Lausanne: Collection de l'Art Brut, 1997.

Stanislaw Zagajewski. Gynia: Epiky; Lausanne: Collection de l'Art Brut, 1997.

Henry Darger: dans les royaumes de l'irréel. Lausanne: Collection de l'Art Brut; Lugano: Galerie Gottardo, 1996.

Made in USA. Lausanne: Collection de l'Art Brut, 1993.

Charles Ladame ou le Cabinet fou d'un psychiatre. Lausanne: Collection de l'Art Brut, 1991.

Hans Steck ou le Parti pris de la folie. Lausanne: Collection de l'Art Brut, 1991.

Wölfli dessinateur-compositeur. Berne: L'Âge d'homme, Fondation Adolf Wölfli; Lausanne: Collection de l'Art Brut, 1991.

Gaston Teuscher. Lausanne: Collection de l'Art Brut, 1982.

Vojislav Jakić. Lausanne: Collection de l'Art Brut, 1979.

Laure. Lausanne: Collection de l'Art Brut, 1978.

Articles and books on the artists in the exhibition

Abrignani, Giovanni
Di Stefano, Eva. *Irregolari: Art Brut e Outsider Art in Sicilia*. Palermo: Kalós, 2008.

FAUPIN, Savine, Christophe BOULANGER, Jaqueline PORRET-FOREL, et al. *Amicalement brut: collection Eternod & Mermod*. Exh. cat., Villeneuve-d'Ascq: Lille Métropole Musée d'art moderne, d'art contemporain et d'art brut, 2011.

PATOCCHI, Lucca, Roger CARDINAL, Elisa FULCO, et al. *Eternity has no Door of Escape: Opere di art brut dalla collezione Eternod-Mermod di Losanna*. Exh. cat. Lugano: Galerie Gottardo, 2001.

THÉVOZ, Michel. 'Giovanni Abrignani'. *L'Art Brut* (20), 1997.

Aloïse (Corbaz)

DUBUFFET, Jean and Jacqueline PORRET-FOREL. 'Aloïse'. *L'Art Brut* 7, (1966; 1989).

LOMBARDI, Sarah and Pascale MARINI. *Aloïse*. Exh. cat. Lausanne: Collection de l'Art Brut, 2012.

MUZELLE, Céline, Jacqueline PORRET-FOREL, Laurent DANCHIN, et al. *Aloïse : comme un papillon sur elle*. Exh. cat. Shiga: Haretari-Kumottari, 2009.

PORRET-FOREL, Jacqueline. *Aloïse et le théâtre de l'univers*. Geneva: Albert Skira, 1993.

PORRET-FOREL, Jacqueline and Marc LAMY. *La Voleuse de mappemonde : les écrits d'Aloïse*, Geneva: Éditions Zoé, 2004.

PORRET-FOREL, Jacqueline, Céline MUZELLE, Sarah LOMBARDI, et al. *Aloïse. Le ricochet solaire*. Exh. cat. Milan: 5 Continents Editions; Lausanne: Collection de l'Art Brut, Musée cantonal des Beaux-Arts, 2012.

THÉVOZ, Michel. *L'Art Brut*. Geneva: Skira, (1975) 1995.

Arneval, Benjamin

DUBUFFET, Jean. *Catalogue de la Collection de l'Art Brut*. Paris: Compagnie de l'Art Brut, 1971.

DUBUFFET, Jean. *La Compagnie de l'Art Brut*. Paris: Compagnie de l'Art Brut, 1963.

DUBUFFET, Jean. *L'Art brut préféré à l'art culturel*. Exh. cat. Galerie René Drouin, Paris, 1949.

OURY, Jean. 'Benjamin Arneval'. *L'Art Brut* 1 (1964); re-edition. Lausanne: Collection de l'Art Brut, 1975.

Bachler, Josef

KATSCHNIG, Nina, KONTRINER, Alexandra, et al. *Der Traum vom fliegen*. Exh. cat. Galerie Gugging, Maria Gugging, 2012.

NAVRATIL, Leo. 'Josef Bachler'. *L'Art Brut* 12 (1983).

NAVRATIL, Leo. *Bilder nach Bildern*. Exh. cat. Vienna: Residenz Verlag, 1993.

NAVRATIL, Leo. *Die Künstler aus Gugging*. Exh. cat. Vienna: Medusa, 1983.

Badari, Fausto

CALICELLI, Cristina, and Paola PONTIGGIA. 'Fausto Badari: figures en vrilles'. *L'Art Brut* 24 (2013).

LUSARDY, Martine, and Gustavo GIACOSA (eds.). *Banditi dell'arte*. Exh. cat. Paris: Halle Saint-Pierre, 2012.

Bertoliatti, Dominique

DEJACE, Anne-Sophie, Michel THÉVOZ, Maurice DELARUELLE, et al. *Connexions particulières: De l'Art Brut à l'art différencié*. Exh. cat. Liège: MAD, 1999.

Blackstock, Gregory L.

BLACKSTOCK, Gregory L. *Blackstock's Collections: the Drawings of an Artistic Savant*. Preface by Darold A. Treffert, introduction by Karen Light-Piña. New York: Princeton Architectural Press, 2006.

LESPINASSE, Philippe. 'Gregory Blackstock, l'encyclopédiste'. *L'Art Brut* 23 (2011).

TREFFERT, Darold A. *Islands of Genius: the Bountiful Mind of the Autistic, Acquired, and Sudden Savant*. Preface by Daniel Tammet. London: Jessica Kingsley Publishers, 2010.

Braillon, David

LOMMEL, Madeleine, Ricardo AQUINO, Daniel LOMMEL, et al. *L'Aracine et l'Art brut*. Paris: Z'éditions, 1999.

Burland, François

BILLETER, Erika, and François BURLAND. *François Burland: im Reich von Mythos und Magie, Au royaume du mythe et de la magie*. Berne: Benteli, Wabern, 2003.

CHEVASSU, Bernard. 'François Burland'. *Création franche* 7 (1992).

BURLAND, François, Michel Thévoz, et al. *Entrelacs 1998*. Staffelfelden: Entrelacs, 1998.

GRIVEL, Florence, Isabelle RABOUD-SCHÜLE, Grégoire MAYOR, et al. *François Burland: poya*. Exh. cat. Bienne: Édition Clandestin, 2011.

JAGFELD, Monika, Philippe LESPINASSE, Florence GRIVEL, Murielle MICHETTI (photos). *François Burland: Space Cowboy – les jouets, die Spielzeuge*. Zurich: Niggli, 2009.

JAUNIN, Françoise, and Michel THÉVOZ. *Les Baleines du Ténéré*. Lausanne: Rivolta, 1998.

THÉVOZ, Michel. 'François Burland ou l'érection permanente'. *Création franche* 7 (1992).

THÉVOZ, Michel, Geneviève Roulin, Lucienne Peiry, et al. *Neuve Invention*. Lausanne: Collection de l'Art Brut, 1988.

Carlo (Zinelli)

ANDREOLI, Vittorino, Sergio MARINELLI, and Flavia PESCI. *Carlo Zinelli: catalogo generale*. Venice: Marsilio, 2000.

ANDREOLI, Vittorino. *Carlo: a Mad Painter*. Exh. cat. Venice: Marsilio, 1996.

ANDREOLI, Vittorino. 'Les dernières années de Carlo'. *L'Art Brut* 11 (1982).

ANDREOLI, Vittorino, Cherubino Trabucchi, and Arturo Pasa. 'Carlo'. *L'Art Brut* 6 (1966).

AZZOLA INAUDI, Maria. 'Carlo Zinelli'. *Raw Vision* 29 (1999).

AZZOLA, Maria A., Lucienne PEIRY, Michel THÉVOZ, et al. *Écriture en délire*. Exh. cat. Milan: 5 Continents Editions; Lausanne: Collection de l'Art Brut, 2004.

BERST, Christian, and Daniela ROSI. *Carlo Zinelli: une beauté convulsive*. Exh. cat. Paris: Galerie Christian Berst, 2011.

GANDLIN, Pierre-Jean, Benoît DECRON, Joëlle PIJAUDIER-CABOT, et al. *Carlo Zinelli (1916–1974)*. Exh. cat. Paris: Somogy Éditions d'art, 2003.

MARINELLI, Sergio, and Flavia PESCI (eds.). *Carlo: tempere, collages, sculture 1957–1974*. Exh. cat. Venice: Marsilio, 1992.

THÉVOZ, Michel. *L'Art Brut*. Geneva: Skira, 1975; re-edition 1995.

Delaunay, Serge

BISET, Sébastien, Pierre-Yves DESAIVE, et al. *Madmusée Collection: 1998–2008*. Liège: Madmusée, 2008.

THÉVOZ, Sylvain, Arnaud MATAGNE, Erwin DEJASSE, et al. *Serge Delaunay*. Bruxelles: Art en marge, 2007.

VERBOEKET, Karin. 'Serge Delaunay: de kracht van techniek'. *Out of Art*, Year 4, no.1 (2009).

Di Giovanni, Curzio

MARANZANO, Teresa. 'Curzio Di Giovanni'. *L'Art Brut* 22 (2007).

Dobay, Anton

NAVRATIL, Leo. 'Anton Dobay'. *L'Art Brut* 21 (2001).

NAVRATIL, Leo. *Bilder nach Bildern*. Exh. cat. Vienna: Residenz Verlag, 1993.

NAVRATIL, Leo. *Die Künstler aus Gugging*. Exh. cat. Vienna: Medusa, 1983.

Forestier, Auguste

DUBUFFET, Jean. 'La fabrique d'Auguste'. *L'Art Brut* 8 (1966).

FAUPIN, Savine, Christophe BOULANGER, Alain BOUILLET, et al. *Trait d'union: les chemins de l'art brut (6) à Saint-Alban-sur-Limagnole*. Exh. cat. Villeneuve-d'Ascq: Musée d'art moderne Lille Métropole, 2007.

OURY, Jean. 'August For'. *Bizarre* VI (1956).

THÉVOZ, Michel. *L'Art Brut*. Geneva: Skira, 1975; re-edition 1995.

Fraisse, Clément

DUBUFFET, Jean. 'Le lambris de Clément'. *L'Art Brut* 1 (1964); re-edition 1975.

THÉVOZ, Michel. *L'Art Brut*. Geneva: Skira, 1975; re-edition 1995.

Hauser, Johann

AIGNER, Carl, Helmut ZAMBO (eds.). *Johann Hauser: im Hinterland des Herzens*. Vienna: Christian Brandstätter Verlagsgesellschaft, 2001.

FEILACHER, Johann. *Johann Hauser: Hauser's Frauen!* Salzburg: Residenz Verlag, 2010.

NAVRATIL, Leo. *Bilder nach Bildern*. Exh. cat. Vienna: Residenz Verlag, 1993.

NAVRATIL, Leo. *Die Künstler aus Gugging*. Exh. cat. Vienna: Medusa, 1983.

NAVRATIL, Leo. *Johann Hauser: Kunst aus Manie und Depression*. Munich: Rogner & Bernhard, 1978.

THÉVOZ, Michel. 'Johann Hauser'. *L'Art Brut* 12 (1983).

Helmut (Nimczewski)

BEECK, Manfred IN DER. 'Helmut'. *L'Art Brut* 16 (1990).

Kernbeis, Franz

FEILACHER, Johann (ed.). *Sovären: das Haus der Künstler in Gugging*. Heidelberg: Braus, 2004.

FEILACHER, Johann. 'Franz Kernbeis'. *Raw Vision* 43 (2003).

NAVRATIL, Leo. 'Franz Kernbeis'. *L'Art Brut* 21 (2001).

NAVRATIL, Leo. *Die Künstler aus Gugging*. Exh. cat. Vienna: Medusa, 1983.

Lecocq, Sylvain

EDELMANN, Claude. 'Sylvain'. *L'Art Brut* 5 (1966).

DUBUFFET, Jean. 'Honneur aux valeurs sauvages'. *Prospectus et tous écrits suivants*, vol. I. Paris: Gallimard, 1967; re-edition 1989.

THÉVOZ, Michel. *Art, folie, LSD, etc.* Lausanne: Editions de l'Aire, 1985.

THÉVOZ, Michel. *Écrits bruts*. Paris: Presses universitaires de France, 1979.

Lemaire, Philippe

THÉBERGE, Pierre, John S. HUNKIN, Maurice FORGET, et al. *Mindscapes: images en tête*. Exh. cat. Toronto: Association canadienne pour la santé mentale, 2004.

Mackintosh, Dwight

DI MARIA, Tom. 'Dwight Mackintosh'. *Raw Vision* 52 (2005).

MCGREGOR, John M. 'Dwight Mackintosh'. *L'Art Brut* 17 (2001).

MCGREGOR, John M. *Dwight Mackintosh: The Boy Who Time Forgot*. Oalkand: Creative Growth Art Center, 1992.

Mayor Francis

DEL COTTO, Sylvie. 'Francis Mayor'. *L'Art Brut* 20 (1997).

Merritt, Gene

STANLEY, Tom. 'Notes sur la mémoire et l'observation dans les dessins de Gene Merritt'. *Création franche* 24 (2005).

STANLEY, Tom. 'Gene Merritt'. *L'Art Brut* 21 (2001).

STANLEY, Tom. 'The World of Gene Merritt'. *Raw Vision* 28 (1999).

DEL CURTO, Mario. *Les Clandestins: sous le vent de l'Art Brut*. Preface by Michel Thévoz. Lausanne: Collection de l'Art Brut 2000.

Motooka Hidenori

PEIRY, Lucienne, Sarah LOMBARDI, Tadashi HATTORI, et al. *Art Brut du Japon*. Exh. cat. Lausanne: Collection de l'Art Brut; Gollion: Infolio, 2008.

HATA Yoshiko, Lucienne PEIRY, Sarah LOMBARDI, et al. *The World of Outsider Art: Art Brut in the East and the West*. Exh. cat. Tokyo: Kinokuniya, 2008.

LUSARDY, Martine, Jean-Louis LANOUX, Céline MUZELLE, et al. *Art Brut japonais*. Exh. cat. Paris: Halle Saint-Pierre, 2010.

Pauzié, Alain

DUBUFFET, Jean, Laurent DANCHIN, Alain PAUZIÉ, et al. *La Ponte de la langouste: lettres à Alain Pauzié*. Paris: Le Castor Astral, 1995.

EDELMAN, Catherine, and Jean-Louis LANOUX. 'Les sentiments distingués d'Alain Pauzié'. *Création franche* 5 (1992).

KARAMANOUKIAN, Jacques. *Le Tube de l'été: les semelles de Pauzié*. Ann Arbor: Galerie Jacques, 1989.

PAUZIÉ, Alain. *Alain Pauzié et les enfants de Touffreville: un regard neuf*. Amdahl: Alain Pauzié, 1987.

THÉVOZ, Michel, Geneviève ROULIN, Lucienne PEIRY, et al. *Neuve Invention*. Lausanne: Collection de l'Art Brut, 1988.

Ploos Van Amstel, Han

AMMANN, Max E., Markus LANDERT. *Collectionneur de mondes: art différencié international contemporain: collection de Korine et Max E. Ammann*. Exh. cat. Warth: Kunstmuseum Thurgau, 2011.

BEELEN, Yvonne, Richard BENNAARS, Ans VAN BERKUM, et al. *Transport*. Exh. cat. Galerie Atelier Herenplaats, Rotterdam, 2000.

BERST, Christian, and Nico VAN DER ENDT. *Made in Holland: l'art brut néerlandais*. Exh. cat. Paris: Galerie Christian Berst, 2009.

BIERLAAGH, Nico. 'Eindeloze serie op vier wielen: Hans Ploos Van Amstel'. *Out of Art*, Year 4, no. 1 (2009).

BISET, Sébastien, Pierre-Yves DESAIVE, et al. *Madmusée Collection: 1998–2008*. Liège: Madmusée, 2008.

VAN DER ENDT, Nico, 'Han Ploos Van Amstel'. *Insita 2000*. Exh. cat. Bratislava: Slovenská národná galeria, 2000.

Pujolle, Guillaume

CARDINAL, Roger. 'Guillaume Pujolle'. *L'Art Brut* 23 (2012).

DEQUEKER, Jean. *Monographie d'un psychopathe: étude de son style*. Rodez: Georges Subervie, 1948.

DUBUFFET, Jean, and Jean DEQUEKER. 'Guillaume'. *L'Art Brut* 4 (1965).

THÉVOZ, Michel. *L'Art Brut*. Geneva: Skira 1975; re-edition 1995.

Ratier, Émile

MAURICE, Jean-François. *Émile Ratier*. Exh. cat. Cahors: Musée Henri-Martin, 2000.

RATIER, Émile, and Alain BOURBONNAIS. *Émile Ratier: articles de bois*. Exh. cat. Rennes: Maison de la culture, 1977.

RYCZKO, Joe (ed.). 'Un bricoleur inspiré. Émile Ratier'. *Plein Chant* 68 (1999).

THÉVOZ, Michel. 'Chiaroscuro: the Aesthetics of Blindness'. *Raw Vision* 39 (2002).

THÉVOZ, Michel. *L'Art Brut*. Geneva: Skira, 1975; re-edition 1995.

WOLFF, A. 'Les manivelles d'Émile Ratier'. *L'Art Brut* 9 (1973).

Robillard, André

DEL CURTO, Mario. *Les Clandestins: sous le vent de l'Art Brut*. Preface by Michel Thévoz. Lausanne: Collection de l'Art Brut, 2000.

GENTIS, Roger. 'André Robillard'. *L'Art Brut* 11 (1982).

JAMET, Christian. *André Robillard: l'art brut pour tuer la misère*. Orléans: Corsaire Éditions, 2013.

LOMMEL, Madeleine, Michel THÉVOZ, and Alain BOUILLET. *André Robillard*. Corbeil-Essonnes: Ar'image, 2002.

RENON, Alain. 'André Robillard: l'art brut à fleur de fusil'. *Hey!* 7 (2011).

THÉVOZ, Michel. *L'Art Brut*. Geneva: Skira 1975; re-edition 1995.

Sawada Shinichi

GIONI, Massimiliano (ed.). *Il Palazzo Enciclopedico: Biennale Arte 2013*, I. Exh. cat. Venice: Marsilio, 2013.

LUSARDY, Martine, Jean-Louis LANOUX, Céline MUZELLE, et al. *Art Brut japonais*. Exh. cat. Paris: Halle Saint-Pierre, 2010.

PEIRY, Lucienne, Sarah LOMBARDI, Tadashi HATTORI, et al. *Art Brut du Japon*. Exh. cat. Lausanne: Collection de l'Art Brut; Gallion: Infolio, 2008.

Stanton, André

DEJACE, Anne-Sophie, Michel THÉVOZ, Maurice DELARUELLE, et al. *Connexions particulières: de l'Art Brut à l'art différencié*. Exh. cat. Liège: MAD, 1999.

Tourlonias, Jean
BILLON, Anne. 'Jean Tourlonias'. *Création franche* 16 (1998).

RYCZKO, Joe. 'Jean Tourlonias'. *L'Art Brut* 20 (1997).

LASCAULT, Gilbert, Roland DUCLOS, and Jean-Paul BLANCHET. *Jean Tourlonias* Exh. cat. Meymac: Abbaye Saint-André, Centre d'art contemporain, 1991.

Vignes, Pépé
DEL CURTO, Mario. *Les Clandestins: sous le vent de l'Art Brut*. Preface by Michel Thévoz. Lausanne: Collection de l'Art Brut, 2000.

MASSÉ, Claude. 'Joseph Vignes dit "Pépé"'. *L'Art Brut* 11 (1982).

RAGON, Michel, Raymonde MOULIN, Michel THÉVOZ, et al. *Les Singuliers de l'art*. Exh. cat. Paris: Musée d'art moderne de la ville de Paris, 1978.

Van Genk, Willem
BROMET, Joop. 'Willem Van Genk'. *L'Art Brut* 14 (1986).

DEL CURTO, Mario. *Les Clandestins: sous le vent de l'Art Brut*. Preface by Michel Thévoz. Lausanne: Collection de l'Art Brut, 2000.

VAN BERKUM, Ans. 'Willem Van Genk'. *Raw Vision* 36 (2001).

VAN BERKUM, Ans, Caroline SATINK, and Nico VAN DER ENDT. *Willem Van Genk: a Marked Man and his World*. Zwolle: Museum De Stadshof, 1998.

VAN DER ENDT, Nico. 'Willem Van Genk: the World as Conspiracy'. *Insita 2000*. Exh. cat. Bratislava: Slovenská národná galeria 2000.

VAN DER ENDT, Nico. 'The Power of Willem Van Genk'. *Raw Vision* 3 (1990).

VAN DER ENDT, Nico. 'Entretien avec Willem Van Genk'. *L'Art Brut* 14 (1986).

WALDA, Dick. *Koning der stations: episoden uit het leven van Willem Van Genk*. Amsterdam: Stichting Uitgeverij de Schalm, Galerie Hamer, 1997.

Widener, George
CARDINAL, Roger. 'The Calendars of George Widener'. *Raw Vision* 51 (2004).

KITTELMANN, Udo, and Claudia DICHTER (eds.). *Secret Universe 4: George Widener*. Exh. cat. Cologne: Buchhandlung Walter König, 2013.

LIDY, Léonore. 'George Wiedener?' *L'Art Brut* 23, 2011.

WIDENER, George. With essays by Colin Rhodes and Roger Cardinal. *The Art of George Widener*. London: Henry Boxer Gallery, 2009.

Wölfli, Adolf
FAUPIN, Savine, Christophe BOULANGER, Daniel BAUMANN, et al. *Adolf Wölfli Univers.* Exh. cat. Villeneuve d'Ascq: LaM, 2011.

MORGENTHALER, Walter. *Madness and Art. The Life und Works of Adolf Wölfli*. Introduction by Aaron H. Esman, with Elka Spœrri. Lincoln: University of Nebraska Press, 1992.

MORGENTHALER, Walter. 'Adolf Wölfli.' *L'Art Brut* (2), 1964.

SPŒRRI, Elka and Jürgen GLAESEMER. *Adolf Wölfli*. Bern: Adolf Wölfli Stiftung, Kunstmuseum Bern, 1976.

SPŒRRI, Elka, Michel THÉVOZ, and Geneviève ROULIN (eds.). *Wölfli dessinateur-compositeur*. L'Âge d'homme. Lausanne: Collection de l'Art Brut; Bern: Fondation Adolf Wölfli, 1991.

SPŒRRI, Elka and Daniel BAUMANN (eds.). *Adolf Wölfli : Schreiber, Dichter, Zeichner, Componist*. Basel: Wiese, 1996.

SPŒRRI, Elka and Daniel BAUMANN (eds.). *The Art of Adolf Wölfli: St.Adolf-Giant-Creation*. New York: American Folk Art Museum, 2003.

THÉVOZ, Michel. *L'Art Brut.* Geneva: Skira, (1975) 1995.

ZEMANKOVA, Terezie (ed.). *Adolf Wölfli: creator of the universe*.Exh. cat. Revnice: Arbor Vitae, 2012.

General Works on Art Brut

CARDINAL, Roger. *Outsider Art*. London: Studio Vista, 1972.

DANCHIN, Laurent. *Art Brut: l'instinct créateur*. Paris: Gallimard, 2006.

DEL CURTO, Mario. The Outlanders. Forging ahead with Art Brut, preface by Michel Thévoz. Lausanne: Collection de l'Art Brut, 2000

DUBUFFET, Jean. *Prospectus aux amateurs de tout genre*. Paris: Gallimard, 1946.

DUBUFFET, Jean. *Prospectus et tous écrits suivants*. 2 vols. Paris: Gallimard, 1967; re-edition 1989.

MAIZELS, John. Raw Creation. *Outsider Art and Beyond*, Introduction by Roger Cardinal. London: Phaidon, 1996.

PEIRY, Lucienne. *Art Brut: Jean Dubuffet und die Kunst der Aussenseiter*. Paris: Flammarion, 2005.

PEIRY, Lucienne. *Art Brut: the Origins of Outsider Art*. Paris: Flammarion, 2001; re-edition 2006.

RAGON, Michel. *Du côté de l'Art Brut*. Paris: Albin Michel, 1996.

RHODES, Colin. *Outsider Art: Spontaneous Alternatives*. London: Thames and Hudson, 2000.

RUSSELL, Charles. *Groundwaters: a Century of Art by Self-taught and Outsider Artists*. London: Prestel, 2011.

THÉVOZ, Michel. *Art Brut.* London: Academy Editions, 1976; Geneva: Skira, Booking International, 1995.

Photo Credits

PHOTOGRAPHY CREDITS

All the photographs were provided by Atelier de numérisation - Ville de Lausanne, Sarah Baehler, Dorine Besson, Amélie Blanc, Julie Casolo, Arnaud Conre, Olivier Laffely, Michael Legentil, Maïna Loat, Lucille Meyer, Sylviane Pittet, Kevin Seiscedos and Caroline Smyrliadis,

except for the pages mentioned below:

p. 7: Jean-Jacques Laeser, Collection de l'Art Brut Archives
p. 13: Jean-François Hamon
p. 10: Prinzhorn Collection
p. 15, lower part: Murielle Michetti
p. 20; pp. 28-29; pp. 76-77; p. 139: Claude Bornand
pp. 60-61: Andrew Edlin Gallery

COPYRIGHTS

This book has been published in connection
with the *Vehicles* exhibition
held at the Collection de l'Art Brut, Lausanne
from 8th November, 2013 to 27th April, 2014.

EXHIBITION

GENERAL COMMISSIONER
Sarah Lombardi
director, Collection de l'Art Brut

EXHIBITION COMMISSIONER
Anic Zanzi
curator, Collection de l'Art Brut

Roxane Fuschetto
Research assistant

THE BOOK

CONCEPT AND COORDINATION
Sarah Lombardi and Anic Zanzi
assisted by Roxane Fuschetto

ADMINISTRATION
Dominique Minder

BIOGRAPHIES
Roxane Fuschetto and Sarah Lombardi

BIBLIOGRAPHY
Vincent Monod

EDITING OF FRENCH TEXT
Anne-Lise Delacrétaz, Chapitre Premier, Lausanne

EDITING OF ENGLISH TEXT
Irena Podleska, IP Communication in English

Collection de l'Art Brut
Av. des Bergières, 11
CH-1004 Lausanne
www.artbrut.ch

5 CONTINENTS EDITIONS

EDITORIAL COORDINATION
Laura Maggioni

ART DIRECTION
Annarita De Sanctis

COVER DESIGN
Giorgia Bianchi

TRANSLATIONS
Isabel Ollivier

EDITING
Andrew Ellis

COLOUR SEPARATION
Pixel Studio, Milan, Italy

ISBN: 978-88-7439-658-0

5 Continents Editions
Piazza Caiazzo, 1
20124 Milan, Italy
www.fivecontinentseditions.com

Distributed in the United States and Canada
by Harry N. Abrams, Inc., New York
Distributed outside the United States
and Canada, excluding France and Italy,
by Abrams & Chronicle Books Ltd UK, London

Printed in Italy in August 2013
by Grafiche Flaminia, Trevi (PG), Italy
for 5 Continents Editions, Milan

Collection de l'Art Brut thanks the exhibiting
artists: Fausto Badari, Gregory Blackstock,
David Braillon, François Burland, John Byam,
Serge Delaunay, Curzio Di Giovanni,
Franz Kernbeis, Philippe Lemaire, Gene Merritt,
Motooka Hidenori, Helmut Nimczewski,
Alain Pauzié, Martial Richoz, André Robillard,
Hans Saletmeier, Sawada Shinichi
and George Widener.

Expressions of gratitude are extended
to Michel Thévoz for his part in producing
the catalogue, as well as to Ans van Berkum,
Denise Bertoliatti, Catherine Cressole,
Filipe Dos Santos, Andrew Edlin,
Nico van der Endt, Johann Feilacher,
Dorothy Frisch, Catherine Froidurot, Mali Genest,
Franko Hansekowski, Rebecca Hoffman,
Patricia Landry, Yujia Zhang Li Hong,
Tom di Maria, Nakano Yutaka, Sophie Petitpré,
Peter Resch, Gianluca Rossi, Catherine Sasseville,
Tom Stanley, Helen Stanton, Elisabeth Telsnig,
Ingrid Traschütz and Alessandro Zinelli.

Special thanks to the project partner

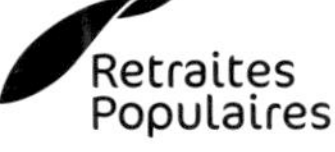